THROUGH THE EYE OF THE NEEDLE:
A MĀORI ELDER REMEMBERS

THROUGH THE EYE OF THE NEEDLE:

A MĀORI ELDER REMEMBERS

MARY KATHARINE DUFFIÉ

HARCOURT COLLEGE PUBLISHERS

Fort Worth   Philadelphia   San Diego   New York   Orlando   Austin   San Antonio
Toronto   Montreal   London   Sydney   Tokyo

Publisher	Earl McPeek
Acquisitions Editor	Bryan Leake
Developmental Editor	Sarah Davis Packard
Project Manager	Andrea E. Archer

ISBN: 0-15-506982-9
Library of Congress Catalog Card Number: 00-106722

Some material in this work previously appeared in HEENI: A TAINUI ELDER REMEMBERS, published in 1997 by HarperCollins Publishers.

Address for Domestic Orders
Harcourt College Publishers, 6277 Sea Harbor Drive, Orlando, FL 32887-6777
800-782-4479

Address for International Orders
International Customer Service
Harcourt College Publishers, 6277 Sea Harbor Drive, Orlando, FL 32887-6777
407-345-3800
(fax) 407-345-4060
(e-mail) hbintl@harcourtbrace.com

Address for Editorial Correspondence
Harcourt College Publishers, 301 Commerce Street, Suite 3700, Fort Worth, TX 76102

Web Site Address
http://www.harcourtcollege.com

Printed in the United States of America

0 1 2 3 4 5 6 7 8 9   039   9 8 7 6 5 4 3 2 1

For Mom and Grandma

ABOUT THE SERIES

These case studies in cultural anthropology are designed for students in beginning and intermediate courses in the social sciences, to bring them insights into the richness and complexity of human life as it is lived in different ways, in different places. The authors are men and women who have lived in the societies they write about and who are professionally trained as observers and interpreters of human behavior. Also, the authors are teachers; in their writing, the needs of the student reader remain foremost. It is our belief that when an understanding of ways of life very different from one's own is gained, abstractions and generalizations about the human condition become meaningful.

The scope and character of the series has changed constantly since we published the first case studies in 1960, in keeping with our intention to represent anthropology as it is. We are concerned with the ways in which human groups and communities are coping with the massive changes wrought in their physical and sociopolitical environments in recent decades. We are also concerned with the ways in which established cultures have solved life's problems. And we want to include representation of the various modes of communication and emphasis that are being formed and reformed as anthropology itself changes.

We think of this series as an instructional series, intended for use in the classroom. We, the editors, have always used case studies in our teaching, whether for beginning students or advanced graduate students. We start with case studies, whether from our own series or from elsewhere, and weave our way into theory, and then turn again to cases. For us, they are the grounding of our discipline.

ABOUT THIS CASE STUDY

This remarkable case study by Mary Katharine Duffié is in the modern vernacular of biculturalism and cultural adaptation. It is not an ethnography in the traditional sense in that it is not about a culture frozen in time, but rather about the process of engagement between an indigenous culture, the Māori of New Zealand, and its colonizers, the British, known locally as the *Pākehā*. This process is dramatically represented in the autobiography of a prominent Māori woman, Heeni Wharemaru, who bridged the enormous gap between the two cultures to become a thoroughly bicultural person. She moved easily and effectively between the two worlds, affecting both with her determined, thoughtful, and compassionate self. Her autobiography, collected and edited by Dr. Duffié, gives the analysis of Māori-Pākehā relationships a personal meaning. The two together, the life story of a woman who experienced the crises and calamities suffered by her people but who took the best of the two worlds she experienced, and the analytic purview by Dr. Duffié, provide an unparalleled look into postcolonial New Zealand society and the relations between colonizer and colonized. But this study is relevant far beyond New Zealand. The situation in New Zealand is mirrored worldwide wherever indigenous people have met with the forces of colonization and Western culture. Confiscation of lands, loss of resources, epidemics of disease, and stunted life opportunities are the lot of indigenous peoples everywhere when they clash with empire builders and colonizers originating from technologically advanced societies.

This case study gives us insight into the complexities of events leading to this condition and into the determined efforts of the people to not succumb to them, and affords an example of what seems to be the ultimate solution to the problem. In her person, Heeni Wharemaru keeps her Māori identity intact and, at the same time, moves effectively in the Pākehā world.

Some form of bicultural adjustment seems to be in the future for most of us as we move from localized and familial identities to transnational, multicultural relationships in the modern world of the Internet and international interdependence.

George Spindler, Editor
Case Studies in Cultural Anthropology

ABOUT THE AUTHOR

Mary Katharine Duffié was born in Philadelphia, Pennsylvania, on June 23, 1963. The eldest of four, she grew up in Glassboro, a small college town in southern New Jersey. She studied anthropology at the University of Arizona and Washington State University, receiving her B.A. in 1985, her M.A. in 1989, and her Ph.D. in 1994. She was the 1993 recipient of the *Society for Medical Anthropology's* WHR Rivers' award, for best graduate medical anthropology paper, nationally. The article proposed a useful model for understanding biocultural illnesses that affect immigrant women in North America. Her dissertation fieldwork was undertaken in Hamilton, New Zealand, beginning in 1993. Her dissertation was first published there as *Heeni: A Tainui Elder Remembers* (HarperCollins) in 1997. She is the author of other academic articles on the culture, religion, and health of fourth world peoples, specializing in American Indians. Previously, she was the Research Coordinator for the American Indian Studies Center, at the University of California, Los Angeles, where her interests centered on postcolonial challenges faced by urban Indian populations in a variety of social contexts. She has recently finished a textbook about the religions of Native North America.

ACKNOWLEDGMENTS

As any writer knows, no book comes to fruition without the support and guidance of a multitude of people: professional colleagues, specialist experts, family members, friends, and others. For almost a decade, since 1991, the following persons have given generously to this project, in one form or another. For their kind acts and expert insights, Heeni and I will be forever indebted.

I owe first thanks to five exceptional people, without whose generosity this book could not have been written. I am grateful to my father, Duke Duffié, who, among many other things, provided the notebook computer on which much of this work was ultimately collected and written; to my stepfather, Dr. Paul Taylor, and his wife,

Hazel, for their hospitality and support during my visits to New Zealand; to my graduate adviser, turned colleague at Washington State University, Dr. William Willard, who above much else, nurtured my mind; and to Dr. Michael King, who not only introduced me to Heeni in the first place, but who really made all of this possible by serving as expert consultant at every critical juncture.

In New Zealand, I am deeply grateful to the personnel at the Māori Studies and Research Centre at the University of Waikato, especially Professor James Ritchie and Sir Robert Mahuta, who gave amply of their time in providing insight during my initial research and in reviewing final manuscripts for the trade version. Likewise, I am grateful to Ms. Nanaia Mahuta, Minister of New Zealand Parliament, who reviewed the final drafts of the academic version and provided editorial changes to ensure substantial and linguistic accuracy. Thanks are also due to those who helped with a variety of editorial details, including Timoti Karetu at the Māori Language Commission and Charlie Fenwick at the Auckland Methodist Mission. Similarly, I am deeply grateful to the late Dave Tūmōkai Pānapa, whose insights into Māoritanga were helpful in building the foundational context for Heeni's remarkable life. I am thankful as well to Mr. Mark Seabrook and Mr. Rafe Potter, not only for their helpful observations regarding Pākehātanga, but for the international friendship that grew out of this project.

In Idaho, I will always be indebted to my friend Carol Hill for lending her creative genius and eternal patience with the "Heeni tapes." Thanks to my friend Yvonne Howard and her husband Terry for their support, and for the many opportunities to house-sit their log cabin in a lovely, inspirational setting in the depths of the country, where I finished the various drafts of the manuscript. Many thanks also to the Hoop, and to my other friends in the States—Thomas J. Yoham and his entire family, Meryl Massey, John J. Marcasciano, Meg Deal, Donna Hickman, Jim Schofield, Deb Parent, Rob Pohndorf, Dianna Rohweder, Michael J. Sage, Louis J. Reynolds, Kathryn and Jay Josephs, Scott R. Zehner, Erica J. Allesio, and Marge Michael for their extraordinary love and support. This work could not have been produced without the support of so many good friends.

At UCLA, I owe thanks to the American Indian Studies Center, especially to staff members Pamela Grieman, Dwight Youpee, and Ken Wade for their collegiality, and for their expertise in locating appropriate resources. I would be remiss if I didn't also express gratitude to my faithful graduate student assistants, who often had to read my mind in order to finish their assigned tasks. I will always be thankful to Angela Mullis, Andrea Viega-Ermert, Benjamin Perez, and Shawn MClendon for assisting with the preparation of the final manuscripts and also for helping with correspondence to Harcourt Brace in the months before publication.

As for my other colleagues in the States, I wish to especially thank Drs. Geoff Gamble and Lewis Carter for their guidance and insight as members of my doctoral committee. Likewise, I am deeply grateful to Professors Vine Deloria Jr., Tom Holm, and the late Robert Thomas, who got me thinking about the relevance of autobiography, while a Master's student at the University of Arizona. Thanks are also due to my other mentors, Dr. Felicia S. Hodge, Dr. Alanna Brown, and Mrs. Peggy Barnett for their superior insight and guidance.

At HarperCollins, I would like to thank my editor, Mark Bathurst, for his meticulous attention to detail and my publisher, Ian Watt, not only for making the trade version of this manuscript a wonderful success but also for helping us bring this version to an international (academic) audience.

At Harcourt Brace, I would like to especially thank Lin Marshall, former Sociology and Anthropology Acquisitions Editor. This case study required extra time, effort, and especially, vision. Her professionalism has been above reproach. Likewise, my deepest gratitude goes to Dr. George Spindler at Stanford University who recognized the reflexive worth of this case study. Last, but definitely not least, I would like to thank Sarah Davis Packard, Developmental Editor; Suzanne Copple, Production Editor; Andrea Archer, Project Manager; and Bryan Leake, Acquisitions Editor for their support and service in bringing Heeni's story to the world.

Final and greatest thanks to Heeni herself, for having led such an extraordinary life and for the aroha that developed between us through its documentation.

Contents

Introduction

Ko te manu e kai i te miro, nōnō te ngāhere;
ko te manu e kai ana i te matauranga, nōnō te āo.

The bird who feasts of the miro berry
shall inherit the fruits of the forest;
the bird who feasts on knowledge
shall inherit the fruits of the world.

TOWARD AN ANTHROPOLOGY OF THE COLONIZED

The idea for this book was first inspired by the work of Marjorie Shostak, who wrote *Nisa,* an autobiography of a !Kung woman, which I read years ago in an undergraduate anthropology class. I have also been influenced by the large collection of American Indian autobiographies written in collaboration with anthropologist others. Of particular interest were *A Yaqui Life* and *Black Elk Speaks,* which created for me a living, personal reality of what it meant to be alive as an indigenous person in a particular time and place. These were richly told stories that provided texture for what I was learning in the classroom about Yaqui and Lakota cultures—in terms of ethnography, history, and colonialism. The combination of subjective and objective perspectives broadened my understanding of the colonial process by illustrating its impact on individual lives. In the book that follows, this kind of pedagogic holism is replicated for the reader, true to Shostak's structure. The life story of a prominent Māori woman is presented in her own words, juxtaposed to anthropologic, historic, and postcolonial analyses that explain relevant themes.

This methodology takes into account the postmodern critics of anthropology. In the 1990s, literary critics and ethnic-studies practitioners accused anthropology of being intellectually colonial, focusing on the objective, scientific view of human cultures, while ignoring important personal and subjective data. In their view, the imbalance distorts the accuracy of cultural presentation in article, book, and/or theory form. Their argument stems from an imbalance in the representation of two kinds of available scholarship used for viewing and interpreting indigenous cultures. My approach is offered to help strike a balance.

The *etic* perspective represents *objective* interpretations of sociocultural data. In this case, anthropologists interpret information collected from direct observation in the field to explain elements of a cultural system ranging from human origins to abstract religious phenomena. These data are also used to construct theories that account for cross-cultural human behavior patterns.

The *emic* view, on the other hand, represents the lived cultural experience of indigenous individuals themselves. Like the *etic* standpoint, the *emic* view also explains aspects of a cultural system, however the details are presented subjectively and in a more integrated manner. For example, indigenous beliefs regarding tribal origins and religious phenomena can be found in oral tradition and are not necessarily separated in the *emic* view, as they are in *etic* schemes of scientific inquiry. Nevertheless, the source of *emic* data is always *subjective,* coming mainly from indigenous literatures (oral tradition transformed into a written genre), biography, and/or autobiography. When transposed correctly, *emic* data can also come from investigative interviews with cultural experts such as shamans, elders, political leaders, and others.

For our purposes, it is important to understand that the *etic* perspective has been used far more frequently than the *emic* view when portraying indigenous realities—especially in classrooms. This problem led to a host of concerns from literary critics, fellow anthropologists, and indigenous people themselves. Their position is that anthropologists, during the latter portion of the twentieth century, have spoken too liberally for the locals. Without prior consultations with indigenous experts, anthropologists have devised intricate theories about specific cultural patterns and beliefs, some of which reflect authentic indigenous realities, whereas others, constrained by the available scientific record, frankly miss the mark. The Bering Land Bridge theory is an obvious example.[1] These theories are thus perceived as artificial, because they are removed from an appropriate context of inquiry and therefore lack crucial aspects of meaningful interpretation. In other words, because most anthropologists are not locals, the critics argue that they not only cannot (and should not) speak for locals without in-depth consultation, but also, in the haste to perform academically, often miss intrinsic information that would lend credibility to their theories. Hence, the tension.

So where does that leave the next generation of anthropologists who want to continue with fieldwork to continue researching and documenting the enormously important cultural processes under way in this world, but who also want to respond ethically to these criticisms? Perhaps a better, more holistic, approach to research would be appropriate. One alternative would be to transform our view of subjective and objective perspectives. We could attempt to see these less in terms of polarized oppositions (the scientists versus the humanists) and more as being opposite sides of the same coin we call *anthropologic inquiry.*

I would like to reinforce the idea that the inclusion of both perspectives—an edited autobiography representing the *emic,* alongside relevant sociocultural and historic interpretation—between the covers of a single book—creates a useful device for diffusing these hegemonic concerns. If authentically portrayed, indigenous meanings remain secure and untainted through time (at least we hope), and therefore can be assessed in a variety of ways by future investigators; whereas the interpretations of the editor are developed in the present to clarify cultural themes and to explain contradictions.

Kathleen Sands has suggested that ethnographic autobiography also has a role to play in deconstructing misguided stereotypes of indigenous people.[2] For example, the only "American Indian," or "New Zealand Māori" of which most people are aware is the common stereotype of one. These representations are constructed and then reinforced by a media complex that uses incomplete information taken from television newscasts, national newspapers, Hollywood films, and literature. According to Sands, these images are "slightly exotic, sometimes fearsome, and highly fragmentary."[3] On one hand, they can be stereotypically negative, such as the poverty-stricken alcoholic or the savage, uncivilized, warrior/militant—bellicose and uncompromising. Or, these conceptions appear unrealistically positive, even romantic (i.e., the noble savage or the shaman with a special connection to the earth and spirit world). These depictions are maintained through time, composed of contradictory traits selected from various cultures even if they are quite different from traditional values and belief systems.

The common denominator among these portrayals is that they are anonymous. Finding an indigenous reality within these anonymous portrayals is complicated and difficult, because the avenues for discovering the required intimacy are few. Sands points out that our high-tech world of telecommunications and long-distance travel has done fairly little to enhance our understanding of indigenous persons. "Until we know (them) individually and intimately, they will remain merely another ethnic type—interesting, mysterious, romantic, but unknowable except as distant figures."[4] Long-distance travel is a means available for personal contact, but not everyone can afford it in terms of both time and money. Moreover, in this day and age of indigenous suspicion of outsiders, who may have ulterior motives for personal or academic gain, who is welcome?

Fiction, written by indigenous people themselves, is another way to establish some measure of intimate contact; however, the work of indigenous authors is relatively recent and therefore limited. Biography is yet another option, affording many good insights into an indigenous life, but biographies are sometimes criticized for being tainted by the cultural filters of the nonindigenous author.

Ethically constructed ethnographic autobiography[5] offers a solution to the limitations imposed by the other genres. Offering both intimacy and depth, the autobiography provides an acceptable entrance into the world of an indigenous person. Many people may come to know cultural worlds this way, who otherwise would not. "Almost universally, the subject of an (indigenous) autobiography tells a story, not merely for his or her own people, but also for the world at large—that is, in practical terms for the nonindigenous, usually white audience who will read the narrative."[6]

As such, autobiography is an appealing method for anthropology, because the narrative exposes the private experiences of an indigenous person—a microcosmic perspective on a human culture that carries weight largely because of its subjective authority. The narrative method embodies a unique collection of subjective insights, attitudes, and behaviors, as well as revelations detailing important cultural, historic, and ethnographic data. These include stories from oral tradition, songs, values, and beliefs, which include particulars about traditional subsistence patterns, religion, and social organization. Autobiography is the personalization of an ethnographic past and present that establishes stages in an individual life, makes links between them, and defines implicitly or explicitly a certain consistency of relationship between the self and outside world.[7]

Ethnographic autobiography is likewise consistent with Clifford Geertz's recommendations that cultural anthropology adopt a polyvocalic posture.[8] He suggested that investigators use "thick description" while obtaining ethnographic data, using both emic and etic voices to expose, layer-by-layer, an authentic indigenous meaning. Geertz observed that these meanings have continued to remain obscure to anthropologists. I would argue that this has been true during the last 2 decades in anthropology—perhaps longer, maybe even since the time of Franz Boas.

Indeed, if we listen to the literary critics and ethnic studies practitioners, it seems anthropology is now faced with the same theoretic stagnation and academic chauvinism that forced the Boasian revolution. To recall, at the turn of the century, he observed that "armchair" theoreticians, using little or no data, had been misguided in their analyses; their ideas tainted with nineteenth century evolutionist inaccuracies and reinforced by a grossly inadequate ethnographic record. One of the worst examples was their notion that the grand scheme of human evolution seats Western society at the pinnacle, whereas indigenous peoples were thought to be working their way up as inferior and savage underlings. Boas disagreed and encouraged his students to carefully detail and record American Indian material culture down to the minutia. By completing the ethnographic record, he eventually suggested a radical alternative—parallel evolution, and with it, cultural relativism. These concepts represented paradigmatic shifts that opened the door for modern American anthropology.

Just as Boas suggested that we collect and document material culture in field to check the hegemony of armchair anthropologists at the turn of the last century, perhaps we are called to weigh in against a similar imbalance at the turn of this century. Only this time, the intellectual problems have arisen from an over-reliance on etic conjecture at the expense of the authority contributed by subjective insights—by the people themselves.

I believe ethnographic autobiography is a part of the solution and should be undertaken more readily by social scientists who are, above all else, ethical. Embedded within a larger, polyvocalic collection of emic and etic writings, autobiography provides a proving ground for our interpretations. An indigenous life history also preserves a context for future cultural analyses—a laboratory that would be otherwise lost to us forever. At the same time, it offers a service to future indigenous generations by upholding an integrated record of traditional behavioral patterns and cultural values. These elements are made available to the indigenous person who desires more information about his or her relatives and/or the intimate aspects of his or her own culture. In this way, ethnographic autobiography serves anthropologic research and preserves indigenous cultural integrity.

METHODOLOGY

I have tried to let Heeni tell her story in her own way and at her own pace, letting her structure its progression according to her personal sense of time and emphasis. During the interview, I made a conscious effort to work from a clean slate, so that I might better understand what she meant to express; however, I kept in mind a clear, predetermined underlying plan of progress. Sometimes I navigated and Heeni steered; at other times, our roles were reversed. The text that follows is drawn from the transcripts of approximately 160 hours of taped interviews, all of which were conducted in English on two visits to New Zealand. The first time I was in the country, January through August, 1993, Heeni and I met regularly at her home in Hamilton for 3 hours at a time, on average three times per week, over the course of 5 months. Often, I had a general idea of how to proceed with a day's topic, but I made a conscious effort to defer to Heeni. I had the impression, later confirmed, that she was thinking very hard about our work while we were not together, about what she should say and how. In 5 months, we covered a lot of ground.

On my second visit to New Zealand, we met 10 times over the course of 3 weeks. These interviews were more intense; Heeni knew exactly what she wanted to say in order to elaborate on what she had discussed before.

Heeni did not tell her story in the order in which it is presented here. As in any natural dialog, we skipped around from one topic to another, beginning with, say, matter relating to retirement and ending with childhood memories. It was therefore necessary to develop a cataloging system, which would organize the material in line with the chronologic plan Heeni herself had made during our initial conversations. I color-coded the transcripts according to the various periods of her life, which she's identified sequentially as "The Early Years," "Preparing for the Church," "The Hostels," and "Reflections." Then, I reorganized the text under each of these headings.

I made three types of editorial intrusions as per Kathleen Sands' advice. First, I introduced changes to ensure consistency in tone and language use, which was necessary for transforming the uneven and incomplete sentences of dialog into readable prose. Second, I made substitutions to compensate for Heeni's challenges with the English language. For example, when Heeni had struggled for an English word or phrase to express a Māori idea or concept, I used the term I came up with myself during the interview. This was always a substitute that Heeni agreed was appropriate to what she was trying to express. Finally, I deleted text that would have generated excessive repetition or that Heeni did not wish to have printed. Fully one-third of our conversations was not included in the final draft.

A HEROINE'S JOURNEY

At age 88, Heeni Wharemaru (Hay-nee Far-ay-mar-oo), whose last name means hardcastle, is the last surviving close friend of the late Princess *Te Puea*. Te Puea is well known in New Zealand for leading nonviolent protest against the New Zealand government and for initiating a cultural revival among her dispossessed and impoverished people in the first part of the twentieth century. At first, Te Puea rejected the Pākehā system because of seemingly profound cultural consequences for the Māori, but later she embraced aspects of it in order to better her people's position. Heeni was to have an active role with regard to Te Puea's vision.

Heeni's early Māori environment, her Methodist deaconess training, and later, her role as one of Te Puea's protégés created an unusual personal capacity for integrating two seemingly disparate cultural worlds, Pākehā and Māori, without compromising her essential Māori identity. Heeni's humble demonstrations of this ability appear across a lifetime of service to New Zealand. Her published life history therefore represents a model for te tangata whenua (the original people) and Pākehā (non-Māori) alike who struggle with the integration of bicultural ideals. The message of Heeni's life is that it can be done, indeed, and with grace.

Heeni was born into an aristocratic family on September 22, 1912, in a small, remote coastal area of the North Island, at the end of the Awakino River gorge, near Mokau. This area borders between the King Country and Taranaki. Governed by strong family ties and traditional religious beliefs, Heeni's elders were experts in Māori culture.

She and her family were also influenced by the Pākehā world. As was typical of rural Māori at the turn of the century, they were drawn into the Pākehā world via a cash economy, because of poverty resulting from the loss of land. Heeni was also influenced by the Ratana Church and prominent Methodist missionaries who journeyed throughout her area holding bible studies and Sunday school classes.

In terms of traditional beliefs, Heeni's spiritual foundation rested on the family's experience with the natural world, the teachings of her koro, and Māori training at home. During her childhood, her family's religion centered on Māori gods who had life-giving and life-taking powers. They saw all nature as having both natural and supernatural properties, believing people should live in harmony with the land, respecting it as property of the gods. Each god was charged with caring for a different part of nature, such as the sea, forest, or crops. Certain proscribed rituals were meant to ensure a continued bounty. In her narrative, Heeni mentions the offering of the first fish of a catch to Tangaroa (guardian spirit of the sea) and the first bird in a hunt to Tane Mahuta (guardian spirit of the forest).

Raised as a puhi (an aristocratic virgin), Heeni was strictly guarded by her family. Ordinarily, her parents would have planned a political marriage as was the traditional custom among the aristocratic class. However, her family made the decision that she was not to marry in the traditional sense, although her alternative "marriage" to the church was indeed a political one. She was given over to Father Seamer at age 15. From this time on, Methodist Church leaders were to assume all financial and spiritual responsibility for her.

Interestingly, marriage to the Church provided political reparations for the transgressions of her ancestors two generations previously—specifically, the mistaken murder of a prominent and loved Methodist Minister, the Reverend John Whiteley, shot down by her great grandfather over an apparent misunderstanding over land. Heeni was thus handed over as a gift to heal the wound created by this murder.

At the time Heeni was given over to the Church, she was unaware of these circumstances. It would be much later in life that she would discover, quite by accident, that she was given away for political reasons. The late Dave Tūmōkai Pānapa explained, "One of the things you do is that you give the blessing of your best. And Heeni would have been what is known as a puhi in Māoridom. What else can you dedicate to God but the very, very best of your tribe?"

As a teenager, then, Heeni left her traditional home behind, as she put it, "to learn the ropes of civilization." She eventually became a Deaconess of the Methodist Church. Deaconesses were trained to dispense spiritual care and to help poor women care better for their children and families. They worked in depressed regions, both rural areas and cities, providing needed services to the economically disadvantaged. Deaconess training was recognized as having both practical and spiritual applications. Deaconess orders in the Protestant churches were instituted in the nineteenth century to enable the spread of "social Christianity." Heeni enjoyed the fieldwork at Deaconess house where she gave sermons and cared for the poor. She was dedicated in 1941.

Before taking up hostel work, however, Heeni enjoyed one carefree, adventurous year as a new deaconess. For Heeni, this period was the fulfillment of all the adventure the dedication to church work had promised from the beginning. The excitement was to be short lived, however, because at the end of the year Heeni was suddenly called down to Hamilton by Methodist Church officials. Her orders were to substitute for a minister who was seriously ill and unable to perform his duties. Heeni remembers feeling anxiety about the conditions of her new responsibility and about the prospect of leaving her new friends on the northern circuit.

Once in Hamilton, she began what became her life's work as a matron of Māori youth hostels. The first hostel was for girls; later there was one for boys. The hostels provided the young people staying in them, some from prominent families, with a Māori home base while they attended secondary schools and/or tertiary institutions in Hamilton. This arrangement complemented Te Puea's vision of young Māori having a Māori base in urban areas while embracing a Pākehā education; Heeni thus took her new role very seriously. She saw it as a moral duty; it was her unique contribution for ensuring the success of the next generation of Māori people.

Te Puea chose Heeni to assume such important responsibilities, because by this time she had been thoroughly exposed to the best of both cultures, Māori and Pākehā. Born and raised in a traditional environment, she bridged the cultural

Heeni and Dr. Michael King, author Te Puea: A Biography.

frontier, assimilated a new and foreign system, and repositioned herself with, as Dr. Michael King put it, "one foot in each world, still standing upright."[9]

Heeni's duties at the hostel included providing a traditional Māori environment for the youth at the hostel, while at the same time dealing extensively with the Pākehā world as it intersected with their lives, such as neighbors, teachers, police, government, and health officials. She was a bridge builder who exhibited the kind of cultural fluency that could only come from the elite training handed down first from her elders and family, on the Māori side, and later by the Church, on the Pākehā side. Dr. Anthony Rogers, a close personal friend of Heeni's during the hostel years, explained that the hostels were not just dormitories; rather, they were places where Māori youth could live together as a cultural unit, learning the ways of the Pākehā from a secure position. "I equated her role to one of a Headmistress of a secondary boarding school for Māori. There is something that boarding schools do. They teach you self respect, and I think she was the ideal person to do this, a perfect example to the (youth) in this regard," explained Rogers.[10]

Heeni was indeed a bicultural woman—and in the early 1940s, long before biculturalism was in vogue. Dr. Michael King elaborates, "Heeni has always believed in the possibility of other Māori being bicultural. She also believes that the Pākehā can be bicultural too. I am not sure that I share her confidence to the same degree, but I do think Heeni has always been ahead of the Kīngitanga on matters of integration and bridge building. Although Te Puea was trying for a long time, certainly through the late 1920s, to bring Māori and Pākehā together at Turangawaewae, that did not necessarily reflect what was going on outside that little microcosm."[11]

Princess Te Puea visited the Te Rahui Wahine, the girls' hostel, quite often in the beginning, lending her support and strength while Heeni adjusted to her new role. Over time, they built a deep and lasting friendship characterized by much aroha (love and affection) and confidence. The late Dave Tūmōkai Pānapa observed, "Heeni was utterly devoted to Te Puea, and to Te Puea's teachings. They were both kindred spirits. Heeni used to chauffeur her around, and in the process, she became Te Puea's confidante. Heeni was someone Te Puea could bounce ideas off, and she needed a sounding board. You need people around you that will tell you the truth. I would like to suggest that Heeni was one of those."[12]

Even after Te Puea's death in 1952, Heeni remained faithful to realizing the ideals of the Kīngitanga movement, enshrined in the belief that all people are one, using the Methodist Church as a vehicle for integrating two cultural worlds within one New Zealand universe. Her work brought her into contact with prominent Māori intellectuals, including Sir Peter Buck and Maharaia Winiata. In her prime, she rose as a respected elder for many long years of dedicated service to the Tainui (and Māori generally) and Hamilton communities. As Professor James Ritchie explained, "Heeni ultimately carved out for herself a role which wasn't pastor and wasn't social worker, you know, it was something quite unique, and it had a Māori flavoring. She was recognized for her special quality of caring, and of course, caring is a terribly important central focus in the Māori scheme of things. Looking after kids in the hostel, she assumed the role of ultimate parent. Even back as far as 1947, I noticed that she received a lot of respect. Hers was like the role teachers had in aristocratic Greek families, where people were given honor because they were in charge of looking after the young."[13]

Throughout her adult life, Heeni has been a trusted friend of the Kahui Ariki, the Māori royal family descended from King Tawhiao. Today, she is the closest female advisor to Dame Te Atairangikaahu, the present Māori queen. Dr. King explains, "In Māori terms this means more than just being a trusted friend; these people are highly tapu (sacred) people. Because when you're working closely with them, you would not be permitted to do things that involve touching them unless you are a very special kind of person. What I'm actually saying is that some of the things that make those people like Te Puea and Koroki awesome—some of those awesome qualities are now with Heeni. Therefore, she is a person who inspires immense respect, because only a very few people could be drawn in as she was."[14]

However, Heeni has provided counsel and confidence to more than royalty. Over the years, she has become acquainted with people from all occupations, Māori and non-Māori. According to Dr. King, "Heeni knew and knows an extraordinarily wide range of people. Not just the people I would expect her to know, like the Methodist Church people, but Māori poets and union activists, like Hone Tuwhare. Peter Buck was another one. When he went off to Honolulu to take the Bishop Museum job, he wanted Heeni to come and to be part of the household. He wanted her to be part of the household because he did not have children of his own. Heeni would have been a trusted friend. She has always worked very hard at friendship. It's always been very important to her, and the consequence is that she's known to and greatly admired and loved by a very wide range of people." There are people who visit her home regularly to receive advice and counsel. Professor Ritchie says, "I think it's been easy for her to open to people and say 'bring me your troubles.' Something like what's written on the Statute of Liberty, for example. Of course she had the model of Te Puea herself, having done that herself."[15]

For reasons that will become obvious, I, like many others in New Zealand, came to have great respect for Heeni Wharemaru. Despite her status and many pioneering achievements, Heeni has remained quite humble and very private. In the course of this research, I had the opportunity to interview members of her social network, including Methodist Church associates, former hostel members, friends, and relatives. I quickly discovered how few people really know Heeni as a person. She later admitted that this was true. Of course, they know "Sister Heeni," matriarch of the Tainui people, and the Waikato pillar, but few know the inner Heeni.

I believe Pākehā (on both sides of the Pacific) and Māori readers alike will be inspired by the story of courage that follows. Joseph Campbell, a prominent scholar and leading authority on mythology, has commented on heroes and heroines as they appear in stories and legends across all cultures. He suggested that for special people—and I am suggesting that Heeni is such a person—hero and heroine stories become a blueprint for real life. The real-life heroine is called to adventure, crosses the threshold between what she has known and what awaits her beyond, goes out to face trials and ordeals, and comes back with a boon for her community. This is the essence of Heeni's life's journey. She found unique ways of distilling what she was taught from her early traditional experience, then transferred this knowledge into a modern, postcolonial context, often at her own expense, to benefit her people. Her life therefore exemplified bicultural ideals long before the idea of biculturalism was conceived. To many, her success in this regard is extraordinary—especially given the plight of fourth world peoples around the globe.

Perhaps Heeni's story can teach us all a little about what is required for bridging the cultural divide no matter on which side we stand.

Woodland Hills, California
March 1, 1999

Notes

1. For example, the controversial Bering Land Bridge theory that details a relatively recent Native American migration (10,000 ya) from Asia across the Land Bridge, where in a very short time the American Indians killed off the Mega fauna and populated both North and South America. The single migration supposedly occurred during the last ice age, through the interglacial pathway between what is now the Rocky and Cascade mountain ranges. Archaeologists created this theory based solely on the available fossil and artifact record. This theory, however, has been rejected by American Indians for decades. In their view, mythology and oral tradition tell them they have been here, quite literally, forever. There is now increasing scientific evidence from the fossil record that, indeed, American Indians may have been here much longer than previously thought, perhaps coming from other places, at many different times and by many different modalities.
2. Kathleen Sands. *American Indian Autobiography: Studies in American Indian Literature.* New York: Modern Language Association, 1983:55.
3. Ibid.
4. Ibid.
5. As outlined in my methodology section taken from Kathleen Sands.
6. p. 56.
7. Ibid.
8. Clifford Geertz. *The Interpretation of Cultures: Selected Essays.* New York: Basic Books, 1973.
9. Personal interview with Dr. Michael King, The University of Waikato, August 1993.
10. Personal interview with Dr. Denis Rogers, Hamilton, August 1993.
11. Dr. King op. cit.
12. Personal interview with the late Dave Tūmōkai Pānapa, Hamilton, August 1993.
13. Denis Rogers, op. cit.
14. Dr. King, op. cit.
15. Interview with Professor James Ritchie, The University of Waikato, August 1993.

Part One

Māori
Beginnings

*Ekuhuna ai te miro mā, te miro pango, te miro
whero. I muri kia mau ki te aroha, ki te ture me te
whakapono.*

There is but one eye of the needle through which the white, black and red
threads must pass. After I am gone, hold fast to love, to the law and to the
religion of Christ.

King Tāwhiao

New Zealand is the largest archipelago in all of Polynesia. With 501,776 square kilometers, it contains more land than the rest of Polynesia combined. It is generally a mountainous country with large, fertile regions of interior plains. Unlike the more tropical Polynesian islands to the north, such as Hawaii, New Zealand lies within the Temperate Zone. The climate is generally mild, but too cold for the harvest of traditional Polynesian plants such as taro and breadfruit.

New Zealand is also unique in terms of culture. Two subcultures, Māori and *Pākehā* (European), each based on a root version of an earlier culture, form a bicultural social universe distinct from other Polynesian Island contexts. New Zealand's population is 3.3 million, about the size of the city of Seattle, Washington. Its ethnic majority is Anglo (80%), mostly from English and Scotch-Irish ancestry. Māori are the indigenous Polynesians there and represent 13% of the population. The remaining ethnicities are other Pacific Islanders (4%), such as Samoans and Niueans, as well as Chinese (1%) and Asian Indians (<1%).

Aotearoa (the land of the long white cloud), is the Māori word for New Zealand. Māori began colonizing the country about 1,500 years ago. The British invaded much later, in the first part of the nineteenth century. Surprisingly little has been written on the Māori by American anthropologists, despite the fact that New Zealand is quite interesting from an ethnographic standpoint. Approximately 40 Māori tribes thrive there and many have evolved as postmodern political entities in a parallel relationship with their colonizers. To defend themselves against the European colonial pattern, the Māori borrowed heavily from British institutions, learned their culture, and embraced along the way, the language of the Pākehā. They also accepted Christianity to some degree. Interestingly, however, the Māori generally did not lose their cultural integrity, as did so many others around the world who endured similar colonial impositions during the so-called Age of Discovery.

Indeed, the Māori are in many ways the envy of the indigenous world because much of their aboriginal culture remains intact, despite two centuries of governmental strategies to assimilate them. The Māori language and English are presently the two official languages of New Zealand. However, this is not to say that the Māori do not suffer disproportionately from the indices of socioeconomic distress as a result of colonial forces. They do, but when compared with other indigenous groups, they have generally fared better as cultural independents. Part of the reason for their success is that the Māori have a long tradition of politically savvy leadership complete with aristocrats who had the protection and salvation of their people at the top of their social agenda. In recent times, these leaders—many educated in New Zealand and Europe's finest schools—have done their legal history homework, applying what they learned toward Māori greater good. As a result, the Māori have been victorious in winning huge compensations from the New Zealand government for illegal land dispossessions in the nineteenth century. The Tainui[1] for example, Heeni's iwi (tribe), are using their settlement monies to build an economic infrastructure for future generations. This includes educational, manufacturing, and fishing enterprises, which will provide culturally relevant employment opportunities.

The subject of this book is Heeni Wharemaru (Hen-ee Far-ay-mar-oo), whose tradition is from this aristocratic class of leaders. Her people are Tainui, a tribal conglomerate that instinctively and collectively took advantage of the Pākehā system to survive economically. They grafted these elements onto an intact Māori cultural foundation to better their people's socioeconomic position.

Throughout her life, Heeni has demonstrated the ability to integrate two seemingly disparate worlds, Pākehā and Māori, without compromising her distinct Māori identity. Heeni humbly demonstrates this ability in a lifetime of service to New Zealand. Her published life history represents a microcosmic perspective on what her people have accomplished on a larger scale. Her autobiography is a model for *te tangata whenua* (the original people of the land), other indigenous groups, and Pākehā alike who struggle with the incorporation of bicultural (or multicultural) ideals. The message of Heeni's life, and those like her, is that it can be done, and with grace.

At age 88, she is the last surviving close friend of the late Princess Te Puea.[2] Te Puea is well known in New Zealand for leading nonviolent protests to win land compensations from the colonial government and for leading a successful cultural revival among her dispossessed and impoverished people in the first part of the twentieth century. At first, Te Puea rejected Pākehā culture for fear of being absorbed by it. But later, she embraced certain aspects, such as education, to promote her people's socioeconomic position. Heeni had an active, integral role with regard to Te Puea's vision. As a matron of Māori youth hostels, she gave young people a Māori home base while they received the benefit of a Pākehā education in the city of Hamilton. Many of these youths grew into leadership positions in the later twentieth century, helping fight the legal battles for economic and social justice in New Zealand. The present-day Māori queen, for example, was one of her young students in the early 1950s.

Like any Polynesian story, Heeni's begins long before she was born, with the traditions and culture of her ancestors. Who her ancestors were, however, and how they arrived in Aotearoa has sparked controversy between anthropologists and Māori intellectuals. Anthropologists look to the archaeological and linguistic evidence in the Polynesian prehistory paradigms to assess origins, whereas Māori know that there is much more to their story. From the Māori point of view, anthropologists tend to view the subject in purely scientific terms, analyzing data that are almost always removed from the context of culturally valued notions of Māori origin. They omit, for example, mythological, genealogical, and other sacred components of Māori oral tradition, which tends to sterilize the story in the view of the Māori intellectual community.

It is important then to review elements of both perspectives, while at the same time setting the backdrop for Heeni's traditional upbringing.

ORIGINS

Anthropologists hypothesize that the Polynesians are the last wave in a West–East migration pattern across the great Pacific Ocean that began from the coast of Southeast Asia some 7,000 years ago. The Austronesians were the first group to set out from the mainland with fully stocked, double-hulled, outrigger canoes and a sophisticated knowledge of the prevailing winds. They have been characterized as expert navigators who were guided by star charts that mapped the sky.

By 5,000 years ago, the coasts of New Guinea and Taiwan were fully colonized. By 3,000 years ago, all of Micronesia and Melanesia and some Polynesian outlier islands were inhabited. The Polynesians arrived in the Eastern Pacific some 1,800 years ago and arrived in New Zealand about 1,500 years ago.

Polynesian peoples such as the Hawaiians, Samoans, and Easter Islanders as well as Micronesian and Melanesian peoples are thus descended from Austronesian ancestors. Each group achieved their unique cultural composite by continually adapting to the challenges of island life. Historically, these adaptations produced certain technical, social, political, and religious innovations—patterns that continue to evolve today.[3]

The strongest scientific support for the migration pattern just described comes from archeological, linguistic, and physical evidence. Archeological evidence comes in the form of Lapita pottery, which has been dated according to the aforementioned time lines. This is a distinctive kind of reddish earthenware ceramic, incised with a characteristic decorative pattern. The Lapita pottery complex ranges from the whole of Melanesia to the western Polynesian islands of Tonga, Samoa, Futan, and 'Utea. The Lapita people were skilled voyagers who had a complex trade/communication network that spanned hundreds, perhaps thousands, of kilometers.

The linguistic evidence comes from glottochronology. Glottochronologists use universally common words (called cognates) such as *thumb, sun,* and *dog* to measure time distances logarithmically between languages that share a common ancestor. The theory states that because Polynesian words are furthest away from Micronesian ones, it is logically assumed the Polynesians are the last wave in a West–East migration.

Likewise, there is evidence from the physical bodies of Oceanic peoples that supports a West–East movement. It comes from dental traits. All Oceanic peoples, differentiating them from another group of Southeast Asians called the *Sundanots,* share dental similarities. The Sundanots started in the same place as the Austronesians; however, they migrated northwest and then east along the Asian continent. Eventually, the archaeologists argue, Sundanots crossed the Bering land bridge; their descendants are Native Americans indigenous to North and South America.

What prompted the continual East–West movement across the Pacific Ocean? Cultural ecologists suppose a relationship between population pressures in the environment and resultant social processes. Their theories are based on the notion that human groups tend to outgrow their resource base until the population is curbed by hunger, war, or poverty. They hypothesize that the colonization of Oceania was compelled by the continual need to renew resources after population pressures made producing an adequate livelihood on the tiny islands difficult. In other words, environmental circumscription (each inhabited island is surrounded by the great Pacific Ocean), coupled with overpopulation, eventually created social turmoil as food became scarce and space became limited. In the view of cultural ecologists, the probable impetus for the great Pacific migrations was the resultant warfare over a shortage of food and the necessity for finding an island alternative.

Marshall Sahlins suggested that upon arrival to a new island, the typical Polynesian social pattern resulted in an increased resource base as native peoples manipulated the environment in their favor, harvesting taro, breadfruit, coconut, and kūmara (Polynesian sweet potato).[4] Almost immediately, a surplus was established, which, almost always, facilitated a population boom. In Polynesian society, political leadership and religious power were fused. Political leaders were the heads of lineage-based economic systems, charged with redistributing the agricultural and fishing surplus that had been pooled by lower-ranking community members. A larger population tended to magnify the status of the leaders and increase their power. With so much at stake, leaders were often in competition with one another. When the resource base became threatened, as it did on nearly every Polynesian Island, so did the legitimacy of the leaders' power. This obliged them to behave in a more dictatorial manner. Thus they constructed a strict code of moral and ritual behavior, which the people conformed to, upholding the tangibility of the leaders' authority.

Raymond Firth's description of what happened on a small Polynesian outlier island called Tikopia serves as an example of this process, which theoretically occurred all over Polynesia.[5] On Tikopia, the population eventually boomed in a disproportionate relationship to the society's ability to produce resources. In this case, the lineage heads were forced to compete with others to maintain both their resource base and the legitimacy of their own power. In Tikopia, however, there was some measure of cooperation to address the problems. The solution was to employ a type of population regulation. First, they killed the pigs because these animals competed with humans for the Island's plant foods. Second, they delayed marriage to slow down the baby booms. In this way, the society was able to save itself from famine and the destruction of warfare.

Irving Goldman has argued that the lineage-based economic system just described was adaptable from the smallest Polynesian atolls to the largest archipelagos.[6] He notes that what happened in Hawaii is an exaggeration of Tikopia, such that competition for resources and status rivalry were taken to an extreme. Ultimately, environmental circumscription and population increases created a Tikopian situation there. Unlike Tikopia, however, Hawaiian "paramount chiefs" aggressively fought territorial wars with other lineage heads for control of a rapidly decreasing resource base. Paramount chiefs were not merely representatives of the people to the gods, as they had been in Tikopia. Rather, they became part god themselves. Part human, part divine, Hawaiian paramount chiefs ruled in a theocracy. They had life or death powers over the commoners, who could be stoned, strangled, or burned for not following rigorous religious protocol (e.g., men and women could not even eat together). Moreover, Hawaiian paramount chiefs used the economic redistribution system for their own ends by financing grand temples and lavish living with communally pooled resources. By the time Captain Cook arrived, the Hawaiians were on the verge of becoming a Polynesian kingdom, unified under one monarchy.

Similar patterns are known to have existed on Easter Island. Goldman has suggested that had the Māori of New Zealand had the time to overpopulate before the advent of European colonization, they would have faced a similar fate as the

Hawaiian and Easter Islanders. It is important, however, to emphasize that no one knows for sure if this would have been the case. Anthropologists should be careful not to combine other island data with that of New Zealand in order to make them fit into meta theories.

The Māori viewpoint is generally congruent with anthropologists' theories regarding a mass Pacific migration, but instead of focusing on overpopulation and warfare as the driving force for colonization, oral tradition points to an ingrained Māori ethos for loving the spirit of adventure. Seen in this light, at least some Polynesian canoes left atolls and islands in the quest for discovery, just as the early European explorers left the mainland during the Age of Discovery.

Moreover, Māori intellectuals argue that to assume that the same circumstances (warfare and food shortages) impelled each of the hundreds, perhaps thousands, of Pacific migrations would be to suggest that the tangata whenua were neither intelligent nor wise enough to learn important past lessons regarding the relationship between population pressures and environmental limitations. Given that it might have taken only two or three generations to deplete the resource base on some atolls, it seems speculative that people with such a sophisticated form of social organization would so quickly forget the lessons of the past, especially ones with such dire consequences.

The initial discovery of *Aotearoa* is credited to *Kupe* some 1,500 years ago. Oral tradition describes the great migration to New Zealand as occurring over the course of several hundred years. A large fleet of double-hulled or outrigger canoes were commanded by brave, aristocratic captains who crossed the Pacific. It was from these voyagers that most present-day Māori claim their descent. The canoes left from different locations and arrived at different times. The Māori therefore question *etic* assumptions that the great migration period occurred in a single sweeping west–east–south flow.

According to genealogy, the *Tainui* (Heeni's mother's tribe) *waka* (canoe) arrived about 1,000 years ago. *Hoturoa*, the chief of the Tainui waka, and his crew boarded the craft and set a course for Aotearoa. They had departed from the mythical place called *Hawaikiki,* which could have been Hawaii, or one of the islands on the way south. On board this craft was *Korotangi*, a mythical bird that acted as guide and protector, ensuring they would arrive safely at these shores. The Tainui waka stopped at many islands during its journey. In Rarotonga, for example, there stands a rock where the Tainui waka was launched on the way to Aotearoa. The Tainui waka landed first on the west coast of New Zealand at *Maketu*, and later at *Kawhia*.[7]

Captain Hoturoa and his crew had two types of navigational guidance. The first were maps of the heavens—star charts mentioned earlier. The navigators were specially trained priests, helping the Captain stay on course, to the right of one or two particular stars. It is said that there are certain people in the Māori community who still retain this sort of knowledge. Second, the people followed the migration of various birds. When a bird was killed or found dead on an island stop along the way, the contents of its intestines would be examined. If foodstuffs not native to the island were found, then the crew would be inclined to follow these birds to another island in the direction of their flight path.

TRADITIONAL SUBSISTENCE

Polynesian culture was originally adapted for much warmer climates in latitudes closer to the Equator and Tropic of Capricorn. Thus, upon arrival to New Zealand, the Māori exchanged a lush tropical climate for a temperate, colder one. As farmers, the early settlers probably experienced hunger and hardship because the Polynesian staples of taro, breadfruit, and coconut would not thrive in the new land. They were no doubt forced to improvise while they adapted to new conditions.

The hardiest food in their lot was the kūmara,[8] or Polynesian sweet potato. "Where the kūmara flourished, so did the Māori. The greater population of the northern North Island is attributed to the abundance of the kūmara as much as to the warmer climate."[9] The Māori supplemented the kūmara with large quantities of birds and fish and other indigenous plants. These took some time to discover, cultivate, and then harvest. (New Zealand plant life is remarkable in that of the 2,000 indigenous species, about 1,500 are found nowhere else in the world.)

With the exception of two species of bat, no indigenous mammals are native to New Zealand. The only meat on the island before the arrival of Europeans was a type of dog and a black rat, both of which were imported by the Māori. Dogs, or kuri, were bred for eating and for use as guards during times of war when enemies encroached. The Māori met most of their protein needs by eating shellfish, deep sea fish, and fresh water fish, including eel. Captain James Cook eventually brought pigs to New Zealand. Pig hunting then became very popular with young Māori men, who would bring two or three home for the women to prepare and store. Heeni has fond memories of her brothers' pig hunts, and the taste of pork prepared in its own fat.

North of Aotearoa, the tapa cloth served as fabric for making Polynesian clothing and mats. The material for tapa cloth is extracted from the bark of a tree and then is pressed into a form of paper. The *oti* tree could not survive in the colder regions of the North Island, so other materials were discovered and used. The Māori substituted flax for tapa cloth. Flax flourishes all over New Zealand. After being specially prepared, it was woven and used for carrying containers, clothing, and mats on which to sleep or sit. Dog hair and *kiwi* feathers (national, endangered bird of New Zealand) were put on cloaks for warmth. Kiwi feather cloaks were reserved for the social elites. Mrs. Rangimarie Hetet was one of the finest traditional weavers in all of New Zealand, and a relative of Heeni's. She has recently died, but her cloaks are on display at the *Kirikiriroa* (Hamilton) Museum.

Mussels: A Māori Staple

One of Ms. Hetet's relatives describes the Māori view of weaving as more than practical: "Weaving is more than just a product of manual skills. From the simple *rourou* (food basket) to the prestigious *kahu* kiwi (cloak), weaving is endowed with the very essence of the spiritual values of Māori people. The ancient Polynesian belief is that the artist is a vehicle through

The Kiwi

whom the gods create. Art is sacred and interrelated with the concepts of *mauri* (life force or essence), *mana* (prestige), and *tapu* (sacred)."[10]

Villages were connected through extensive trade networks that reached to the opposite tips of both islands. Cloaks, canoes, carvings, dogs, prepared foods, fishing technology, basalt, greenstone (jade), and just about anything else conducive to Māori life were traded throughout New Zealand before European arrival. Trade continued to expand after contact.

SOCIAL STRUCTURE

The smallest social unit in Māori society is the *whaanau* (family). As the numbers of families increased, certain groups broke off, forming extended kin networks called hapū (clans or subtribes). Although tracing genealogical connections through males was favored, membership was recognized if a line of descent included several females, so the hapū was not unilineal. In effect, a person could opt to claim hapū membership through the father, through the mother, or through both parents. Subtribes were a smaller unit of what ultimately became the *iwi* (tribe). The whaanau, hapū, and iwi share a common ancestor aboard one of the major canoes. Traditionally, loyalty ran deep, so even though rivalries and disagreements might have broken out among relatives, the people willingly cooperated in the face

Traditional Fishing Hook

of other iwi threats and aggression. The population of Aotearoa included 40 iwi, which developed based on ancestral descent. The existence of iwi relied strongly on kinship links and was upheld by the continued tradition of reciting genealogy, or whakapapa at hui. In this way, people were inextricably connected to their ancestral lands.

Traditionally, the Māori lived in a fortified village setting called a *pā*. Very high fences, usually milled from local timber surrounded many pā sites. Deep ditches were dug close to a watercourse to provide access to fresh water springs during times of siege. Pā were always near rich food sources, such as shellfish beds, and land suitable for growing kūmara. "Pā were usually built on high ground, palisaded, and where possible, moated."[11] In her narrative, Heeni mentions her father's family's pā, one never taken by enemy forces. Situated off the coastline down from her parent's house, this pā is now a national landmark.

A traditional village depended on its situation and size for security from other iwi aggression and depended on its proximity to food and water for supplies. Family dwellings were built around a village common called a *marae*. This is a courtyard in front of a main meeting house where important political discussions are held during the daytime, and where songs, dances, and celebrations are held in the evening. "Visitors were greeted here and then entertained with food."[12] An ancestral marae was (and still is) the focus of community ritual,

Ponga Fern

where hapū and iwi social bonds are cemented through kinship gatherings.

Traditionally, daily life centered in buildings constructed for specific purposes. These were built out of the small trunks of *Ponga* ferns (along with Raupo, the national tree of New Zealand). There were structures built specifically for sleeping, cooking, and storing food; these activities were never mixed. Combining food and body accoutrements is *tapu* (forbidden) in Māori society because doing so might contaminate the essential purity of each.[13] An entire family would use a sleeping house for dormitory purposes only. It was well insulated to shut out the dampness and cold characteristic of Aotearoa's winters. Meeting houses were sometimes added on to sleeping ones and used for discussions or entertaining visitors. The cooking house was typically a Ramada set over an oven pit. Storehouses were also built to be used as pantries for surplus foodstuffs collected in woven flax containers. A station platform was built high above the pā[14] where sentries stood guard, watching for signs of encroaching enemies.

Of course, most modern Māori no longer live in traditional houses encircling a marae. The Māori of today live in Pākehā-style homes, but this does not in any way detract from the continued spiritual and ceremonial significance of marae across New Zealand. Marae activities have united Māoridom in myriad ways before and after colonization. For example, all Māori decision-making, which is conducted according to rules for consensus building, and much of Māori entertaining, celebrating, and grieving are still conducted on ancestral marae or in auxiliary meeting houses.

One belongs to a particular marae based on ancestral lineages linked to iwi and hapū ties. Indeed, it is possible to view the intricate network of marae in both the North and South Island as the cultural infrastructure that, in a sophisticated manner, maintained the solidarity of the Māori culture, despite two centuries of colonial impositions. "The marae are central to the concept of *Māoritanga* (Māori culture). Māoritanga consists of an acknowledgement of and pride in one's identity as a Māori. While Māoritanga has a physical base in ethnic identity, it also has a spiritual and emotional base derived from the ancestral culture of the Māori. Māori oratory, language, values, and social etiquette are given their fullest expression in the marae setting at *tangi* (funerals) and *hui* (ceremonial gatherings)."[15]

Heeni grew up near the ancestral home of the anchor of the original Tainui waka. Heeni's mother was of the Tainui waka and the *Maniapoto* iwi. Heeni's father's iwi was *Taranaki*, and his hapū was *Te Ati Awa*. Heeni felt no pressure to choose a particular hapū or iwi loyalty, although she lived and worked more closely with Tainui as an adult. Early in her training, elders told her both groups would know her equally, depending on where she traveled in New Zealand. Heeni's ancestral marae was *Te Maniaroa*, near the place of her birth, but the one with which she was most active as an adult is the famous *Turangawaewae* marae. The late Princess Te Puea initiated its construction in the 1940s. It represented the fulfillment of a prophecy from an earlier Māori king—King Tawhiao—who predicted at the end of the nineteenth century that Tainui would someday reclaim the land on which the marae is built from the New Zealand government, who had stolen it in the land wars of the 1860s. *Turangawaewae* translates literally as "foot stool." It is now host to the Māori queen's coronation anniversary *hui* (ceremonial gathering), an annual rite solidifying Māori unity. Numerous heads of states and dignitaries have been entertained there, including Queen Elizabeth (also, more recently, Prince Charles).

As mentioned previously, Māori society was hierarchically stratified—split into two sections or castes—which were determined by inheritance. The firstborn of an elite marriage had the most mana. Termed the *rangatira,* these children were raised in a chiefly, or royal, atmosphere. Superior families of lesser chiefs assisted the highest ranking elites, or *ariki*, in upholding the sociopolitical process. "Rank and leadership went by primogeniture (first-born) in senior families and purity of descent was jealously guarded by selection in marriage."[16]

Heeni was born to the *ariki* caste; however, it would be an offense for her to draw attention to this fact because this would be incorrect status behavior. In Māori society, one never brags about one's *whakapapa* (genealogy), which is usually kept secret anyway. Throughout her life, she remained humble—as she should—and never wanting to appear close, although she was, to *Te Ariki Nui*.

Traditionally, rangatira status meant different roles for males and females. Chiefly status was so ascribed because he, almost always a man, could trace his ancestry back to a leader of one of the iwi's canoes. He was considered *tapu* (sacred); the special status ensured he would be treated with the utmost respect. This deference extended to his hair, eating utensils, and sometimes to the ground on which he walked. When he visited other marae, a woman would be sent in the evening to bed with him, as Heeni said of her father, "to keep him warm."

Females in an aristocratic line were raised as *puhi* (virgins) and given in marriage to someone of similar status. The daughter was vigilantly watched to make sure she remained virginal for the ultimate plan of a political marriage. In higher society, marriage was a political instrument, and the girl's parents made the decision as to whom she would marry quite early in life.

Brought up as a puhi, Heeni was strictly guarded by her family. Ordinarily, her parents would have planned a political marriage. Her family, however, made the decision she was not to marry in the traditional sense, although her alternative "marriage" to the Methodist church was indeed a political one. Church leaders assumed all financial and spiritual responsibility for her at age 15; the union was consecrated in a small ceremony at her home in Mokau.

Marriage to the Church provided diplomatic reparations for the transgressions of her ancestors two generations previously—specifically, the mistaken murder of a prominent and loved Methodist minister, the Reverend John Whiteley, shot down by her great grandfather over an apparent misunderstanding over land. Heeni was thus handed over as a gift to heal the wound.[17]

The assault happened on February 13, 1869, near Heeni's home in Mokau. Whiteley, in his thirty-eighth year of ministry, had established himself as a peacemaker during the time of the land wars, earning respect from both Pākehā and Māori, even those who were traditional enemies such as Taranaki and Waikato peoples. A series of events led a war party from Waikato to take a blood oath to sacrifice anyone who might oppose their resolve to attack and destroy New Plymouth.

"Hearing the threat from the North and the reports of violence, Whiteley rode out hoping to be able to restrain and reason with the Māori forces and their leaders. As he rode up the sunken roadway near the Blockhouse, he was challenged and warned to go back, but replied that he could not do so when his 'children' were doing wrong. At this a shot was fired, by whom is not clear, and his horse fell under him. Whiteley dropped to his knees in prayer, and when further shots rang out, this fine old servant and friend of the Māori was killed."[18]

It was a terrible accident. When the Maniapoto leader, Wahanui, heard at Awakino the news of Whiteley's death, he said, "Here let it end, for the death of Whiteley is more than the death of many men . . ."[19] At the time Heeni was given over to the Church, she was unaware of these circumstances. It would be much later in life that she would discover, quite by accident, that she was given away for political reasons. The late Dave

Tūmōkai Pānapa explained, "One of the things you do is that you give the blessing of your best. And Heeni would have been what is known as a puhi in Māori Māoridom. What else can you dedicate to God but the very, very best of your tribe?"[20]

For both genders, marriage was viewed as a formal agreement between two family groups, not between two individuals. The Māori were patrilocal, so the newly married couple usually settled in the groom's village. In Heeni's case, the Methodist Church and its various mission locales became her new home. Also, it was the people of the Church who became completely responsible for her, as a groom's family would have if she had been traditionally married. This was a family of Church elders with whom her parents and *Kaumātua* (male elders) had already established a binding relationship.

A special class of experts held a different status outside the elite and commoner categories. *Tōhunga* were priests or shamans who had various degrees of religious specialization. They were skilled as artisans, such as weavers or carvers, or in the healing arts, such as specially trained doctors.

Heeni speaks candidly about her koro who was a healer, a seer—a tōhunga. As her first mentor, they shared a special relationship. His teachings left an indelible impression as he could see far in advance what life would be handing her, and he saw to it that she would be spiritually prepared for a world he, himself, could only imagine. Never did she wander far from the advice and counsel of her koro, even long after he was gone. His healing abilities also drew him to her. Early in life, she had contracted tuberculosis, and later she accidentally broke her arm in half. He treated her tuberculosis in a traditional manner and set and healed her arm as well.

Traditionally, childbirth was experienced differently depending on one's social status. For both castes, however, blood associated with menstruation and childbirth was considered extremely *tapu* (forbidden, polluted), so it was necessary to isolate the expectant mothers from the rest of the village. Commoners were born with little ceremony in a rough sort of shelter. The mother's mother and related women, as well as the husband, would help with the birth.

Among the aristocracy, however, childbirth was very elaborate. A special house was built where female attendants waited on the expectant mother. The most significant characteristic differentiating a commoner birth from an aristocratic one is the protocol for properly handling the umbilical cord. Among the aristocracy, it was handled in a very special manner. "The cutting of the cord was usually achieved with a sharp piece of flint and the cut was smeared with oil pressed from seeds of the titoki tree. The area was then dressed with the inner bark of the lacewood tree soaked in titoki oil. The dried cord after it separated from the navel, was placed in a cleft of rock, in a tree or buried on a (tribal) boundary, a method common throughout Polynesia."[21]

Because of the economic impact of colonization, on the surface, Heeni's birth was much like a commoner's birth, except for the special treatment of her umbilical cord. Heeni's father delivered her and all of her siblings, and he was the only one to know where the umbilical cord was buried. It can be assumed that it was most likely a tribal boundary because boundary issues intensified in the King Country after the great land confiscations.

The institution of adoption was practiced all over Polynesia. On some islands, 30% to 70% of households were involved with it in one way or another.[22] Parents who gave up a child or two to another family would accrue mana for doing so, especially if they were among the aristocracy and gave up their firstborn. According to Polynesian anthropologists, adoption is carried out for at least three reasons, all of which have to do with redistributing child wealth so that all families benefit. First, adoption serves as a "distributive mechanism, helping to equalize major imbalances in family size," because childless couples are seen as disadvantaged and even pitied in some circumstances.[23] Second, adoption offers a means for balancing the labor needs of a household. Children "serve as long-term economic insurance" because they eventually become important contributors to the family's economy.[24] Third, adoption is also a strategic means of maintaining cooperative relationships with other groups such that a network of interdependency is built and maintained. This is much like the political marriage discussed earlier that took ". . . priority over the wishes of individuals, even such strong wishes as attachments to one's natural children."[25]

John Terrell and Judith Modell have suggested that anthropologists have tended to apply Euramerican biases when analyzing adoption in Oceania, arguing that there is more to be said about the self-conscious gesture involved in creating kin and its diverse manifestations.[26] This is probably the case in Māoridom as none of the aforementioned reasons apply. Among Heeni's people, noble adoption was carried out to strengthen tribal and subtribal bonds in order to *secure bloodlines*. So important was the need to ensure the aristocratic pedigree of related marae that adoption would most likely be decided on before the child was even conceived. Over the years, Heeni's parents gave up their eldest son, another son, and a daughter. Her eldest brother was given over to a marae in Taranaki; eventually, he became a leader there. Heeni's father, who was a chief from Taranaki, had been more involved with the Tainui people as an adult. So his eldest son, the one with the most *mana*, was sent back to her father's iwi so that the family's precious bloodlines would not "move too far out," as Heeni puts it. In this way, the marae remained deeply connected through the generations. Now, whenever one of her family visits her brother's marae, they feel they are at home. The metaphorical importance of noble adoption becomes apparent when examining the meaning of the word *iwi*. Literally, it means *bone*. A child is adopted out to keep the bloodlines intact so that the bones, which represent the body of an iwi or hapū, are bound together forever. "Just as tribes are closely linked by a network of genealogical connections, so are the peoples related spiritually to their ancestral lands (including marae). And these relations have ethical implications."[27]

James and Jane Ritchie have called early Māori socialization the golden world of childhood.[28] Indeed, Māori children "grow up with a carefree abandon typical of Polynesians. They swim, run, dance, and play a host of different games."[29] At the same time, however, Māori children constantly learn from powerful elder influences in their family, extended family, and community. "The behavioral guidelines of the ancestors were monitored by living relatives, and the wishes of an individual were constantly balanced against the greater (good) and the concerns of the group."[30]

In traditional Polynesia, kinship terms were very often applied to a wide variety of friends and other relatives. "The words for mother and father generally applied to all relatives in the parental generation. Since children are considered to belong to the community, everyone in it is expected to act parentally—to comfort, to instruct, to admonish, to punish. This distributed pattern of parenting leads children to develop a range of emotional ties among adults, rather than investing almost exclusively in their biological parents."[31]

Thus, Māori kinship can be classified under the Hawaiian system, insofar as cousins were referred to as *brothers* and *sisters,* whereas aunts and uncles would be referred to as *mothers* and *fathers.* As Dave Tūmōkai Pānapa explained, "We don't have a very nuclear family, as do Pākehā. We have quite a wide family relationship and all my cousins, 26 cousins in fact, I refer to in Māori terms of either my brothers or my sisters. And this is where you get the term 'cuzzy bros' in New Zealand. He's my brother, but he's my cousin. So the relationships in Māoridom are very broad."[32] While Heeni was growing up, parental kinship terms extended not just to Māori elders, but also to Pākehā ones as well. Pākehā neighbors who owned ranches adjacent to Heeni's homestead were frequent visitors who bore food and gifts in the traditional Polynesian manner.

We have seen that adult Polynesian society is hierarchical; peer relations, however, are more horizontal than vertical. Having a common status with one's peers is a socialization principle, which tends to reinforce the consensus nature of Polynesian politics. "The capacity to drop yesterday's conflicts for today's cooperation is learned in children's activities, is reinforced in the games adolescents play, and is carried over into the political arenas of the adult world. It is not that conflicts do not matter, but they cannot be allowed to persist, and certainly should not be allowed to interfere with long-term social commitments."[33]

Girls and boys traditionally had different chores to do around the home. "Girls generally had more domestic responsibilities. Boys were permitted to roam farther from home, take more risks, and appeared to assert more authority within the peer group. In effect, the pattern of sex role specialization is as much a consequence of peer influences as of parental modeling."[34] In some ways, Heeni bridged both roles. On one hand, she was an avid sewer, making clothes for the family as well as for her dolls. On the other hand, she would be inclined to fix the sewing machine if it broke down. She also liked to tinker outside with old bicycles, guns, and other machinery, which was the role of a boy. Heeni worked a good bit outside with her father as well. She enjoyed helping him milk the cows and feed the animals. Both sexes in Heeni's family collected driftwood along the beach. However, it would be most accurate to say that for the most part, the boys did the fishing and pig hunting, while the girls did the food processing and cooking.

At puberty, boys and girls (commoners) were allowed to experiment with premarital intercourse. Freedom of intercourse between unmarried people was permitted until a young man or woman formed a more permanent attachment. "Among commoners this was particularly so. A couple lived together in a trial marriage and when they were satisfied with each other, they continued as man and wife officially."[35] This was not the case with Heeni, who, because of her puhi status, was strictly guarded. Her father was very fussy about whom she dated and how she spent her leisure time. Heeni accepted this without resentment, preferring pals, never lovers. She did not experiment sexually.

In terms of gender, the traditional status of Polynesian women is paradoxical. On one hand, they were viewed in terms of their essential moral and physical inferiority. Many anthropologists have made a strong case for male dominance in this region, which emphasizes male strengths and female weakness. "Traditionally, restrictions upon women were often formalized in the form of taboos and were backed by supernatural sanctions. In many Polynesian cultures, women were barred from sacred places, from contact with men's fishing gear, and from consuming certain kinds of food. Menstruating women were generally considered unclean, and were secluded to a greater or lesser degree. The common notion was that women are especially vulnerable to capricious supernatural influence when menstruating; hence, they must be confined in order to avoid accidental disruption of supernatural-human relationships."[36] Anthropologists have observed indicators of low status for women, including enforced virginity and a marked subordination of wives to husbands within the domestic sphere. Goldman, for example, provides a summary of gender relations among Māori: "By associating women with childbirth—a passive sexual role—and with darkness and misfortune, the Māori inevitably stigmatized descent through females. Masculine-feminine was viewed religiously as complementary and antagonistic. The masculine represented the sky, light, and divine descent; the feminine represented darkness, the earth, and the underworld."[37]

These analyses, however, may be more or less true in the present. Contemporary Māori would consider the role of men and women as complementary; there is a fine balance between the male–female elements and corresponding roles. Heeni's narrative seems to confirm that the traditional Māori conflict between the sexes is passé. Although Heeni resented the limitations imposed on her because of her menstrual period, she never spoke of her private parts as obnoxious or polluted. Heeni's narrative also suggests that Māori wives can and do enjoy high status. Her father treated her mother with the utmost respect and caring. In one example, Heeni tells a story about how her father saved the prized piece of the family's fish for her "mum" on a regular basis. As far as enforced virginity goes, Heeni saw this as a positive with nothing restrictive about it.

Moreover, Māori women of high status play active political roles in modern New Zealand. Indeed, the two most influential indigenous political leaders of the twentieth century have been women—the late Princess Te Puea, and Te Arikinui Dame Te Atairangikaahu, Te Ariki Nui, the present-day Māori queen. Princess Te Puea courageously fought the New Zealand government about enforced conscription measures during World War I and almost single-handedly built a cultural renaissance in the Waikato after her people suffered intense poverty, famines, and disease brought on by European land confiscation and warfare of the 1860s. Te Arikinui Dame Te Atairangikaahu is most noted not only for cementing alliances between the Māori and the Pākehā of New Zealand, but also for using the power of her office to build alliances with heads of state, activists, and others all over the world.

Some Māori women play more passive, but equally powerful, roles. Heeni would fall into this category. She provides quiet, behind-the-scenes counsel to the queen and other Tainui leaders. Panapa describes her purpose: "From my perception, the role that she has with Te Ariki Nui is like a confidante, someone who's there but isn't there. Heeni is someone Te Arikinui Dame Te Atairangikaahu can turn to and talk with at any time. One of the Queen's daughters was named after her, after all. The eldest. So that's the kind of mana Heeni's holding, the Queen's first born named after her."[38]

As one of the senior matriarchs of her people, her presence is sought after at ceremonial events such as tangi and hui. Heeni remains quite visible sitting quietly and humbly as a living conduit—a bridge between the old ways and the new and as a symbol of all that it means to be a Māori woman—kind, humble, and serene. Dave Tūmōkai Pānapa again: "To me she portrays and embodies all that is wonderful in womanhood. She's the living personification of human humility. She certainly never pushed herself to the front of things, but has always been there in the background, to help, to advise, and to counsel. We know that things are well because of her presence. By sitting in the meeting house, she keeps us warm."[39]

RELIGION

Two concepts are essential for understanding traditional Māori religion. These are *tapu* and *mana*. Tapu has two distinct usages: one active and the other more passive. In an active sense, *tapu* suggests a contained *sacred* potency that inhabits some thing, place, or person, meaning that the subject is connected to the divine. It refers to the deference, respect, and reverence associated with a great ariki, for example. Likewise, the *whakapapa* (genealogy) of an ariki is considered tapu: "Whakapapa is one of the most prized forms of knowledge and great efforts are made to preserve it."[40]

Paradoxically, *tapu* refers to something that contaminates some essential purity. As mentioned previously, mixing body and food elements is considered tapu. Likewise, the blood associated with menstruation and childbirth is considered polluted, dangerous, and *forbidden*. In this more passive sense, tapu orders the Māori world by establishing categories of behavior that ensure divine protection. Bodily well-being among traditional Māori actually depends on the social world, governed by laws of tapu. "Any transgression of the laws of tapu lead to the withdrawal of divine protection. (One's life force) is then exposed to the influence of malevolent spirits. Illness with a non-observable physical cause was attributed to an attack on the life force by the spirits."[41]

The other term is *mana*, loosely translated as prestige. The Polynesian concept of mana, although often used with reference to chiefs, is usually tied to the powers of the gods. An elite ancestry is therefore linked to powerful mana. However, mana can also be a benevolent influence that intercedes between divine and human affairs. Therefore, those who are not ariki can also demonstrate high mana levels. In this way, *mana* refers to the positive effects created by some intrinsic, vital force, not necessarily the force itself, but rather the quality of its magnificence as it manifests in the world. It becomes visible and then attributable to certain people in terms of outstanding achievement, generosity, intelligence, beauty, and other qualities of abundance. Mana is not fixed; indeed, it can be quite fickle. One can gain or lose mana, modulating according to a person's relative success or failure in maintaining good social relations. Heeni's mana stems both from her aristocratic ancestry and her good deeds.

During her childhood, Heeni's family's religion centered on Māori gods who had life-giving and life-taking powers.[42] They saw all nature as alive, containing hidden and mysterious supernatural powers. They believed people should live in harmony with the land, respecting it as property of the gods. Certain proscribed rituals were meant to ensure a continued bounty of food from the sea and the land. In her narrative, she mentions offering the first fish of a catch to the god Tangaroa. To Māori, a fish in the sea is a child of this god, watched over by potent local guardians. "Tangaroa is (also) the god of lakes and rivers, with dominion over all creatures which live in them. Tāne Mahuta is lord and master of the forests and the birds of *Rehua* (caretaker bird of life)."[43] Māori thus had a responsibility to protect the life force of the animals in each god's dominion: "The resources of the natural world were not to be abused. Even essential food resources were to be approached with care and used with respect."[44]

Encounters with *kēhua*—ghosts, spirits, and visitations from ancestors—are part of Māori life, especially in traditional communities. Heeni discusses personal encounters of this kind. In her tradition, a ghost-sighting heralded the news of a relative's death. Her father saw ghosts, and her mother could hear them, while Heeni herself was sentiently aware of them. They applied pressure on her clavicle and shoulders at different times throughout her life.

As discussed earlier, tōhunga were Māori religious practitioners most directly concerned with spiritual matters. Tōhunga were ranked hierarchically according to various criteria and training levels. Among the senior class were fully trained doctors, military leaders, craftsman, and agricultural experts. They knew ventriloquism, hypnotism, and telepathy and used these to heal and otherwise help their communities.

Tōhunga doctors used a combination of herbs and rituals to produce cures. In more difficult cases, they would meet with a collection of elders to discuss the psychological reasons for someone's illness. This was a special discussion called a *muruhara*, where emphasis was placed on discovering the psychosocial imbalance that created the illness and making things right, orderly, and correct again. "Intrafamilial conflicts were especially likely to be seen as a cause of ill-fortune, and steps were taken to resolve them, and to restore the harmony that is a precondition for health and prosperity. The notion is that interpersonal entanglements are a major cause of illness and bad fortune, and that clearing up entanglements—setting things straight again—is a necessary condition for healing to occur, especially in instances where the malady is persistent. In her narrative, Heeni mentions such a ritual that occurred early on in her childhood. She remembered that tōhunga and koro would often determine that a ritual would be required to clear away the anger and hostility that obstructed the patient's road to recovery.

Heeni's elders were experts in Māori culture. Her spiritual foundation thus rested on the family's experience with the natural world, the teachings of her koro, and Māori training at home. However, Christian ideas were to texture her traditional upbringing as well, because she and her family became increasingly influenced by the Pākehā world.

Heeni was exposed to Anglo culture because, like many Māori, her family was drawn into a cash economy due to poverty resulting from land losses in the nineteenth century. Methodist missionaries had also long been active in Heeni's iwi area. They journeyed throughout the Waikato holding bible studies and Sunday school classes. By the time Heeni was ready to leave home, she had become very familiar with the mission work of Sister Margaret Nicholls (1894–1967) and the Reverend Arthur John Seamer (1887–1963). Both made a great impression on her as a young girl and were loyal friends when she became an adult.

Sister Nicholls was a pioneering deaconess who became a legend in Church circles. "For many years she was a familiar figure in the Waikato and King Country, covering vast distances (alone) on her horse. She would carry a rolled up blanket attached to the saddle so that she could spend the night wherever she happened to be. When she acquired a gig, she could take her mother's little sewing machine so that she could help women to sew. Taking Bible in schools, holding women's meetings, gathering children for Sunday school, wherever she went she experienced warm hospitality."[45]

Heeni's family also held Father Seamer in high esteem. He was sensitive to the political problems brought on by the land confiscations and utterly devoted to ameliorating Māori poverty. Many admired his work with Māori youth. He organized a mixed choir, which toured the country and overseas, performing traditional Māori music for eager Pākehā audiences.

After about age 10, Heeni attended the local Ratana Church—where Christian, Māori, and mystical elements were merged simultaneously. Heeni's koro was a leader there. The Ratana Chuch was founded by Tahupotiki Wiremu Ratana. In 1918, he had a vision in which he saw the angel Gabriel and his message was that Ratana should be a mouthpiece for God's work. Ratana began work as a healer, and the movement evolved into a political and religious movement to unite all Māori. His vision immediately allowed him to perform curing miracles, which drew him a large following at a time when Māori were enduring cultural and humanitarian crises. "This movement first developed as one centered on Divine Healing. . . . Underneath all Māori restlessness lay their unhappiness about land, and their dissatisfaction with the handling of the Treaty of Waitangi by successive Colonial Governments. Many Māori had also read much of the Old Testament as reflection of the experiences of the Māori Race, and there had been those who had used this to expound a doctrine of the Māori being one of 'The Lost Ten Tribes of the House of Israel.' From this there eventually rose a steady expectation of a Messianic deliverer . . ."[46] People came from all over New Zealand to Ratana pa to hear his teachings and to receive the grace of a cure.

By 1924, Ratana followers, who had begun ministering their own weddings and baptisms, were putting pressure on the Reverend Seamer to help them create their own legitimate church. Ratana leaders, like Heeni's koro, were chosen as lay ministers. They came from very different folkways and backgrounds, and their preaching drew upon the traditions from which they originally came. By the late 1920s, the Ratana Church, based on a syncretic blend of Christian and Māori teachings, with the official backing of the Methodists, had become the church of choice for a large proportion of Māori people.

It has been suggested that some Māori, such as Heeni, who have been meaningfully exposed to both cultural traditions, have few problems negotiating between traditional Māori religious forms and Christianity. The late Dave Tūmōkai Pānapa explained, "Similar Māori concepts were already well in place with the arrival of Christianity. For example, we had a belief in a supreme being (in addition to lesser gods). Sister Heeni's spirituality not only comes from the church in which she became a very, very strong Christian, but also from the Māori side of her; that spirituality was all around her, and with her all the time. She carries that well, as do most Māori people."[47]

WARFARE

Institutionalized warfare is a hallmark of Polynesian and Māori culture. Traditionally, insult, adultery, or revenge could provoke war. Or it could be brought on by trade disputes or battles for territory. For example, if the resources in one area became depleted, the village would have to rely on other resources nearby, which may have been the exclusive territory of another village. This would provoke attack and bring the demand for *utu* (retribution), which would eventually lead to war. "War was a military science to the Māori. The experienced leader had a number of formations and plans of attack and defenses to choose from. The use of ambush and surprise attack was a common strategy. Generally, an attacking party made its way into enemy territory and attacked fortified villages. The villages were contrived such that the defenders could stone and stab at the attackers from a height advantage. In this way the force of attack could be checked and the strength of the enemy dissipated."[48] Some pās were unusually strong and never taken. To have succeeded, the enemy would have to scale huge cliffs or some other major obstacle to gain entry.

Like other Polynesians, the Māori were cannibals who ate the flesh of dead enemies as part of a tradition of ceremonial warfare. After battle, the victors used the slain for food. Cannibalism served two purposes in Māori culture. First, it satisfied a hunger for meat, which was extremely scarce before the arrival of Europeans. Second, it served a psychological purpose by reducing enemy chiefs to the lowly status of food.

Unlike the heavy clubs and spears used in the rest of the South Pacific, Māori weapons were lighter and easier to handle. Like all of the material culture among the Māori, they were crafted with intricate carving designs. Battling opponents sparred using short, quick blows. "Only when an opening was offered would a spear be plunged into its target, or the heavy end brought down in a hard blow."[49] In Māori combat, the opponents watched not the other's eyes, but rather, they would watch their big toes because they could ascertain by the movement of the toes, the direction and timing of a coming wallop. A severe blow came from the shoulder after the opponent took a firm stance by gripping the ground.

The Tainui have been critical of the anthropological tendency to glamorize Māori warfare. They suggest instead that warfare in which people actually died and then were eaten was far less frequent than anthropologists tend to imply. Proof of this lies in the sophisticated development of Māori arts. The intricate development of musical and other artistic achievement requires prolonged periods of peace. If the Māori were continually at war, how would they have had the time to develop these art forms? The Tainui suggest that there was perhaps an equal balance between peacetime and wartime, so peaceful undertakings could develop and prosper. A culture that was perpetually fighting would not have been able to survive. The people would have been paranoid and focused on survival, unable to create the kind of sophisticated material culture found among the wealthy Māori.

MUSIC AND ART

With no written language, their tribal history was passed on in story-telling, but also in a rich tradition of song, dance, and arts and crafts. Their musical tradition is full of allusions to Māori mythology, past and present. "If ever humans sang and made music to fulfill themselves, it was the Māori, and any man or woman who could do both well was assured of respect . . ."[50] Each song, instrument, and dance expressed a certain purpose. "Every song had its point—an orator could drive home an argument, a pleader could sway his listeners into compliance, each one with a culminating point; a telling illustration; a flash of revelation."[51] For example, a particular song or dance could summon help with some special project or to gain courage to face enemies before battle. Hence, the famous *haka* performance before modern rugby games.

"The most impressive dance of the Māori was, and still is, the haka, which would be used for either welcoming guests or defying enemies. It is a posture dance and may be described as a series of rhythmical movements of limbs and body,

Haka Dancer Carving

accompanied by song or by a number of short refrains. Both men and women took part. The most striking features of the haka are the distortions of the face and the incredibly good timing of song with actions. A skilled haka party moves and sounds as one man."[52] The purpose of the haka in war was not only to intimidate the enemy (the tongue was ejected wildly according to the rhythm of the chant), but also to energize the warriors to give them the courage necessary for enduring the hand-to-hand combat typical of Māori warfare. The haka was composed by a war chief—Te Rauparaha—during a flight from kawhia. It has been said that it was composed above the ranges of Maniaroa Marae, where Heeni is from:[53]

Ka mate, ka mate, Death, death,
Ka ora, ka ora: Life, life,
Ka mate, ka mate: Death, death,
Ka ora, Ka ora: Life, life
Tenei te tangata puhuruhuru: This is the hairy man
Nana i tiki mai i whakawhiti te roa: Who causes the sun to shine
Upane, kaupane: Up and up,
Upane, kaupane: Up and up,
Whiti te ra The sun to shine.

Another traditional type of dance is called the *poi* dance. It is just as striking, but not as dynamic. This dance is traditionally performed by young women who gracefully twirl two balls attached to short lengths of string—one in each hand. All the while, the women sing with balls twirling, while their bodies move gracefully to the time of the music. It is very pleasing to watch.

Musical instruments carved from wood accompanied song and dance. The carving of musical instruments and other artwork required expert care. Carvers used special adzes, useful for trimming and smoothing wood. An adze was also an everyday utensil for doing such activities as hollowing canoes and building houses. Because it was so important, it had another meaning as well; it was also a symbol of ownership and tribal pride. Carvers also made *tiki* out of *greenstone* (jade). Some anthropologists have described tiki as grotesque squatted figures, but to the Māori, these are living spiritual entities that represent certain ancestors. They hang around the neck of a relation. They were also seen as fertility symbols revered for sentimental reasons.

Whatewha: Traditional Adze

Carved musical instruments included drums and gongs, wind instruments such as the native flute, and stringed instruments. "The Māori had no skin drums, but used large wooden gongs and castanets. The war gong was constructed out of an oblong piece of wood about six feet long with a groove in the centre. It was suspended on the watch tower platform and beaten by a sentry who called the watchword of alarm after every stroke. The sound travelled about 12 miles. Castanets of wood or bone were made and used with a pair in each hand."[54]

Wind instruments included a native flute and a trumpet. Trumpets, called *pū*, were made from shells, flax, wood, and composites of wood and shell. Pū would be used to assemble the people, to announce the coming of visitors or the news of an aristocratic birth. Flutes were called *putorino*. These were about 18 inches long with stop-holes for playing a tune. In the trademark Māori way, all instruments were lavishly decorated and elaborately carved. "Wooden instruments would be carved and often inlaid with glittering *paua* (like abalone) shell."[55]

Even though European melodies have replaced many of the traditional Māori ones, music has remained an integral part of Māori community life. "If you ever go to a Māori settlement, or to a place where there is an active Māori community these days you will be able to appreciate

The Tiki

what an important part music plays in their lives. From earliest childhood, they sing, whether at work or play. From the introduction of radio to the advent of television, Māori voices have had great success in competitions, song quests, and other performances."[56] Small Māori groups perform everywhere in the world, and certain Māori individuals, like Inia Te Wiata and Kiri Te Kanawa, have left an indelible mark on the arts in New Zealand.

1 / The Early Years at Kamate

After the child is born, the umbilical cord is taken and buried on the land, along tribal boundaries. A very important concept in Māoridom; you are a part of that land forever; it is a part of you forever. That is why the land could never be sold.

Dave Tūmōkai Pānapa

MY FATHER BROUGHT us all into the world. It was September 22, 1912, when I was born in a mud-floor ponga house in Kamate, just south of the family cemetery.

After a baby was born, the umbilical cord would be wrapped in several layers of material and immediately taken away and buried. It was given back to the earth, and its burial place was considered very special. Up and down the land, and all along the coast down there, there would be special sort of tapu places where cords were buried. And that is why there is such a fuss about Māori land. This was a traditional custom, and that is why women didn't go to hospitals, because they knew that the medical people there would flush that special part down the sink, and that sort of thing. My father was the only one to know where my cord was buried.[1]

A Māori birth happened in the home. The mother would know pretty well when the time was near, and then these ladies would come, sometimes with their husbands, and everyone would just sort of help. Birth would be attended by older women, who would do this sort of thing for young mothers, the young girls. But my dad did most of it for my birth. Māori women didn't often have a prolonged labour, because they'd be active up until the last minute. They'd just move around the home, doing chores.[2]

It didn't always run smoothly. My dad's first wife died while giving birth to twins. Dad remarried my mum. It was an arranged marriage. He was a good bit older. Perhaps a good eight or so years older. My mum was tall, taller than my dad, but slight of build. She grew up in the nearby town of Te Kūiti in a good, clean, yet Māori way of life. My mum and dad, my dad especially, were experts in Māori culture and traditions. My mum and my koro always emphasised that we should never forget our Māori culture. And they made sure that we didn't. Mum had very good manners. She was also very keen for us to learn the European way of life. She was part European herself, her great-grandfather being French. Her last name was Hetet. Yes, my great-great-grandfather was a Frenchman. Mum was always neat. Whatever she wore—it was always just a skirt and then something over to keep her warm— was always neat and clean. She thought we should always be polite and clean. She wanted us to be tidy, tidy, tidy about our personal appearance and everything. She taught us to be gentle and kindly, no matter where we were or what we were doing.

A mud-floor ponga house like the one I was born in.

Mum only finished Standard One at school, but that was very common for Māori women in those days. Her English was fairly good, but her reading and spelling were poor. She'd often pick up the newspaper and pretend to read it as if she were an expert. I didn't know this at the time, but I found out from my brother Paddy much later. It shows how much she valued education, and had we had the money I think Paddy would've gone to Wesley College. I think he had the mind, but we just didn't have the money. We had lots of land, but no real cash to speak of.

What I remember most about my mum is that she was a very caring person, and many people sought her company. Lots of relations would come by to spend the day with her. They'd chat away or sew together. I loved my mum, and I can quite honestly say that I never ever got any growling from her. Whenever I was naughty she'd just pull my ear and say, 'No, no, no, you mustn't do that.' If I was being cheeky to the others, she just took me aside and said no; that was enough for me.

Like in most Māori households, there was a special emphasis placed on honesty. Mum always stressed the importance of leaving things alone that didn't belong to you. Always be honest. Dad backed her up on all of that too. They were fairly united in their way of life and in their outlook, I think. I can remember on several occasions seeing money sitting on the mantelpiece. It was about half-a-crown, I think. In those days we used a different kind of money from today. I'm sure those coins were put there to test us kids. They'd lie around there until they were needed, but no-one ever failed the test.

My father was an upright sort of fellow, and all of us kids respected our dad. Quite early on in my life I remember sitting down to tea on woven flax mats laid out on the floor, although later we sat at a table. My father was always at the head at mealtimes. And I can remember the staple of our diet was always seafood. I remember having fish, fish, fish. Seafood was always a wonderful meal to us, and the head

My mother, Mahora (left), and maternal aunt, Tira Tumoha, at Otaki in the early 1950s.

of the fish was the most valued part. The best part really, in the Māori years. And Dad would say to us, 'The head part of the fish goes to your mum; she'll have that part of the fish.' Oh, he really loved her. That's how we would begin the meal. Yes, I've said this many times, I've said it in Papa's presence too. Never did I hear any cross words between my mum and dad. We never heard our parents argue. They seemed to us to be a very loving sort of couple. They worked together, and they moved together; they were partners in everything they did.

I grew up in a chiefly Māori atmosphere, I guess you could say. Though it wasn't talked about a great deal, I had an idea my dad was recognised as a chief from his home tribe, Taranaki. Because of this, I was brought up in that very guarded Māori traditional way of life. Anybody can say they were a princess. I wouldn't like to be labelled that, but there was some nobility there, coming through the lines of life. I was raised as a puhi. Dad was always very fussy with me.[3]

When the boys came in from work, sure they'd been working hard all day, they'd tidy up and put on something clean, and we'd all sit around together. I think my mum was very precious to my dad. And they worked together out on the plantation. To my mum, when we were growing up, my dad was the only man around. I think she simply adored him. They were never too far apart. They'd go down to the beach to pick up mussels and they'd carry the catch together.

My father, Ihakara, in the early 1900s. J. Bragge

Dad was average height, not a big man like most Māori men. As I say, when I was a young girl I had an idea that he was a chief, but I didn't know for sure until his death. At his tangi, I overheard women-folk from Taranaki talking. They said that when my dad was alive and travelled among his people, he was treated as a big chief. In the traditional way, they would build up a bed for him, one mattress on top of the other—very special.[4]

In those days when a chief came to visit a marae, they would arrange for a woman to share his company on the evening of his arrival. Even if he was married. Moving around in those days was heavy going, on horses—very little in the way of cars in those days. If they were moving down the coast, they'd have to wait according to the tides before they could cross over the river. They'd arrive there really tired, and this was just the thing to revive them. An elderly chief would be provided with someone to keep him warm and cosy and nice. In bed, you know, the bed made up specially, and in the very private part of the meeting house, and it would be known. That was the highest sort of honour for a chief. This is real Māori tradition. I had an idea about this sort of thing, because I used to hear them talk—'and when Dad stayed over they'd build up a bed for him on very high mattresses and he'd be given a young woman of very high rank'.

Now, if the girl became pregnant, the child would be adopted out. I mean, adopted out by *her* family. The child wouldn't come into *our* family. But he or she would be recognised. And it would be fine. He or she would be raised by another family and the child would be considered well connected. My grandparents were the last generation to do this. There are some of those children still around.

My mum and dad were a good couple. She always treated him as a noble person, and I think he treated my mum the same, because she was also from a prominent family from her tribe, which is Maniapoto.

I grew up in a large Māori home. There were ten of us kids, although three were adopted out. It was the custom among the elite for a Māori family to give up some of their children to other couples.[5] Babies were taken immediately at birth so that it would be easier on Mum, and also on the child, I suppose. I know it must have been difficult, very difficult, but this was Māori custom. The child was usually given to someone fairly close who wanted a child but didn't have one. This is something very deep. It was done to tie up links between people, to connect families if the relationship had become too far out. Two of my brothers and one of my sisters were taken, yes. One of my brothers was given over to the Parihaka marae at Taranaki, my dad's people. He became a leader on the marae. It was to bring in the connection again, because Dad got away from that marae, where he was brought up. It's done so that any one of us can now go that marae and still feel that's our marae too. It's done to keep our communal tradition alive. With my eldest brother it was the same sort of thing. He went to Wellington. These were connections on my father's side. From my father's family's point of view, he had become very involved with my mum's people, Tainui. They thought he'd gone too far out.[6]

I think my parents were marvellous. They were very dedicated and steeped in Māori culture, absolutely steeped in it. There was a great deal of aroha in our home. It was a little wee home, but we were surrounded with a great deal of care and aroha. My koro, Tainui Wētere, was another source of caring and wisdom. I adored him, really. I think that, quite possibly, I was very close to my koro because he healed my arm after I broke it when I fell from a horse.

One day there were several of us kids playing on horses. We were climbing around on them and pulling their tails. I think I was about eight years old. Well, a few of us got on one horse. We fell playing on that horse. I wasn't alone, but I was the one everyone fell upon, you see. It happened along in Mōkau at the old gathering place. There was a hui on, so we were all outside playing while our parents were there at the hui. When everyone fell on top of me, it was noticed fairly quickly by the parents. The other kids didn't get hurt, but I did. I blacked out. When I came to, my arm was sort of wrapped up, and I'll never forget the pain. It took a long time to heal, but my koro attended to it in the Māori way, and this cemented the bond between him and me. There has always been a sort of weakness in this arm, and it is becoming more apparent today. As I get older, it is becoming more distinct. Last night, for instance, I woke up and the whole arm was numb. When I was young, I sometimes had to be excused from school activities, such as swimming or other exercise, because I couldn't do it. But the Pākehā people knew that Janey (as they called me) had fallen off the horse and her arm was broken at the elbow, here.

My koro—and there were other elders involved too—bound up my arm; and it took quite a while for it to come together. What they did, I don't know. While it was healing, my koro told me to keep my mind on my work and to look above. My koro could do certain things; he knew that there's a greater power to help with the healing. I think for him to tell me that was quite something, because it reinforced what I'd always known—that my koro was a very great man.[7]

My arm took a long time to heal, but I know my koro did do a good job of setting it. Later, when I went to have it examined by a specialist, this doctor complimented my koro's work. He didn't want to do anything further with it, just wanted to leave it as it was. He did a pretty good job, I guess. That's what the doctor said.

While my arm was healing, I used to go and see my koro for therapy. I think there was beginning to form in my mind a notion that there was something beyond what the body alone could sense and observe. He used to take me into his very small, tiny, little house where I would find lots of things that would puzzle me. He was our tohunga. He was also an āpōloro, which is the Māori word for a minister, mostly used in association with the Rātana movement. I would go into his place there on the beach, because I had great affection for him even at a very young age. I knew he was healing my arm, and I was drawn to him. And I listened very hard to the things that he'd tell me.

The first thing he tried to instill in my mind was not to be afraid of anything. Fear not. Because in those days people were still afraid of silly things. They were afraid of the dark, for example. But I used to listen to my koro, and the things my parents told me, and this brought me up not to be afraid of anything. He told me that when I grew up my hands would not be the tools of the Pākehā, but rather the instruments of te runga rawa. He said all this to me in Māori. I'm translating it into English, which sometimes loses its real power. But I think what he meant was as long as I knew where true power emanated from, then I had no reason to fear. Fear not.

My koro would talk to me about old Māori custom. He himself was very old at that time. He must have been eighty, and was a little blind, I used to help him along. So he'd tell me about certain things. He was a believer in the highest being, and he knew that his own healing power came from this source. The Pākehā can't say that they brought the notion of a supreme creator here to New Zealand. Some would like to believe that, but it isn't true. Since I've moved away and travelled around various circles up and down this country, talking to folks, I am sure that my people already had a notion of a supreme creator. We call it te runga rawa. The tohunga knew their power came directly from te runga rawa, from a wāhi, or from a very deeply hidden and secret place.

My koro knew that I would be going into many strange and unfamiliar situations when I grew up. He was preparing me for the future, when I'd be going into situations quite different from my home background. So the second thing he instilled in my mind was to lift my thoughts up to te runga rawa before I entered a strange marae, or a strange house outside my own area. He said, 'Always stop for a minute or two and say a little prayer for guidance and protection.' Later I knew the reason for this.

It was to connect myself with my Māori thoughts, even in Pākehā situations. My Māori thoughts would come uppermost and forward in mind, before I went into new or Pākehā situations. It was good training, because even though I've been deeply involved in the Pākehā world, my Māori thoughts have never wandered from me. I've kept that sort of contact always. I've never wandered from my beginnings. I've never talked with others about this. I believe it should be said, though, because most people don't know Heeni.

The first time I went into my koro's house, I saw rats running around. He said to me, 'Don't take any notice of what you see around here.' At that stage, I didn't ask what these rats were doing. But I knew later that a rat could talk to my koro, and rat actions could mean something quite special. He lived right down on the sea coast, right near where the tide came in. He lived very close to nature, and this was just his lifestyle.

My koro had a lot of other things lying around that were old Māori taonga. A taonga is what you Pākehā might see at a museum. It's something fairly precious. It could be a piece of greenstone, or it could be a piece of carving. He had a carved walking stick too. All of these things would be hanging around in his house, which I didn't dare touch. I knew they were very special. I knew they were tapu taonga. In his house there were other special things that you could hear. Unusual sounds and so forth. But I was brought up in a traditional way, so I did not see these things as strange. I knew they were spirits of power. I knew right from the time when I was only eight, even younger, that my koro was a very powerful, special man. He was the spiritual leader of our people; no-one tried to be above him.

When people got sick, he took care of them. Oh yes, I wasn't the only one that he was attending to. Don't get me wrong there. It was just that he made such a great impression on me at a very young age. When he healed my arm, I sort of felt—well, that my koro was part of my body now.

My koro helped me quite a bit in other ways. He helped me to understand things in my own mind. He knew I'd be joining the Church and living by Christian love, but he also knew that I knew about a time way back—way, way back—when the people were very warlike. It didn't bother me, really. I knew my own people were essentially good, but I did find out that they did some cruel things to each other.[8] Way back then, it was different circumstances, so my koro helped me to understand this. He told me, 'I know you already know that your people ate one another. But forget about that; forget about all of it. Don't let that cloud your mind.' This was impressed upon me very much, to the point where it became like a statement in my own head.

And, of course, at the time I knew there was still a lot of mākutu. *Mākutu* means to bewitch someone or to cast a spell. Something like sorcery, when you're using supernatural forces to hurt others. Yes, my koro said that it would so cloud their minds that it could mean instant death to the one casting the spell. He warned me that a spell could be cast on someone by another who was jealous. Sometimes, he said to me, you might find yourself among those who were hateful and would resort to mākutu to keep you from moving along with your calling. My koro believed it was necessary to clear the minds of the people who still dwelt in that time. He thought we had to become more reasonable. My koro would invite people to bring their magical items to be cleansed. Any evil spirits that were associated with those taonga would be purified. Of course, he gathered a tremendous following.

There weren't many people living around us in Kamate. We were there on a small farm. The house we lived in had a mud floor and was built from the trunks of ponga ferns. It was rectangular, not too wide but fairly long. One area was designated for eating, one for sleeping and one for important discussions, which were often held at our house.

The eating area was the main one, down at one end of the house where there was a fireplace and a chimney stack made of galvanized iron. Around the fireplace hung a big kettle and other pots; this was where all the cooking was done. We had one table, but no chairs. At Kamate we mostly sat down on the floor to eat, on woven flax mats.

Flax played a big role in our lives.[9] One of its uses was cleansing the inside of the body. It was taken to clean your tummy and intestines. The roots of flax plants would be scraped and boiled, and, boiled and boiled. We were then given a dose of this stuff, which we had to drink obediently. I think it was about a teaspoonful. This was a ritual which was done fairly rigidly in my home. It was horrid stuff. Someone said it was comparable to quinine, with the same effect. I can remember it being horrible to take. We must have been fairly obedient kids, because we did what we were told, even though it was miserable. This potion was supposed to help with tuberculosis, which I contracted at age seven.

My mum and dad had a great knowledge of herbs and natural remedies, because there were no doctors. Mum would just go into the bush above the home there and get the right kind of herbs for whatever was the problem. I missed out on all that, because I left home at an early age. The right kind of shrub or other plant would be put on a cut, and no more pain. Today I can't feel comfortable with what the Māori people are telling the Pākehā about our botanical uses some ninety or a hundred years ago. Because my mind goes back, and I wonder if it's the right kind of plant they're preparing in the right way as my mum did.

Well, we used flax for weaving kits too. Kits are containers for holding things. Some would be like purses, used to hold your handkerchief or powder puff on very special occasions. Others would be used for weeding, or for carrying potatoes. All of these would be woven from flax. The tightly woven ones were for a special occasion, the loose ones for helping with the harvest. All the different kinds of kits were kept separate from one another.

You see, we didn't mix things in those days. For instance, mussel kits would be hung up outside, and washed in basins that wouldn't be used for clothing and body cleansing. Totally different. Kits and basins were kept quite apart from each other, depending on their function.[10]

Before I was born, people made their clothes from flax. Mrs Rangimarie Hetet has just had her hundredth birthday, and she's known to be the finest traditional weaver in New Zealand alive today. She still makes piupiu (skirts) and korowai (cloaks). I had one or two skirts, but I've given them away. The flax used for skirts and clothing is very, very fine. It's gathered from special places, or it's grown specially by the weaver herself. You gather it, and then you prepare it by boiling it if you want your clothing to last. You boil it for so many hours and then you hang it up to dry. After it's been processed, a special dye is used to add colouring. This is a traditional dye, not a bought one. The dye comes from a certain kind of mud in the South Island. You bury the flax in that mud and leave it there for several days. Then you take it out of the ground. After it's been stained black, which is traditional Māori, you weave your garment. Kiwi feathers might be added as well. Traditional clothing was made of flax and kiwi feathers.

Traditionally, skirts and cloaks wouldn't have too many ornaments on them. In the days before the Pākehā came, the clothing of chiefs would be just dead plain. Not too many of the tassels you see hanging on the ones today in tourist areas. But there were certain cloaks for working in, and other ones for sleeping in, and still others for gatherings and social events. There were certain cloaks for bad weather, ones which would make the rain just fall away.

The women did all the weaving, and they'd spend hours making clothes and mats.[11] Though my mum didn't weave our clothes, she did weave huge mats which we used like carpeting on the floor when we lived at Kamate. First the floor would be lined with old flour sacks, and then layers of woven mats would be piled on top. These mats were woven from wider strips, so they could be constructed in a very short time. In Kamate we slept on these layers in rough sort of mud-floor sheds, which were next to the main house. Yes, that part was reserved for sleeping. We slept in there, two or three people to a bed. Sometimes we just slept in our clothes, the ones we went around in after we got home from school.

We had several layers to sleep on; I can't ever remember being cold. Of course, we had blankets in those days, because civilisation was just coming in. Before that, the people might have used dried ferns and flax to cover up with. At marae meeting houses, at hui, people slept in the same room. In those days it was very, very tapu that you had your own mat and slept on it by yourself. You could only step over another's mat if it was one of your own family group. That was fairly strictly kept until just quite recently, that you keep to your own individual space.

Our life at Kamate sort of revolved around animals. Mum and Dad were farmers I suppose, but on a very small scale. I can't remember how many cows we had, but probably less than twenty. I can remember seeing one of those cows calve, so there must have been a bull around somewhere. I just stood there in amazement and thought, now what's the matter with this cow? Because she was grunting, and she was out there on her own. I could see there was something strange, and then suddenly I think I saw legs, and this fascinated me. So I just stood there and watched the whole thing come out. And then she was licking it; it was just lying there. I don't know how long I stood there on my own out in the paddock watching this. I remember the colour, and the long legs, and I thought, fancy this thing coming out of there. The cow didn't seem to mind me, but I didn't get too close. And then I saw this little ugly thing with long legs begin to move quietly, very quietly. And then it tried to stand up. It was so feeble, absolutely. At that stage I wondered if I should go up, then I thought, no—I'm not going to interfere here. By the time that calf stood up, the cow had licked it pretty well, and it was sort of clean. And her mind was on this little calf. I can still see it today. I was fascinated really, and quite curious. It was a couple of my aunties who explained these things to me later on.

One of my chores was to be up at dawn to milk the cows. You see, we had to send the cream to the factory at about six a.m. I helped Dad bring the cows from the paddocks, and then we milked them by hand. The other kids were around too. I wasn't the only one, but I think I was Dad's girl. I moved around with him, and enjoyed the kind of work that he was doing.

In those days we had no machine for milking; it was all fairly primitive. The cows' legs would have to be tied to a post, I suppose to keep them steady, and then we had to wash them. We especially had to be sure the tail was clean to keep the milking sanitary. That was a problem, you see, because the cow depended on its tail to keep flies and other things away from its body.

We had a separator which isolated the milk from the cream. The cream would then be sent off to the factory. Special vans or trucks travelled around our area on a regular route to collect the cream. We weren't the only farmers there, of course. There were others who were into big business in farming, even in those days. Those people had lots more cows to attend to, and lots more cans of cream to send to the factory at Mōkau.

The money we earned from the cream helped keep the family going. I can't remember how much it went for, but probably not much. We only sent away a small can. We bought things at the shop with that money, things we couldn't produce ourselves. Because we only had skim milk, we rarely had butter. Sometimes we'd use the money to buy a pound of butter, buying back our cream I guess. I can remember drinking and enjoying skim milk. I didn't get a taste of rich milk until much later, when we moved south to Mōkau. To this day I prefer skim.

After we'd milked the cows, I'd get ready to go to school. We didn't have a great deal for breakfast; we certainly didn't have toast or any of those sorts of things. Mostly it was just porridge. We were brought up on porridge and plenty of skim milk. It was very filling and hot. Sometimes we'd have fried scones, and maybe there would be some lard around to put on top. Mum kept the lard in big ceramic jars, collected from the pigs after the men had been hunting.

After breakfast we were off to school. We walked with the other kids and carried only what we needed for school. One of my old schoolmates is still alive. His name's Alan. He's about a year younger than I, and he still comes around to see me. He might tell you how he used to come around and pick Heeni up for school. We were usually a little bit late, but the teacher didn't mind. Not much homework in those days. It was a small school with one Pākehā teacher. There would only have been about twelve or fourteen of us there. A very small country school indeed. Of those, there would have been about five or six Māori kids, and the rest Europeans.

Our teacher always had a hot cup of cocoa for us after we swam or walked during recess. I remember how I enjoyed looking forward to that. She was a real honey of a teacher. She lived just around the corner. She was so kind to all of us, so caring. We often didn't have much in the way of lunch to take, and I remember she'd always keep some biscuits for us, too. 'Have you got lunch?' she'd ask. 'Yes,' I'd think, but sometimes I'd say, 'No, no no.' Mum couldn't afford to buy biscuits you see. Sometimes we just went off and 'forgot' about taking lunch so we could get some nice biscuits.

We really enjoyed sports at school. If it was a fine day, we swam before our lunch hour. There was a river which ran behind the school. It was a clean area then, suitable for swimming. Of course I enjoyed swimming very much, and I got a certificate for swimming a distance competition. Swimming was also good for my arm, I think. We used to have a lot of fun teasing each other—'You cheated!', and so on. But we weren't, well, competitive. We were all just one big family. Then we'd sit together in the sun and have lunch in the same way. In those days, I felt there was no difference between the Māori and Pākehā kids, especially at that school. I don't know about other schools; maybe other Māori have had experiences that would be foreign to my thinking.

There was one incident. One day I was working with my cousin, and I stood up abruptly and said to the teacher, 'I want to go to the toilet'—in Māori. We weren't allowed to speak Māori in school, and I got a wrap on the knuckles for speaking Māori that day. We were allowed to do so out in the playground, but this was in class, you see. Yes, she said, 'Hold out your hand, Janey,' like this. She had a strap, like a belt with cuts at the end, and I got a strap for that.

This upset me. On my way home I thought why, why was that? When I returned home from school, I told my dad about it. And he inquired why I had got the strap. I told him exactly why, because I'd yelled out in Māori that I wanted to go to the toilet. And then my dad told me that it served me right. Dad differentiated between home and school: 'We send you to school to learn all you can about the English way of life, the English language; but when you come home here, you are coming to your Māori circle, and you can talk as much Māori as you want to talk here. So when you are at school, you keep to your lessons, and honour what your teacher says.' He supported this, he did.

A lot of rubbish is coming out today about how horribly treated the Māori were in New Zealand schools. But I don't go along with that. I believe that having been taught English was a wonderful opportunity. I praise my dad and mum for sending me to school. Never again did I disobey the rules. But as soon as I got back home, well, I began to speak Māori again. I had the best of both language worlds, you see. I'll never forget my Māori; and English helped me when I left home.

No, I've always appreciated the education that I got in those days. I only wish, as I've said many times, that it had been possible for me to pursue higher education. I was mechanically minded. I think if I hadn't been a deaconess, I'd quite possibly have been a mechanic with the airlines. I was always toying around with the boys' bikes and old trucks and things around the place. Sometimes with their guns. I always press upon our young people how important it is to stay on at school, and go on as far as they possibly can. It's so important to be fluent in both languages, and both cultures. That's what the world is all about these days—jobs. You need a job to get the good things in life.

After my dad told me this, I was much more keen to learn at school. I think his advice was good for me, and of course I was quite impressionable at that young age. So I began to become more interested in my subjects. I remember volunteering to work out math problems on the blackboard. There would be several columns of figures, and I'd add them up (but don't ask me to add them up today). Math was easier than English. English was something I had to concentrate very deeply on. It was heavy work for me, another language, you see.

Writing and history were a bit easier. I loved them, but they were a bit foreign. My teacher said I had good penmanship. 'You've got that flow,' she'd say. As far as history went, it was mostly European and a little American. No Māori history at all. We learnt about the old kings of England, and were taught quite a lot about old Abe Lincoln. I remember he was a big, strong fellow sitting there in the pictures in the atlas.

School was out around three p.m., and then we'd make our way home. Often we'd play along the way somewhere. The area was forested with kahikatea, pūriri and miro, so there were plenty of trees to climb, and things to watch. Sometimes our walks home were like a nature study. Where we lived the trees hadn't yet been cut down, and the bush was still wild and untouched. I used to love playing around the ponds and catching frogs. They were slimy like eels, and I used to try to hang on to them as long as I could before they'd slip out and jump away. I don't know, I guess I was always after frogs, and the tadpoles intrigued me too. I guess I was drawn to any animal or bug that was sitting around, like spiders and things. I'd never kill a spider, just play with them. I have a lot of respect for nature. Even today, I'd never kill an ant or a spider. I keep them out of my house by putting dried mint leaves in strategic places. Rats and insects and things don't like the smell of mint. When they do get inside, as they sometimes will, I just sprinkle curry, pepper and salt near them, and they scuttle off.

Along the way home, my schoolmates and I would discuss our schoolwork. We wondered a lot about what the teacher meant about this and that. I had lots of friends, both boys and girls. We might stop and play with marbles, or with the toys my dad used to make for us. We especially enjoyed tops. He would plait strips of flax prepared by scraping the outside part until the fine fibre was revealed. These would be used like ropes, and tied to the head of a top to make it spin. The top was made of scraped wood. It would be spun using the flax strip to keep it going. We had a lot of different games using tops. In one game, you'd keep the top spinning off the flax rope and then hit it along the ground to get it through your opponents goal. If it stopped, you had to go back and begin again. You had to keep hitting it with the flax. I think I was pretty good at those games, I won a lot, but my cousin was really the best.

Marbles were also fun. Dad used to buy them for us, and I remember how important we thought it was to look after your marbles. We kept them in little bags that Mum would make for us. You looked after your marbles. There were many times that I cried over my marbles because somebody else had pinched them or I'd lost them, or whatever. We didn't cheat; we'd play strictly by the rules. But the others would steal mine . . . oh, I guess I did too. I'd better own up. We were given so many, but then, you see, you kept losing one until after a while you were left with not enough to play. Then you had to bargain: 'I'll give you something, and you give me . . .' There were a lot of us kids, and luckily our parents always brought marbles home from their shopping trips.

We had our arguments, just like all kids do. Sometimes we'd accuse each other of cheating, and then we'd argue and argue. But never any real fighting. I think I can remember having my hair pulled pretty hard, yes, and pulling someone else's hair too. You know, those sorts of things. Of course, that's all part of the growing process. I think I argued more with the Māori kids than the Pākehā ones.

I can remember a Māori kid cheating me out of my lunch, I always had sandwiches. I sat next to this fellow and looked at his lunch. When he pulled out what looked to me like an egg sandwich, I said, 'Oh, Philip, what have you got for lunch today?' He said, 'Oh, an egg sandwich.' I told him that I had an egg sandwich, too, but his looked better because it was yellowy. So I said, 'I'll change you.' And he said, 'OK.' But his sandwich turned out to be a pumpkin one instead. You know, yellow. I could have flared up a bit there. I thought, you big cheat, you big liar. But I did enjoy his pumpkin sandwich, even though I got cheated. I guess he enjoyed my egg.

Sometimes we'd stop for a game of rounders. We also played hide-and-seek a good bit. At our house we had lots of places to run and hide. But after we returned home from school, we had our own sort of jobs to do. One of our chores was to collect firewood. We preferred to gather driftwood, because it was easiest to find. All of us kids collected the wood. We used a dray, which was like a sled. We'd all go down to the beach, and it would sort of be like a picnic. In those days there were the most beautifully shaped pieces of wood.

But there were also different jobs for boys and different ones for girls. Of course our parents grew almost an acre of potatoes and kūmara, and we girls had to help with the cultivation by weeding, and with the food processing by peeling potatoes, etc. Of course we had to make our own beds, and change out of our school clothes, which were to be kept nice. Mostly we lived in old things and, sometimes, sandals. Once we were changed, we'd go down to the beach and gather mussels and things.

Mussels grew on the rocks below our home. We'd be told just to gather enough for a meal. None of this going down and picking bucket-loads or sackfuls of seafood as they do today. No, we just took what we needed for dinner, and we were told not to eat them immediately. It was customary to let them lie for a little while before plunging them into water. We didn't believe in cooking seafood or vegetables while there was still a good bit of life in them. All seafood, and even potatoes and kūmara, would be left out on the ground to dry. They wouldn't be used for eating until the next day, because it wasn't correct to eat instantly something which still contained its life force. I still believe in all that sort of thing. By letting the life force drip away from the mussels before you eat them, you're letting the Creator take the life back, so that it can continue. The harvest from the previous day would then be shelled. We took the shells down to the beach again and scattered them around, so that when the tide came in, the sea would take them back.

The sea to us kids was a great source of sustenance. We loved the sea, because it was a mighty provider. But we were also afraid of it. This was all explained to me when I was quite young. The sea is clean, very clean and tapu. Later, when I began menstruating, we understood that to go down to the sea was forbidden. If a woman was having her period, she was not to collect mussels because she would contaminate the sea with her blood. For the same reason, one would never think of urinating in the sea, because that would contaminate all the food you would be gathering from the ocean. The sea is a pristine body, a clean provider, bigger than life itself. And, of course, the same also applies to the bush.[12]

The boys' duty was to go fishing off the rocks, because that was a little bit more difficult. The first fish that they caught at the beginning of the season would be thrown back into the sea. The first of everything of that season, whether it was fish or fruit or vegetable, would be given back to the Creator. This is a tradition handed down through many generations. It's still done today. The Creator gives the people these things. We don't create them, they're given to us. So, by throwing a fish back into the sea we're showing our thanks. It's a way of showing appreciation and aroha to the Creator.[13]

Of course we didn't have electricity then. In the evenings Dad would play his kōauau,[14] and the boys had banjos and ukuleles, and we'd sing. He was quite an entertainer. Sometimes before we went to bed he'd play a shadow game with us. This is where you put your hand up in front of the lamp light and make shadow images on the wall. I can always remember a rabbit, a rabbit's ears in fact. I think it was a rabbit sort of munching on something. Then Dad would begin to tell a story. 'Oh, there's his mate running along,' and so on. We also did this during wet weather.

Before bed, we folded our school clothes, which were kept neat and tidy at the bottom of our bed. We had just two or three changes of clothes, that's all. Most times we slept in our clothes.

I remember elder adult influences on me early on. Now this is slipping back to my very early upbringing. It was very much a custom of my people for the old people to get together when someone became ill. They'd talk about what had been done wrong that would bring this illness on. If it was a child, perhaps it wasn't the child's wrongdoing, but the parents who might have done something wrong. The elders called it muru hara. *Muru* means to solve a problem, and *hara* means maybe you've done something wrong to cause a problem and need forgiveness. So the elders would get together and have a karakia or a kōrero about it, and try to determine what had gone wrong. And then they'd ask for forgiveness. After a mura hara session, the sick one or the injured one would always get better.

There was an area in our house where elders would come to meet and talk. It was partitioned off from the main area, and we weren't usually invited into it. I remember my dad being fairly busy with these meetings. They'd come to our house for serious discussions. It would all be in the real Māori style that I think we were kept away from, but I think they'd have been talking about the many issues of that day, many of which are similar to the ones facing our people today. I know there would have been discussions about the boundary between the Maniapoto and Taranaki people. There are proper Māori boundaries. I think I knew at a very early age that the Mōkau River wasn't the accepted Māori boundary between the Waikato and Taranaki provinces. That was a Pākehā boundary. The accepted Māori boundary was a sticky point because of disputed land areas.

My dad would go off to tangi and hui, just as we have tangi and hui today, but Mum didn't travel with him. She'd stay with us. He sometimes went down Taranaki way, New Plymouth and Waitara. Even though we lived in a remote area, our family wasn't isolated from the people. My dad was fairly well connected down the Taranaki area, and I remember him being away a lot. He'd be away at meetings, and it took longer to get to places back then, because you went by horse of course. There were no telephones, but there was mail to get word of a tangi or a hui. The news always came through very quickly. A big bus might deliver a message in the little township of Mōkau, and someone would ride over to where we lived and pass on the message. I think my dad's opinion was sought after quite a bit.

2 / Growing Up in Māoridom

We have a saying in Māoridom: 'You see a face and you remember a name.' When I see Sister Heeni, I see my parents. I see that she's a link with the past. We are living symmetries. We are the parents who have gone before us. Life is a continuum.

Dave Tūmōkai Pānapa

AS I GREW up, I became quite strong and grew away from my chest problem and my broken arm. We moved south, past Mōkau, when I was about ten. When we moved from Kamate, milking wasn't our focus anymore. That all went. We had lots of animals and a large garden, and by this time the boys were grown up and hunting for other kinds of food. The house we lived in was handed down through my mum's family, from my mum's great-grandmother, and of course others in my family owned it through a system of multiple ownership.

There's an old Taranaki pā, Te Kawau, on the coast just down from our old house. That pā was never taken. It was a stronghold then, and now it's a historical landmark. Our ancestors last lived there in the 1830s. My nephew lives in a house there now, and he's happy to be looking after the area. Our ancestors' spirits are still there, and we're very careful to say our prayers before we go down to the beach.[1]

Back then, warfare was fairly frequent along the coastline. Of course our house sits right on the border, in Taranaki at the southern tip of the Waikato. I reckon the worst part was when the muskets came. It was a terrible slaughter. The Tainui people would come down here to fight against Taranaki people there on the pā. The Tainui—Maniapoto people, their boundary was Mōkau. The enemies would come along the beach, and soon they'd come to this pā. It was situated atop a huge cliff site, totally surrounded by rough sea water at high tide. The only way you could get up there was by using a flax rope. It was an unusually strong pā. Perhaps 400 or 500 people lived there, and there were freshwater springs and plots suitable for cultivation. They had all the shellfish they could possibly want, and birds and wild pigs. They dug right into the ground for their living quarters. My nephew's son has been up there, and he's seen those whakaruru, or dugouts. People are buried up there. When I say buried, I mean he saw their skeletons in the burial grounds.[2]

We have a huge prickly pear cactus in front of our house there. It's been there forever. Someone tried to steal it one night. They drove by with a noose and a rope, and lassoed it. I don't know what happened; I suppose it didn't want to be moved, because it's still there, thriving.

Dad and Mum planted all kinds of gardens around our new house. It was just a bare place when we moved in, but they planted many different kinds of trees. To

The front (top) and back (bottom) of the house in Mōkau where I was raised, as it is today.

protect the house from the sea breezes, they planted a delicious fig tree and other fruit trees. And they had kūmara and potatoes, which were alternated by season so the soil wouldn't become depleted. Dried plots of potatoes would be turned back into the ground, and the area would be left for at least three years before it was planted again. They didn't do any top dressing in those days. Everything was done completely naturally.

At our new house, the boys did all the hunting.[3] They'd go over the hill looking for wild pigs, and there were plenty of them around. It would be a whole day's event, a day full of fun for my brothers and their neighbour friends. They'd make a party of it. They were after pigs, never birds. They used their own special hunting dogs, and rifles to shoot with. The boys also had the duty of preparing the pigs for cooking. When they got home, they'd light a fire outside and begin to singe and scrape off the pigs' hair. Plenty of hot water would be used to clean—absolutely clean—each pig. They used very sharp knives for processing the animal, knives that were to be used only for this purpose. We girls wouldn't be allowed anywhere near these knives. They'd be carefully put aside so that no-one could get hurt. After it had been prepared, the meat would be equally divided among the friends in the hunting party. Our neighbours would go home with their lot, and our lot was handed over to my mum, who would prepare it for cooking.

Te Kawau, the pā near home that was never taken.

After it had been cleaned, the pig would be hung out in the sun for a while to dry out properly. It would be wrapped in a muslin cloth to protect it from flies. There were lots of flies around, and we had to make sure they didn't get to the meat. After it was dry, the meat would be stored in a pātaka, a little place outside Māori homes with openings to catch the sea breeze. The meat would be preserved, and cooked as needed. It would keep for a long, long time.

We'd use the fat from that pig on many things. It would be delicious on bread or on fried scones. We'd even put it on potatoes and kūmara and pūhā. It was really lovely, and I often wish I could go back to that way of life. I miss the taste of pork preserved in its own fat, and cooked until almost dry. But I guess I don't miss the porridge. When I left home, I didn't want to see porridge ever again. Or eggs.

Eggs were another of our staple foods. We had chicken and duck eggs. Yes, chicken and ducks were all around. We also had geese, but they'd try to escape quite often into the bush. We lost quite a few. When they left, we used to go hunting for their eggs in their nests. And turkeys. That's how we were brought up, so that Mum and Dad didn't need to buy any food. Dad always knew when the fowl would be laying. He could hear the hens clucking away when they were about to lay an egg. There were times when we collected quite a lot of eggs. Of course we couldn't eat them all, so Mum would give them to friends and neighbours. Sometimes we had more chickens, ducks, geese and turkeys than we really needed, so Mum would give them away as well. We always had plenty of fried eggs. As I mentioned before, we took fried-egg sandwiches for lunch, or boiled eggs sometimes. After I left home, I didn't want to look at eggs for a long time.

Sometimes we'd let all of the animals out of the pens. Oh, how we used to love chasing them around. We often let them out purposely just to have fun with them. They were our friends. There were a lot of kiwi birds around too. They were protected birds, so the boys weren't allowed to shoot them. I can remember one coming near the house. It had been wounded; I think the dogs had got hold of it, and of

On the farm. With my sister Huirangi (left) and cousin Amy
(centre) at our home in Mōkau, when I was about thirteen.

course the kiwi's bare below its knee. I can remember Dad patching it all up and caring for it. It was OK when he let it go. For a long time he had it in the house, and in
one of the sheds. We didn't get very close to it, because we were told it had very
strong talons; it could grab, scratch and make quite a mess of you if you weren't
careful. Dad made a special little pen for it. When he thought it was well enough to
go back into the bush, he just took it up to the hills, and we never saw it again. We
often used to hear kiwi at night-time. They make quite an unusual sound that you
recognise immediately. But you'd only hear it at night-time.

Dad had a special way with animals. He had a horse that recognised his voice.
His horse would be grazing up in the hills, and Dad would just call him to come
down, and down it came. This was a special horse. It was one we weren't allowed to
ride. Dad also had a special dog that would only work for him. Its job was to get the
newspaper from down the road. His name was Churchill, and he was around until
just before I left home. He lived to a great age, because he was a very special dog.
Everybody knew that dog—the bus drivers, the neighbours. Everybody loved him,
but he was loyal to my dad. I remember one day I went out searching for the newspaper, when Churchill came galloping up with it in his mouth. I knelt down to re-
trieve it, but Churchill wouldn't give it up. He wouldn't let go. I followed him around
to where Dad was working, and Dad asked him for the newspaper. Churchill dropped
it in front of Dad.

Occasionally goats would wander down from the hills. They were naughty, because they'd climb everywhere. They'd come into the house and climb on everything, and want to chew up any item they could find. If you had clothes hanging out on the line, they'd get up on them and chew them up, so we didn't keep them very long. We'd kill the goats for their skins, which we used for mats on the floor. There might still be one or two mats out in our house at Mōkau.

We also had a pet lamb, you know, running around the place. We also had pet pigs which the boys wouldn't kill. We had dogs that were pets and were allowed to walk around, unlike the hunting dogs that were kept in the kennel. You see, we had animals all over the place. We sheltered animals that were friends, and ones that were for food. And we fed them all. We had to.

All of us kids would go whitebaiting at certain times of the year in the Awakino River. Back in those days, there were no restrictions on whitebaiting. Whitebait are tiny fish, and are quite a delicacy around here. They're the tiniest little wee fish. They have little dark-brown rings around the eyes. We eat the whole fish, many of them at a time. You'd need about a hundred to make a meal. We'd put the proper whitebait net down, and watch for these little fish coming along. Then we'd scoop them out, just enough to fill about half a kerosene tin. We weren't greedy. Mum and Dad would just cook them up with a little bit of milk, just for a minute or two. You don't overcook them.

To get to the place where we whitebaited, we walked along a traditional Māori route. This was tapu country. You had to be fairly clean and tall in yourself.[4] You couldn't be fooling around with nature here. No damaging anything, or pulling out ponga. This was where my ancestors moved up and down. I felt comfortable and cosy and at peace. Before the main road was built, I used to love to pass through this area. It was just bush, bush, bush.

Not too far from our house we'd go eeling. Eeling, that was a lot of fun. You got into the little creek there, which wasn't terribly wide. You had to go to another river for the huge ones, but I didn't take part in that. These were the little ones. We got into a little creek, and waded a bit. All at once we'd tramp through the water at a certain spot, and the noise would bring the sleeping eels out. I used to jump down into this area myself and feel these wiggly eels all around my legs. That was great fun.

There is a lovely lady who made a great impact on me for much of my life. That would be Sister Nicholls, a lovely lady. She helped me decide to go into church work. This is a woman who made a great impression on my mind. My mum and dad knew her family, who owned a grocery store in Te Kūiti. Our families were well acquainted, and she was very accustomed to things Māori. She grew up among Māori. My mum's sister lived in Te Kūiti, and Sister Nicholls grew up with my cousins. She grew up to do tremendous work for my people.

Sister Nicholls was in charge of a huge Māori area in the Waikato. She was a missionary for the Methodist Church, and she'd visit our area two or three times per year. She travelled on a bicycle, spending a few days in Piopio and Kāwhia, making her way slowly down to Mōkau. Mōkau was the end of her travel boundary, and when she arrived she'd stay with us in our home. My earliest memories of her are when I was about nine or ten.

She'd arrive and be full of fun. I felt there was something special about her, even at that very young age, that I loved very much. And I think my cousins and all of us kids were very attracted to her. Since we lived about six or seven miles away from the shop, there was no running there for sweets or drinks or anything like that—none. We had to make our own sweet drinks, but only when the blackberries were in season. Anyway, she'd bring us sweets sometimes. And we thought, 'Oooohh. We'll take the sweets, how lovely.'

Yes, she'd stay with us, and I don't know what we gave her to eat. We didn't have very much, but I can't ever remember starving, because no matter how bad things got, there were always fish and mussels down on the rocks. She'd take us swimming, swimming, swimming. Of course we had no togs, although she did. And we'd go down to the beach and she'd swim with us for hours. Afterwards, we'd sit on the beach and she'd tell us Bible stories. Her caring for us is what I liked most about her. When she came, she just sort of took over the kids, all of us kids, and almost had complete control. I think when we went blackberry picking, she'd join us. She was just full of fun.

At this point I think she was already a deaconess, and I think that quite possibly she thought it was her calling to visit Māori with ideas from the Church. Yes, she seemed to concentrate on me. I'm sure she watched me quite a bit over the years. I knew she was observing me when we had Sunday-school lessons. Her teachings centred on values, which is what the younger ones today are missing. Sister Nicholls used to gather us up, you know, and would have short evening devotions in our home. And I can remember her saying, 'Oh come over here, Heeni, and sit beside me.' She was the one who was really responsible for my getting a job in church work. A lovely lady. Our devotions were very simple. We were inside, of course, and all who were in our home would join in, including Mum and Dad. They began mostly with singing, singing choruses and things. It wasn't really a service as one would think of a Christian service today. It was mostly just singing, and would maybe close with a short prayer. No sermon or anything like that. I can remember singing: *Wide, wide, is the ocean . . . Deep, deep is the deepest sea Like my Creator's love for me . . .* You know, those sort of things. Easy and simple. There was another song that made an impression on me. It was a song about God riding on top of a storm, seeing all of life in a grand way, despite the storm's destruction. *He plants his footsteps in the sea And rides upon the storm. . . .* Lovely. Singing has always been very important to me, and of course Māori have a rich tradition of song and dance. We were always singing, and at that time most Māori people would gather and sing some of their own songs.[5]

There's another wonderful lady who also made a great impression on me later on. The late Princess Te Puea came into our home one day. She was no stranger, dear. I would not like to presume that theirs was a special relationship, but she did know my parents. Long before she arrived, I became aware of her impending visit. We kids were told three or four days before that she'd be arriving with her husband, Tūmōkai. We were told these were special visitors, and Mum and Dad both indicated they would prefer that we kids didn't come in and out too much and get in the way. Well, the very first night they were there, Heeni was very inquisitive about all of the special preparations. I watched Mum set up the front room. The beds were taken out, cleaned up and remade, then brought back inside. That was the way they entertained in those days—on mattresses made up with sheets and pillows on the floor. Mum and Dad didn't say you can't go in there, they'd never say that. But they did say they'd prefer that we didn't. It was all very interesting to Heeni.

In the evenings we sometimes sat and listened to our mum and dad tell stories about kēhua, or ghosts. These stories would be told after the evening meal in the sitting room in front of the fireplace. The road through the Awakino River gorge into Mōkau used to be quite lonely, and the word *Awakino* means 'dangerous', so you might have tricks played on you on this road. As my father made his way home, he was often stopped suddenly along the road by ghosts. If he and his friends were riding horses, they'd have to stop and get off.

I can remember quite distinctly my dad being held up by a group of ghosts who were sitting right across the road, blocking his way. He had no choice but to get off his horse and talk to them. Yes, he talked to them as though they were really natural people sitting there. He said to them, 'Now look here, you people, I've got to get home to my wife and kids. Open the way and let me get through.' He hopped on his horse, who had by this time become quite nervous and was jumping about (they do sense unnatural things). So it came to my dad's mind to charge right through them, which he did. He did, he jumped straight through, and got home to us. I don't know if they were ghosts of our ancestors, but he'd recognise some of them. We weren't afraid of ghosts, we knew how to interpret them. Usually seeing ghosts meant that a member of your family, or a member of your wife's family, would soon be passing on.

Some of the other elders would talk about moving along that road and hearing singers. They would see ghosts who were jumping head over heels on the other side of the river. There's a stone tunnel that you must pass through on your way to Mōkau. There would be a lot of tricks played on them there by these kēhua. They'd be jump-ing around above the tunnel, dancing and flipping round. At the same time you'd hear beautiful singing in women's voices. They'd be dressed in beautiful flowing gowns. But if you didn't get through the tunnel before nighttime, they'd hold you up. If you went through at night, you'd have to stop there for a while until all of this sort of thing came to a pause. They'd stop and do their karakia, because naturally they'd feel just a bit hesitant about going through the tunnel with all of these ghosts around. Of course, there was no danger to anyone. The ghosts were just having fun.

It wasn't only Māori people who were held up by ghosts. I knew a reverend in the Methodist Church who was travelling along the same road around midnight one night. Quite suddenly his headlights just went out. (These kēhua can't stand bright lights.) So, naturally, he had to stop, and he thought, 'Well now, what's the matter with this car?' He got his flashlight out and checked everything, and all seemed OK. But his lights wouldn't work. He thought, 'Well, this is funny.' Then he began to feel eerie and strange. (I wasn't the only one in the room when he was telling this story.) He remembered the stories about people passing through there and being held up, so he thought, 'Oh my golly, I'd better get back into the car.' As he tried to get back in, he felt a tremendous pressure on his shoulders, as though there were a path of people pulling him back, preventing him from getting in. So he quickly said a little prayer, and was able to get into his car. The headlights came on straightaway, and he went on his way. He never forgot that experience. There are others who will tell you similar stories. Even many of my Pākehā friends would want to get through this area before darkness falls, even today.

Mum used to talk about her experiences with ghosts. She didn't see them, she heard them. She knew when someone would be passing on, because she'd hear a whistle, one that would come fairly clear to her. My mum had great faith. She'd say to us when waking us in the morning. 'Oh, I heard that whistling again.' I used to listen and wonder, 'What's Mum talking about?' Dad would ask where it was coming from, and she'd point this way. My mum belonged to this area, King Country, and my dad belonged that way. And Mum used to point in the direction of her people. 'I wonder who it is that has died,' she would say. She'd listen to the tone of that whistle, and if it was strong and powerful, coming from the Maniapoto area, she'd know it was from someone close to her own tribe who was either very, very ill or on the verge of passing on. She'd also know whether it was a man or woman. It was beautifully talked about in the most reverent sort of way. And I can distinctly remember my dad saying to Mum, 'There was a pressure on my chest last night,' and he'd point in the direction of his people. Mum used to massage my dad's body, and he'd do the same to her. And Mum would say, 'Who?' and Dad would say, 'I know, I know . . .' and sure enough, word would come through. The message would reach us about two or three days after that, sometimes a bit longer, that someone had passed on.

My mum and dad weren't tainted by the Pākehā world. Absolutely, they were real Māori, the kind you would not find today, anywhere.

Long after my dad had died, my brother Paddy (who was very close to Dad) saw him standing at the foot of his bed. There he was, plain as day, looking at my dad. Paddy quickly hopped up and went up to grab him, and of course his arms were empty. This was just after the war.

I haven't seen any ghosts myself, but I have felt the pressure, sometimes, like my dad did, on my shoulders. One day I felt that pressure, much later in my life when I was living in Auckland. I was just stepping out of the house from the back door when I felt something holding me back. I felt someone applying pressure on my shoulders, and it felt a bit eerie. I had a funny feeling all day that I just couldn't shake. It wasn't very long after that I got the news—one of my lady tohunga had passed on.

We were very poor by today's standards, because we had little money. But we always had food. I can never remember going hungry. And there was always plenty of pūhā. These were a type of greens which grew out among the potatoes and kūmara, but we never pulled them out as if they were weeds. I know people used to think they were weeds, but they weren't really. We ate them and that was a good source of vegetable nutrition.

What little money there was spent on flour. Flour, yes. At certain times we'd purchase a huge sack of flour to last for months. We'd also buy a huge sack of rolled oats for porridge, and some sugar and tea. We didn't drink very much tea, though. Mostly it was milk or water. We had never heard of coffee, of course. Bread would come along once in a while. Mostly Mum made her own scones because there was plenty of fat around and flour had been purchased. Māori bread doesn't contain baking powder, just milk, flour and a bit of fat. You knead it for quite a while, and then bake or fry it. It's still served on some of the marae today, but of course it takes a lot of time.

We loved what Mum cooked. Now and again I think maybe she'd think we kids weren't getting enough lollies, so she'd make us some toffees. I don't know how she made them, but they were delicious. I can remember in the summertime having a lot more variety in our food, like jellies and custard. We had plenty of fruit trees, which Dad had planted. There were apples and peaches, and we also had a strawberry patch. Mum wouldn't let us anywhere near that, but we wouldn't think of pinching anything anyway. We waited until the strawberries were properly red. We were not to go too close to the watermelon garden either. Dad would know when they were ready to pick. He'd take us over and instruct us. When the curly part of the watermelon is quite dry, then it's ready for eating. So, he'd then cut it, and we'd all have the water-melon, or share it with others who might be coming in to see us. I grew up with a lot of knowledge like that. Even if I want to buy a watermelon today, if that curvy piece at the end isn't dry, I won't take it. And it's the same with the kūmara and the pota-toes, and all that sort of thing.

We didn't spray any kind of pesticide on our fruit like they do today with all those sorts of things to destroy them. Blackberry juice was quite a treat in season. We mushed the berries and added water. It was a delicious drink, and natural, you see. They were in season in late March, at the end of summer. Sometimes we'd gather them, and Mum would make a delicious jam. Most people down that way did, and we kids were always going from paddock to paddock gathering them. We'd eat a lot on the way home, naturally.

We cooked outside a good bit. There were big pots with round legs that you could stand over an open fire. You could bake bread or roast meat, or whatever. You see them in very old museums. We called them oumu.

There was no pressure on the young to say grace or that sort of thing. Mum just told us not to forget to say thank you to te runga rawa for blessings, first thing in the morning or evening, during the day or during the night. That strain sort of went through my life as I grew into adulthood. We didn't say grace or thanks together. I remember my mum gathering us on the verandah at home and just reminding us to give thanks privately for things like a good meal, or a good rest during the night. She'd instill this sort of idea into our minds, that there was a higher being, a supreme being to which we should give thanks to our own way.

Sometimes I wasn't quite sure how to do that. It became a lot more definite in my mind after many talks with my koro Tainui and Sister Nicholls. But it was only later in life that I got a much clearer conception of what my mum was talking about. Nevertheless, her words were always in the back of my mind, and I can remember as a kid sometimes going off on my own to contemplate these things. I would go and sit on the banks or on the cliffs at the beach. I'd look out toward the sea—and by this time I was beginning to grow a little bit in my mind—and I'd say to myself, 'I won-der what's beyond that big sea.' This is what helped me get an idea of something bigger and greater, something supreme. Yes, I used to sit quite a bit and look at the bush, too. I remember going up a hill where my brothers would go pig hunting, and I'd sit at the top. All I could see were trees, trees, trees, the wild bush country, and I'd wonder, 'How far does this stretch?' It was the same sort of thing. These were ways in which I began to formulate a conception of something that was bigger and greater than myself. Yes, I was spiritually minded even way back then.[6]

It was quite fun going to the store with Mum and Dad. Maybe we'd get a sweet treat. There were clothes for sale in that store, but we couldn't afford to buy them ready-made. Everybody made their own clothes in those days. I can remember making myself a nice top and skirt out of a flour sack. The porridge sacks were made of linen, so I'd use them too. From a very early age, I was always very fond of making things for my mum, my sisters and myself. We'd make aprons out of the sugar sacks. Sometimes we had to buy our own material, especially for warm things. Flannelette material was fairly cheap in those days. We'd just make a straight sort of skirt and top, with a little bit of fancy work, not like the full skirts we wear today. The skirts would be stitched down two sides, with a long piece of elastic around the middle. Sometimes we'd just use string and gather the waist from underneath.

Mum had a sewing machine. It was an old pedal-driven Singer, with a lid that opened and pulled out. When you closed it down, the top could be used as a table or something. Mum did a good bit of sewing. The older one's clothes would be passed down to the younger ones, so there was lots of mending to do. She was always sewing up my dad's socks. Sometimes clothes would be given to us by our neighbours, who knew we were the only large Māori family around.

I was always fiddling around with the machine. I knew all about the machine by the time I was able to sew myself. If anything went wrong with it, my mum would ask me to attend to it. I used to make little gowns for the dolls we played with at school. Just little suits and frocks that would be miniature versions of the larger pieces I had in mind.

We didn't wear shoes much, even in the wintertime. No, I think we were pretty hardy. And of course no bra. I didn't wear a bra until I left home. I was fairly big, and going to school on a horse without a bra really helped develop that part. We did wear knickers. I remember Mum just buying material, and we'd cut it up and put elastic here and elastic there, and that was it. We were quite happy with that. Mum did buy us singlets, but these got a bit ragged because we wore them when we went down for a swim. As I said before, we had no special swimming togs or anything like that. We couldn't afford those things.

I remember the beggars who would come along to our house. We called them swaggers in those days. These were people who just walked around and slept anywhere. They went from place to place without any real sort of purpose. Really, they just walked. I think that as far back as I can remember I was afraid of them. We kids were all afraid of these tramps. But Mum wasn't. Mum would always give them whatever she had in the house. They'd carry their own billy, and they'd light up a fire

My ancestral marae, Te Māniaroa, home of the anchor of the Tainui canoe.

along the way somewhere. They didn't come around very often, but when they did, Mum always gave them some food, even if it was only a bit of crust or a hot cup of tea.[7] We kids would run behind the house and peer round the corner to get a good, but safe, peek at them. They were never brought into the house. They'd be given food or tea on the verandah, and off they'd go. They weren't Māori. These were Pākehā. No, there were never any Māori tramps in those days.

I was raised in a home that was quite far away from the marae.[8] It was a few miles from our home, just before you get into Mōkau. It's called Te Māniaroa marae. Māniaroa means open space. On a clear day you can see Mount Taranaki, which is the sacred mountain of my father's people. It was renamed Mount Egmont in 1769 by Captain James Cook. The meeting house faces the sea, and just next to it is the graveyard. This is enclosed by a concrete fence, and the anchor stone of the Tainui canoe lies there. That canoe brought the original ancestors of our iwi. It's been placed there for safe keeping. The stone is difficult to move, because it weighs about two or three tons. It's rounded and has a very deep hollow portion in the centre. Its placement here symbolises the southern boundary of Tainui. When you look at the cardinal directions in Māori terms, north is actually the opposite to what Europeans regard as north. What is thought to be south in a Māori sense is actually regarded as the north among Pākehā. In that graveyard is buried my koro, Tainui Wētere. His association with the anchor symbolises how special he was.

Back at home, there was a station owner who lived nearby. His name was Jim O'Halloran, an Irishman. We called him Granddad because he was very old. He named my brother. I'd forgotten about that. He asked my dad if he could have the honour of naming the boy while my mother was pregnant with him. Granddad named him Patrick, and we called him Paddy. When he was born, old Granddad gave us two cows as a gift for the new baby.

As my brothers got older, they got jobs on the adjacent farms. Freddy Wardel owned the farm next to us. They were Pākehā, with plenty of money. It was a huge station, so there was lots of work for the young men. They kept sheep and drystock, I think, mostly. We called the owner Uncle Freddy, but we didn't see a great deal of his wife. Uncle Freddy used to call at my home to see Dad. When he called, he nearly always had something in his hands in the way of food. Yes, they were on friendly terms, and sometimes he'd bring over a slaughtered sheep for the family. In season, Dad would oblige with a part of our harvest of potatoes, kūmara and other vegetables. They exchanged food, but without any sort of words being said. There was a lot of that among different families while I was growing up in those days. There seemed to be just caring—caring in the way of food, vegetable and meat. We shared our good fortune with one another, but we'd also extend caring to those who couldn't reciprocate. They and their children would come in and out of our home, and we'd do the same at theirs. We all went to school together. They didn't look at us differently because we were Māori. Our mum and dad were Mum and Dad to them, and their mum and dad were parents to us.

When I turned thirteen, I got my period for the first time. My mother had instructed me about all of this sort of thing, but I didn't understand until it started. When I first began having them, I thought, 'Oh golly me, This must be it. How awful.' I was a good bit frightened, really. For me it was very alarming. I said to my mum, 'What do I do?' In those days we didn't have pads or tampons or anything like that. She said you have to save up pieces of clean material, old material from some of your old bloomers. I think that was the word she used. She told me to cut them up and be prepared by having a stock of them ready for each month.

She told me to keep myself very clean during that period, and not to let any man know about this sort of thing. That's because this part of the body is tapu; all this idea of tapu was talked about quite a bit in those days.[9] It's just something very personal and very private. A man's tapu part is more his head and hair, while a woman's tapu is her period and all of her female parts. Yes, in those days Mother would quietly bury cuttings from haircuts, in the same way as we buried cloths from our periods. Mum told me never to have intercourse at this time. Yes, to Māori it wasn't clean. A woman is never clean during that period, and this is the reason why she's restricted from gathering seafood, and going near where food is growing. I had to keep away a good bit.

I disliked myself when I first experienced periods, especially during the first few years. I thought, 'Oh, fancy having to go through all of this.' Mum said, 'Yes, you have to go through all of that, and you are not to worry about it.' I didn't have too much pain with it at first, but then I can remember how it changed. It really upset me. I can remember standing up and feeling very intense twinges, and I thought, 'What is the matter with me? What is this all about?' And it really took me a good while to get used to it. My mother explained that this was the natural way of life. Women reach a certain age, and then they begin to bleed, until one day it just stops.

Mum told me I might have problems with it, and I did—lots. She had suggestions about what to do for the pain. On the first and second days, I was to take it easy and not participate in any sport. I wasn't to go horseback riding or anything like that. Of course this upset me, because I was a great one for horseback riding. Mum told me that when there was pain, I was to keep myself warm. I said, 'How can you feel warm with all that yukky stuff coming away?' She said it had to come away: 'Don't ever do anything that you think might prevent it. And you are never to go swimming!' Of course, that's exactly what I was wanting to do to get rid of it. She used to point down to the beach and say, 'You are not to go anywhere near that area. You keep well up here.'

She instructed me to find a place on the farm where it would be possible to dig a little hole and bury the soiled material. We buried them every month; they were never washed out and used again. We couldn't wash them, anyway, because they would contaminate the basins we used to wash our faces with. Every month, we buried our material, pretty well in the same sort of area, and far away from where food and things were kept. It was quite far from the house. It had to be where there was no possibility of food being planted or things which would be gathered. Nowhere near the sea, or near flax, and away from the river.

We had several basins to wash our faces, and of course we kept our bodies fairly clean down at the sea. Dad had made a pipe to carry riverwater to our home, and we used to rinse our faces and clean our cooking materials. So we really didn't have hot baths. We had a huge tub outside, and every now and again we would all have a soapy bath, and that was our way of life really.

The hair of a man is particularly tapu, but even we women were told be careful about our hair. I think it was Mum who said, 'Be careful about your hair. Don't go to the hairdresser's too often!' She knew very little about hairdressers, but she knew to stay away from hair dryers. The first time I went to one, I asked to sweep up the hair myself and take it home with me. I took it home and went out and buried it. And Mum told me not to sit under those hair dryers. She said that it would make my hair turn grey earlier. So I think that since that time, I've rarely done that. I'm lucky to have very little grey hair at my age.

I remember lots of boys who were friends. It was always just a friendship though, because I was fairly well protected. There were different fellows coming in, because my brothers were in sports. Rugby, rugby, rugby. It was the main sport in those days; my brothers were mad about it. Every weekend there would be a test. All of the boys would arrive at our place on horseback, and then would go off to wherever football was being played. There was drink around in those days, sure. Mostly beer, some wine. Mum didn't drink, but Dad did. He enjoyed it with the boys, and he'd go off with them to rugby matches.

Women didn't really drink in my day. Well, they had to go way over to another township to get it from people who were sly grogging. These were dealers who were secretly selling drink to the Māori people. There were no pubs around there, so that was the only way you could get a drink, because this was King Country. It was the king's area, which had been proclaimed a dry area by the Māori people. So it was not only difficult to get hold of, but very expensive to buy. Some women did drink though, I guess. Because I can remember this auntie of mine. I noticed how happy she was. She said, 'My dear, you know what I got under here?' And I said, 'I wouldn't have a clue what you have under there, auntie.' Then she pulled out a bottle of wine that was popular to drink. Not so much beer, it was mainly wine. 'Oh,' she said, 'it's lovely. But I'm not going to give you even one sip. You won't get any, because if you do your dad will throw me out of the house.' There she was, sipping out of the bottle. Yes, I missed my auntie when she passed on.

Sure, I became a bit friendly with some of my schoolmates, but my dad was always very careful; I was well guarded. There were two boys from fairly wealthy farming families down the road. I can remember one of them coming around and asking if he could see 'Janey'. He wanted to take me to the pictures that night. He was a fine-looking fellow, but I didn't think too much of him. Dad would hesitatingly say yes, but he'd add, 'Should I hear anything, well, no more coming here for you in this home!' Dad was particular. But I enjoyed this boy as a pal. He had a nice new car. Not too many of the folk down there had a car. So we would go along to the pictures, and that was OK, and then we went home.

I went with other boys to dances, schoolpals mostly. I first went to dances when I was about fifteen, just before I left home. But I'd come back on holiday when I was older and go to dances then too. I loved dancing, and I would enjoy the company of these boys. We danced in an old hall in Mōkau. In those days it was a very old building, but today a new one has replaced it. I wasn't really restricted too much as long as we went along in a group. We all enjoyed the dancing. We are musical people. That's what we enjoyed together, because we didn't have a television or anything like that. There were always guitars and instruments that the boys would play, and everyone would dance. Mōkau Hall would also be the place where the pictures were shown.

My social life wasn't really separate from my family life. It was fairly free and natural to do different kinds of things, but with friends, cousins and siblings. I didn't single out anyone special. Many of them were friends of my brothers. Sometimes I remember they didn't always want a sister tagging along. That's because they knew they had to be responsible for me. Sometimes they'd try to toss me around. 'Here's a scythe. Now you go up there and cut some of those blackberries,' or 'You go and feed the dogs'—or the ducks, or whatever.

I remember my eldest brother, Ngatai; he was very attractive and had a few girlfriends. He'd want to take one of them to a dance in the evening after he'd worked all day. I remember him saying just before he went to work, 'Do you think you could wash my shirt out? I have a date tonight.' And I said, 'Oh, you wash your own!' And he said, 'I'll give you half-a-crown if you'll do it.' Of course, half-a-crown, well. It was a lot of money in those days. And another thing, I knew he meant it. We didn't take anything that didn't belong to us, and were raised to be truthful. 'OK, yes,' I said. And I did! He gave me half-a-crown and I thought I was rich. It's worth about twenty-five cents. Oh, but it was a lot of money to us then.

Even though they teased me a good deal, I had a lot of time for my brothers, and they did for me. They'd always ask if I was OK. There were real Māori foundations here, which you don't find so much today. That kind of loving protection and staunch loyalty would be very difficult to find today. In those days, a woman didn't have the same kind of mana as a man did. You had to listen to your brothers, and do what they wanted you to do. But in exchange for that you got love and protection. Even today the man is really the head of the family. It's started departing a little from that recently simply because so many younger people aren't being taught the things that I grew up with. For those who are traditionally Māori, it will always be there, and I think there are still a lot around who would regard the man as the head of the family.[10]

Anyway, sometimes I'd be trotting along with some of my schoolmates and cousins. Once we came upon some other girls who were smoking, and they said, 'What about you, Heeni? You know, want to try some?' 'Oh no, no,' I said. And they pushed on, 'Here, take this. Don't be so old-fashioned.' One time I picked up a cigarette and smoked. I must have been about fifteen, just before I left home. My dad, yes, he caught me smoking. So he had a good punishment for me. He came to me and said, 'I've seen you smoking with the others, Heeni. I've got a pack of cigarettes, and I want you to smoke them.' And I had to smoke the whole pack, one after the other. I became absolutely sick. I got really ill in my head. I didn't know what was happening to me. So, never again after that did I care to smoke cigarettes.

Before I left home, my mum and my dad and my koro called me in to have a kōrero. In those days your whakapapa wasn't talked about a great deal—in Māori circles, anyway. It was tapu. The whakapapa was kept a secret in the family. Now everyone talks about it. Back then, your family knew who you were, and everyone else around you knew who you were. That was good enough.[11] I remember once or twice my dad did sort of cut me. I think he had some idea when I was growing up that I was going to be a conceited girl. So he said, 'Well, we won't tell her who she is.' I used to hear them talk, you know. And of course Mum comes from fairly high up in the Waikato.

But there was another reason why they didn't tell me, of course. My elders told me that because I was going into church work I should keep my mind on that. 'Your whakapapa is to remain back home here with us. We aren't going to tell you about your whakapapa.' People would ask me, 'Do you know anything about your whakapapa?' And I'd reply, 'No I don't know a thing.'

But my elders did tell me that wherever I went on my travels, I'd be known. My dad was very well respected in Te Āti Awa, and my mum was very well known in the Waikato. I knew my mother's sister and her brother were Maniapoto. They were all of the chiefly line, my mum's. And they told me, 'When you go south, you'll be known because of your mum.' So I didn't question that. Not a bit. Nor did I question who I was or where I was going. It didn't worry me. Even right to this day, I respected what my parents and elders said.

My whakapapa was sort of secret for another reason too. The Methodist Reverend Whiteley was a great missionary, and very well known. You might have seen his name but you probably wouldn't have connected him to me. He was stationed a good bit north of Mōkau, and he was in charge of the Māori mission. So he had to travel a good bit up and down the coast visiting Māori families. The main route in those days was along the beach, along the coastline. Anyway, I don't really know exactly what happened. Something just went wrong; I think there was some misunderstanding between my people and the Church.

Reverend John Whiteley. Methodist Archive

Anyway, you see, one day it was my great-grandfather who shot and killed the Reverend Whiteley, along from my home near White Cliffs. As Whiteley was moving past there, he saw a Māori group along the beach. The reverend was warned they didn't want him to go through (this is where I can't put my finger on what the problem was). But it turned out that my old koro warned him not to go one step forward, and to immediately dismount from his horse. I don't know if this had something to do with land, but the old reverend came closer, and my old koro shot him dead.[12]

It was kept quiet for a long time. The family knew about it, and of course so did my elders. But they've all passed on, you see, and it's beginning to come out quite a bit today. So I'm the great-granddaughter of the man who shot the Methodist minister. My koro is his great-great-grandson, you see. (I mean my koro today, grandson of my childhood koro. He is also Tainui (or Koro) Wētere, the former minister of Māori Affairs.) I've talked with him just recently, and just a few days ago he gave me permission to tell you this. That's why my elders said to leave my whakapapa back in the home where I grew up.

So without really understanding why at that time, I was given over to the Methodist Church partly as an offer to make reparations. I think they saw something in the future, and I was the one they chose. They could have chosen my younger sister, but I think my parents and koro thought that, well, there's something about Heeni, about this girl who has bonded so well to Sister Nicholls and the church folk. I think they accepted that without a good deal of fear.[13]

Now there were things that led up to my leaving home for the Church. The iwi of that area knew for some time that something was going on. It wasn't a secret

*My mother, Mahora. This photograph hangs on
the wall of our family home in Mōkau.*

thing; they knew that quite possibly I'd be going away. It was no surprise to anyone, including myself. I knew I'd be getting away from home. I had no hesita-
tion whatsoever, no fear; I trusted Sister Nicholls totally. She had been coming
down to visit for a long time, and was really like family to us. And I always
trusted the Reverend Seamer, who was head of the Māori mission. I knew him
less, but felt close to him because of his association with Sister Nicholls. When
he came through our area with a choir of young people, I was quite clear in my
mind that I would be going. It was the adventure that appealed to me. I was
looking for adventure.

There were arrangements that had to be negotiated with Sister Nicholls and
Father Seamer. My koro, Mum and Dad discussed with them what provisions would
be made for me, and what would become of me. These talks went on for some time.
The Reverend Seamer had been visiting quite often and talking with my people. It
was finally agreed that the Church would take full responsibility for my welfare and
financial arrangements. But I wasn't just sort of picked up and taken away. No, no,
no, a proper ceremony was initiated.

If I hadn't gone into the Church, my mother and father would've arranged a marriage for me. Yes, that was the custom. In lots of cases the arrangement would've
been made while the girl was still with her parents. She would've been watched, as
I was watched a good bit. No sleeping around, none of that. The man to whom she'd
be engaged would be someone in the family. Even a first cousin was OK, although
usually it was a little farther away than that. But there was a good bit of value put on

marrying your own. The reason was so that if you and your husband had fights and arguments and this sort of thing, then the elders could take care of it because it would all be in the family. If you married someone outside your family, well, you see, there was no recourse.

But marriage and this sort of thing didn't enter my mind. I was hoping I'd go away, you know. The idea of adventure. And I had already got the idea in my mind that I didn't want to settle in such an isolated area. When the opportunity came to leave, truthfully, I forgot all about marriage and children. I just didn't think about that again until much later in my life. It was when I was about twenty-seven or twenty-eight that I wondered if perhaps it was time for me to get married.

I remember my mum's advice as I was about to leave home. She started to talk to me about the proper ways to be with menfolk. You know, I mean how to behave in their presence. She told me not to let myself become flirty with a man, because, well, then you encourage him. Later on in my life, my thoughts went back to my mum's advice. There were some men whom I really enjoyed being with, enjoyed their company and that sort of thing. But I always knew when to turn off and not encourage fellows. Early on, my mother warned me about that sort of thing, and talked to me about having respect for sex. It should be done within marriage only. My mother came from the old school of the olden days. Once a woman begins to have sexual intercourse with a man, she keeps that man and no other.

I think that is why there weren't the same sort of diseases and things running around that there are today. I remember one time, just before I left home, there was a woman known to have been with several men. She was the carrier for a Māori boy who contracted gonorrhoea. He was taken away by the parents. They went to find some Māori medicine from the bush. Still, one had to be careful.

Anyway, Mum told me that the first time with a man could be quite disastrous. She said, 'Be careful. No matter how much you want to get with that boyfriend of yours, always be careful.' It could be a problem; it could produce a child. And I had some people confide in me later in my life that their child was indeed conceived on the first time. One lady said, 'I want to talk to you quietly, just the two of us. My child isn't who you think it is. I went out with a young man just before I married my husband, and we were around together, and I became pregnant immediately. Then I married my husband.' That made me think very carefully about all this sort of thing.

PART TWO

PREPARING FOR THE CHURCH

He wahine, he whenua ka ngaro te tangata

For women, for land, men will die

As a teenager, Heeni left her rural Māori home to "learn the ropes of civilization," as she put it. From the age of 15, she grew up under the custody and care of Reverend Seamer and the Methodist Church, who assumed all financial and spiritual responsibility for her. Ultimately, she would become a Methodist leader herself, a deaconess who brought both Christian and Māori philosophic systems together under one umbrella in her service as Matron of Māori youth hostels in Hamilton.

Methodism was logical for Heeni because a solid relationship had already been established between the elders of her hapū and leaders of the Church, such as with Seamer and Nicholls. It also made sense because the reparations needed to heal old wounds were still lingering over the mistaken murder of the Methodist Reverend John Whiteley by her maternal great grandfather and a Waikato raiding party. Heeni could not have known at the time she was handed over that, 60 years after Whiteley's murder, as an adult, she would in many ways pick up where Whiteley, an established and respected peace maker, left off. She was to become a missionary of peace herself, who would build important cultural bridges between two races to help heal the legacies of the misguided colonial program.

In contrast with many parts of the colonial world, where missionaries worked in tandem with colonial governments to ethnically cleanse indigenous people, and in the process convert them to Christianity, certain New Zealand missionaries took a more independent, culturally relevant approach. They did so by putting indigenous welfare ahead of conversion priorities. With Māori lifestyle continually threatened by land conflicts, the Church worried about the ensuing disasters as impediments to conversion. The missionaries were thus thrust into an activist role as a way to build trust and loyalty because their agenda could not proceed unless land and lifestyle issues were being addressed. In this way, they won the respect of the Māori by helping offset some of the social damage posed by the colonization program, which had the acquisition of Māori land at the top of its political agenda. The Methodists, for example, lent spiritual and mediation support during the "Māori Land Wars," a time of great cultural crisis for the tangata whenua.

The Methodists were also better able to devise a culturally sympathetic program because they had more freedom to develop one than did the Anglicans and Catholics due to the vast distances separating them from the major evangelical power centers in Europe. "In the United States you were a matter of a week's sailing from continental Europe. By contrast, in New Zealand, you were a matter of months, or even years. It took a long time, and therefore the missionaries were very much on their own, left to their own devices, except for the two dominant churches (Anglican and Catholic) because they had the power of Canterbury and Rome transferred nearby from the colonies in Australia. But, you see, the smaller religious sects did not have the same degree of authority coming from a central proximate base."[1]

The Methodist program also won Māori allegiance because it emphasized a personal relationship with the divine, a structure already well in place in Māori cosmology before the arrival of the missionaries. "Of course the Methodists and Presbyterians were very radical in that one of the most important things was your personal relationship to God. You see the Anglicans did not have that. With them, you had to go through bishops and priests. To the Māori, the Methodists' program had strength, because they emphasized the link among God, the tribe and individuals."[2]

These two factors, the development of a culturally sensitive conversion program that rested on a concern for Māori welfare and an emphasis on an individual connection with God, ultimately brought the Methodists much prestige among many of Heeni's ancestors. To understand how Heeni found herself as a teenager in such a unique position with the Methodists, it is necessary to summarize New Zealand colonial history to set the backdrop for her launch into the Pākehā world.

COLONIAL NEW ZEALAND

The colonial pattern in New Zealand followed a similar trajectory to the ones initiated all over the world, during and after the Age of Discovery. For the better part of 300 years, European voyagers set sail from places such as Britain, Spain, Holland, and France for distant lands, in search of natural resources that could be sent back to increase the wealth of the mother country. Shortly thereafter, European settlers arrived in the new lands, exploiting resources while making their new homes in the colonized territories.

As the colonists settled, usually there grew an immediate culture clash with the indigenous peoples. Europeans perceived the natives as obstacles in the way of progress, and the natives viewed the Europeans as invaders disconnected from morality. The cornerstone of their ensuing difficulties rested on cultural differences pertaining to the land's intrinsic value and how it should be used. Europeans saw land as spiritually dead, as an economic resource that could be bought and sold, individually owned, and exploited for personal gain. By contrast, indigenous people traditionally saw land as sacred and alive, the property of the gods, and something that could never be sold because it was corporately or communally held. Indigenous people did not view themselves as "owners" of the land in the European sense, although territories were definitely *theirs,* but rather as stewards who took seriously their supervisory role, with all of the ritual duties and responsibilities necessary to ensure that nature would continue to provide an adequate livelihood for them and future generations.

This kind of culture conflict was remarkably similar all over the world with tragically comparable consequences, from North America to Oceania to Australia to Africa. It was no different in New Zealand. Unconcerned with long-term repercussions, Europeans sometimes stopped at nothing to maintain the growth of their agrarian subsistence pattern. Agriculturally rich indigenous land resources were stolen, sometimes on the battlefield and sometimes with the stroke of a pen. Violence was often used to maintain control of the lands, justified according to the "substantial use" rationale—that the natives were wasting valuable land resources by letting large areas remain unproductive.

The New Zealand colonial government did indeed confiscate more than 25 million acres of Māori lands through bloody conflict and subsequent unlawful legislation. The laws were illegal because they ignored the stipulations of the *Treaty of Waitangi.* Besides being the founding document of New Zealand itself, the treaty represented an official agreement between various Māori tribes and the Crown guaranteeing them; in the Māori version: (1) separate independence, (2) full rights and privileges as equal British subjects, and (3) retention of sovereignty over their land and other natural resources.

In May 1840, the Treaty of Waitangi was signed. The idea to treat with the Māori was conceived of by the British government, who was anxious to officially colonize the new land. Colonization was inspired by considerable poverty in the British Isles, exacerbated by inheritance traditions in which the eldest son was the only sibling entitled to the family's wealth.[3] Thus, the Crown saw the potential for mass migration to New Zealand as a mechanism for lessening the stranglehold of indigence gripping the empire at this time. Treating was also an expedient solution to the costly prospect of sending soldiers to take the new land from the Māori by force. Britain was burdened by the exorbitant expense of sustaining its empire at the time and simply could not afford to engage the military. Early in the nineteenth century, the Māori outnumbered Europeans nearly 50:1. Claudia Orange has argued that the idea "was to establish the independence of the country under the protection of the British government [which] would be the most effectual mode of making the country a dependency on the British Empire in everything but name."[4]

Alan Ward has suggested the treaty was to be an opening that would provide the colonizers with breathing room—or space and time to get them established and organized while they populated and settled the new land.[5] To this end, the Brits commissioned Captain William Hobson in 1839 to serve as the first lieutenant governor of New Zealand. Hobson called a panui (an invitation) to all Māori chiefs in the Bay of Islands to discuss a possible treaty. Three points were added, which became Articles 1, 2, and 3, summarized previously.

It is commonly recognized that the hired missionary translator assistants were not competent to effectively transliterate the Māori language. "The translator's Māori text failed to convey the full meaning of the national sovereignty being conceded. Adequate explanations could have overcome this, but failed to do so."[6] Added to the confusion was the fact that it had to be translated very quickly, in one day, to keep up with the schedule. On the following day, 600 Māori had been invited to gather, feast, and discuss the terms of the treaty. Whereas signing was recognized as the most important part of the treaty negotiation for the Europeans, it was discussion that was most important for the Māori, who have a long tradition of consensus building politics.

The missionaries couched the treaty in terms of the queen's act of love: "The Māori then viewed the document as a special kind of covenant with the Queen, a bond with all the spiritual connotations of the biblical covenants; there would be tribes, including the British, but all would be equal under one God."[7] But, an act of magnanimity it probably wasn't.

Another element adding to the confusion was that two versions of the treaty were ultimately signed that day—one in English and the other in Māori. In the end, 40 chiefs of the lower echelon signed the English version of the treaty. Eighty copies of it were then made and extended by missionaries and government officials to the rest of Māoridom. In all, 500 more chiefs signed the Māori version of the document. Heeni's mother's people, the Tainui, never signed the Treaty of Waitangi.

Ultimately, the Māori understanding of the treaty left much to be desired. The older chiefs probably thought their communities would remain monoculturally Māori, while a few nearby Pākehā "would open the way to trade in much desired European equipment, agricultural, domestic, personal and warfare materials."[8]

Instead, the Māori quickly found themselves defending their way of life against land-hungry settlers. The great Pākehā migration continued steadily from the British Isles, such that the Māori to Pākehā ratio weakened from 50:1 in 1840 to 50:50 in the 1850s. The flood of Europeans into New Zealand was a shock to the Māori, as they saw a future of cultural disaster if things were allowed to continue as they were.

The economic imperialism of the invaders was also destabilizing the Māori. For example, they were forced as novices into a new economic system that included a cash economy. They traded with unscrupulous tradesmen who often took advantage of the inexperienced Māori. Most of this new trading economy focused on timber and flax. "The discovery that trees and flax were a means of gaining trade articles had meant a revolution in the life of the people. The movement away from the (traditional Pas) became accelerated, and the primitive unhygienic camps near work became the rule. Many people completely neglected the usual seasonal planting of essential food supplies, and when winter arrived there was widespread hunger and undernourishment. This left the people physically unprepared to meet the subsequent series of devastating epidemics of whooping cough, measles and severe influenza."[9]

At this point, the Methodists intervened on behalf of the Māori. "They found it essential to bring instruction in arithmetic, and the proper method for estimating the timber content of logs into their school classes, and this, with reading and writing, was felt to be a Christian obligation for the protection of the people."[10]

The clearing of the land and selling of timber gradually made the Māori realize that in their eagerness to trade, they were losing their main resource—the land itself. Land losses extended as well from Earl Gray in England, who, in 1847, instructed the colonial government to take over all "surplus," unoccupied land and offer it for sale to prospective settlers. The settlers then increasingly put pressure on the Māori to sell their land, especially in the much coveted, agriculturally rich Waikato, Taranaki, and Bay of Plenty regions of the North Island. The rationale for forcing them to sell was that much of it was forested and not being made productive. It was therefore lying in waste. However, the Māori refused, and those in Reverend Whiteley's district held him in high esteem for offering support for their position.

He initiated many letters of protest to mission and government authorities alike, pointing out that the integrity of the missionaries was at stake because they themselves had urged the Māori to sign the Treaty of Waitangi. "A further point made most strongly was in a country where communal ownership of land was governed by a long-established code of procedures, there was no part of the country that did not belong to one or another tribe, and the fact that forest land was not cultivated did not necessarily mean that it was not vital to the economy of the people as a source of their traditional food supplies. Moreover their system of cropping of the land, and then moving to new areas so the land could rest, meant that large areas were left to lie fallow to recover."[11] In his pleas, Whiteley was expressing the Māori position that, in their worldview, there is no such thing as surplus or unoccupied wasteland, an inconceivable concept to the European invaders.

During this time, Whiteley began to establish himself as an esteemed pacificator. The Māori had begun warring quite heavily among themselves because native warfare had been exacerbated by the introduction of the European musket. As a result, Whiteley was often called in as an arbiter, and thus began proving himself as a dominant force among certain tribes as a peacemaker.

Because of his growing influence, he was chosen Chairman of the Southern Waikato Methodist. "In his own district Whiteley was consolidating his work with steady progress, as far as his frequent calls to distant places permitted. His reports showed a far-reaching concern for the whole of the Mission. There was a states-man like quality about his mind that drew leaders, both Māori and Pākehā to him for advice . . ."[12]

Although it won him much prestige among the local Māori, Whiteley's protests were ignored by the government. For their part, the Māori refused the forced sale of "surplus," corporately held tribal land. Tensions grew as the rhetoric of the period claimed that "land confiscations would have great benefit to the Māori people be-cause of increased land values brought on by settlement" and hence the end justified the means.[13]

To the Māori, February 22, 1860, is remembered as the historic occasion when the Pākehā took steps to deprive them of most of their best land. On this date, the new colonial government declared martial law in the much-disputed Taranaki region. With the declaration of martial law, many settlers drew within their safety and the defensive points, the Māori grouped into factions, some favorable and others bitterly opposed to the Colonial government.[14]

It was in this sociopolitical climate that the New Zealand "Māori Land Wars" began. Nine years of bitter unrest and periods of violent conflict followed the decla-ration of martial law. The Māori who defended themselves were dubbed "rebels"; their "rebellion" then justified land confiscations.[15] In all, three million acres were confiscated before 1860.

By 1867, there had been frequent battles between the militia of the new settler government and Taranaki Māori. Everyone was war-weary, including Reverend Whiteley. Despite the fact that he had won the respect of many Māori in both the Waikato and Taranaki, by caring very deeply about Māori concerns and despite the fact that he was often involved with negotiations for peace between them and the gov-ernment, he was killed on the beach in a freak incident just as "the war was dying down and farmers were returning to their land."[16] Ironically, the death of this peace-maker was the virtual end of the Taranaki wars.

By the turn of the twentieth century, the two cultures remained practically for-eigners to one another. Most Māori lived in rural areas subsisting traditionally with the addition of dairy cows to their small homesteads. The caste divisions of Māori society were intact; however, they were invisible from an economic standpoint be-cause most were dispossessed of their lands and therefore poor and disenfranchised. The majority of New Zealand cities were inhabited mainly by Pākehā containing few Māori until about 1950. By the time Heeni was ready to leave for the Te Kūiti School of Domestic Science and Hygiene in 1929, "their paths seldom crossed except in ca-sual business contacts, as each world was almost sealed off from the other."[17] Hence, the culture shock Heeni discusses in her narrative.

Heeni left for school as a teenager. At the time, she was a self-possessed adolescent girl, a bit sad about leaving home but absolutely ready for a big adven-ture. She knew doors were opening for her—that she was "on a road going to somewhere." Her first stop would be something like a finishing institution for Māori girls, an interim Methodist school for those who would be going on to do Church work.

The school had come in response to the perceived need for providing education to older Māori girls, as well as reports from missionaries about an increasing Māori population and growing health problems, which appeared to them to be the result of a lack of hygiene in Māori homes. It was under the direction of Mr. and Mrs. Strand, who opened it in what was formerly a cottage hospital.

After Te Kūiti, Heeni moved to Auckland, where she provided a leadership role as Senior Girl in the newly established Kuruhana Māori girls' school, a 10-room girls' hostel, on almost 2 acres of land purchased by the Methodist Women's Missionary Union on January 26, 1931. This school had the primary goal of reaching potential Māori mothers to assimilate them into mainstream Pākehā life. For example, to teach them all aspects of domestic work, the rudiments of hygiene, and infant care. The curriculum at Kuruhana included sewing and first aid, as well as some general school subjects. In addition, keeping hens and cows and learning to mend shoes were all a part of the training. The girls also attended Bible classes and took part in Christian activities. As Senior Girl, Heeni was preparing for a role she would later play as matron of Māori youth hostels in Hamilton. Heeni spent approximately one more year at Kuruhana and another in Father Seamer's home in Auckland, meeting church people and "having fun" before her application to attend Deaconess House in Christchurch was accepted.

The revival of deaconess orders was largely to enable the spread of social Christianity. Deaconesses were trained to dispense spiritual support while helping poor women care better for their children and families. They worked in economically depressed regions, both rural areas and cities, providing needed services to the economically disadvantaged. Deaconess training was recognized as having both practical and spiritual applications.

The New Zealand Methodist Order of Deaconesses was established in 1907 in Christchurch, although deaconesses had been active in New Zealand much earlier. The training at Deaconess House was more challenging for some, less so for others. Heeni found the Old Testament quite heavy and hard to work with. However, she enjoyed the fieldwork at Deaconess house where she gave sermons and assisted the poor. She was dedicated in 1941.

Before taking up hostel work, however, Heeni enjoyed one carefree, adventurous year as a new deaconess. She worked alongside Sister Ivy Jones traveling on a circuit north of Auckland. The two looked after Māori women and children in Northland, much in the same way Sister Nicholls had done for Heeni and her family in Mokau. For Heeni, this period was the fulfillment of all the adventure that dedication to church work had promised from the beginning.

The excitement was to be short lived, however, because at the end of the year, Heeni was suddenly called down to Hamilton by her Methodist Church officials. Her orders were to substitute for a seriously ill minister who was unable to perform his duties. Heeni remembers feeling anxious about the conditions of her new responsibility and the prospect of leaving her new friends on the northern circuit. As it turned out, the responsibility of substituting for this ailing minister was to be the least of her worries. His illness served primarily as a catalyst for getting her to Hamilton, where she began what became her life's work.

3 / Culture Shock

One of the truly extraordinary characteristics of Māori culture is that change is not a problem. Change can never overwhelm you. After all, you know, these people had everything taken from them that could possibly be taken. But in the end, there was that hard ideologically adaptive core that saw them through. Clearly, one part of this for them is that there is one sort of universal spiritual system which can incorporate whatever else comes along.

Professor James Ritchie

MY MUM AND dad and my koro gave a ceremony as I was leaving home. I was fifteen then, going on sixteen.

The ceremony honoured my being given over to the Church, sort of like an adoption. My elders were recognising that the church people would become my new family. From this point on, my people had no further say about the direction of my life. Unofficially, it was as if the Reverend Seamer, who was at that time the head of the Methodist Church on the Māori side, was becoming my new father.

The ceremony was held in the front room. It was a fairly small affair, just Father Seamer, Sister Nicholls, my parents, my koro and myself. The furniture had been removed; we were just sitting on mats. Most of it was conducted in Māori, because, of course, Sister Nicholls and Father Seamer spoke Māori fairly well. First of all, there was a mihi, with the proper Māori protocol for those who were there from the Church, and after that some prayers. Then the final blessing was given by my koro, who spoke on behalf of everyone in my family: 'We give Heeni over to you, and she is to become your adopted daughter; and there will be no problems from our people. We will have no further say about her future.' It was just a special sort of karakia, recognising a formal gift to the Church. I was the gift.

It wasn't like I was officially married to the Church. If we were to say it that way, some people might think I was restricted, which I wasn't. I could go out later, which I did do—I went out with friends to the pictures. I went dancing too. The Church didn't put any limitations on me in that regard. My only requirement was that I had to give four years of service to the Church; and after that I knew that if I did meet someone, I was going to settle down. At the end of my four years, I was told, if you want to get married or anything like that, you are free. And that was fair enough. I think it was also the way with theological men. I think they were trained by the Church, cared for by the Church, and then they did their service and got married. I don't think the word *promise* was ever impressed upon me. We weren't told to make a formal promise.

The transition brought mixed emotions for me, but mostly I was completely willing. I was absolutely excited about the opportunity to move around, up and down the

Father Seamer, President of Conference of the Methodist
Church of New Zealand, 1933.

country, doing my training. I knew there would be vacations, holidays and such coming along, when the Church would send me home. For me, it was a wonderful adventure to anticipate. But at the same time, I had some doubts. I began to think, 'Oh golly me, I'm actually going away from here. Have I made the right decision? I wonder when I'll be coming home again,' and that sort of thing. I don't think I cried when I left home, because my koro had been preparing me for my departure, so I knew it was coming.

Sure, there was a lot of sadness leaving home. I was quite homesick at first. It was really hard the first night in that great big house in Te Kūiti, and the first few days away. I wept in my strange bed, and naturally I felt very alone, having had such a loving sort of home. At first I was terribly lonely and homesick. That homesickness didn't leave me for some years, but because of the variety of opportunities that were being offered to me all the time, I was happy. There were always some moments, still today, when I wished I was back home. Right through my whole life, really.

I was taken to the Te Kūiti School of Domestic Hygiene, which had the primary goal of teaching students how to conduct themselves in such a manner that they'd become ladies. It was like a finishing school. This was a school for Māori girls who were going to become involved in the Church. Before we could do anything with the Church, they had to teach us the ropes of civilisation.

When we first arrived, I did what my koro said to do. Yes, that has lived with me to this day. After I got out of the car, I looked around a bit and saw the house—it was a huge, rambling place. At one time it had been a private hospital. Before I stepped into the house, I remembered the words of my koro. He said, always remember te runga rawa, wherever you go, and don't be afraid. So I lifted my thoughts above, and I tried not to fear my new environment.

Everything was so different at this new house. I remember walking inside, into the dining room. The tables—I remember sitting at the table and I didn't know quite which knife to use, or fork, or things like that. At home, well, maybe we had a spoon, and we'd just share a fork or a knife or something. In the summertime, we just used mussel shells that had been cleaned for eating utensils, and one or two other good knives or forks would be shared by all. But here in this new house, everyone had their own set of knives and forks and spoons. And they were absolutely clean—nice and shiny.

The first night of that type of living, in this very modern type of Pākehā dining room, well, I was a bit puzzled. At home we'd quite often sit on the floor and eat, because there wouldn't be room enough for all of the kids to eat at the table. We'd just sit on the floor to eat. But here, you see, we all sat around this big table. I thought, 'Well, I'm not going to say anything, just watch what the others are doing.' I think there were about nine of us there, just a small family. The matron and her husband were quite senior people. The husband was partially retired. He'd been the minister of the local church. He was also a builder, and was still sort of puttering around. She was quite a loving sort of woman—grey-haired and elderly, but that didn't worry me. But it was the neatness of this woman that I really remember; my first impression of her was tidy, very tidy, with her grey hair all nicely done, and dressed in nice clothes. And I thought, 'What a nice Pākehā'—because I'd been mixed up with Pākehā people before. I just sort of sat quietly and watched everything, and I began to think about this woman's hair. The other kids and I had long, straggly hair, while Mum had straight hair which she used to keep nice. And she didn't grey—even at my age she didn't grey. But this woman's hair was nice and wavy. I'm sure she had it done in Te Kūiti. I remember looking at her hair, and looking at everything about her. She was so tall. We grew to like her very much.

The first thing served to us was soup. We didn't have soup at home. I thought, 'Oh golly me, what's this? This is just like some kind of watery thing.' So I watched the others, you know, and I thought, well, soup is soup, so I'll use this spoon. But I wanted to pick my plate up, you know, and drink it like a civilised person. I found it was nice. I think it was like tomato soup. Then I think we had a roast. It was a special meal, because I can remember the matron's husband carving it up. Roast seemed sort of familiar, because we had roast pork at home. And then out came ice cream, and I thought, 'Oh, this is the way. You start off with soup, and then get a big meal, and then sweets,' which we didn't get much of at home.

There were four of us assigned to one big room. It was a sort of dormitory, and the matron's room wasn't too far away from ours. It was a big change for me, you know. It was such a large house. I lived there for a year. I don't think I was afraid, I don't think I felt that kind of fear. But I looked around and. . . There was a beautiful view, yes. I remember peering out over the rise, looking down on Te Kūiti one of the first evenings there. But I wondered. I was a bit apprehensive. Sure, I questioned things at that stage, wondering, well, what had I come into? But I never doubted my parents. And they'd prepared me, after all.

But I sure didn't sleep very well. How I missed the sound of the sea, and looking out on it first thing in the morning. In Mōkau, we kids would be tired at night. As soon as we got into bed, the sound of the sea would come into my ears. I was asleep in no time. I missed that sound the most the very first time I was away from home. How I missed the crashing of the surf and the constant waves and the closeness of the bush.

The town of Te Kūiti wasn't as big as it is now; it was a much smaller place. But it did look out on a different setting from what I was used to. A totally different outlook. I went from a natural world to a civilised world overnight. That was what my people were wanting me to do. They always talked to us about the importance of learning all you can about the Pākehā way of life. I think with my dad travelling all over the country they were alert enough to realise, and had enough foresight to see, that Heeni would be living in a different kind of world, and that she'd need to be trained for that type of world. It was very hard on them to move me out of the family, for me to go away from them. But they sacrificed me for the future good.

I remember getting up early at Te Kūiti, but that was no problem for me. That's because I always had to get up early at home, to walk the long way to school. At Te Kūiti, we had to be out of our beds by about seven o'clock, I think. And then we had to tidy up our room and make our beds properly. This was the first time I'd had a bed of my own, and proper sheets and that sort of thing. So I was learning. We had to be ready and dressed nicely for breakfast at about seven forty-five, so that there would be time for a Bible reading before breakfast was served. Sometimes it would be the minister, other times it was Sister Airini Hobbs, who would do the reading and the prayers.

We had to learn all of the Bible passages. The first one was the twenty-third Psalm. 'The Lord is my shepherd. . .', we had to learn that, then recite it to the minister without the Bible. But there was no pressure; we took our time. We recited it to him when we were able to. Slowly, I understood what these passages meant, because the minister explained them. I'd been to Bible lessons with Sister Nicholls, so I was a little bit advanced, but often it was a struggle, especially with the Old Testament.

The minister would explain just a little bit at a time. There was a shepherd with his crook, and he'd be over the hills. He would never bribe his sheep, but led them to shady places. That became very much what I had to follow on with and teach myself much later in life. The twenty-third Psalm always stood out in my mind, because I could see this man with a crook, a walking stick sort of thing to pull on the sheep, steering them. He explained it in such a way that no-one could not understand. 'I shall not want' took a bit longer to understand, because I couldn't see it in my mind. But I could see the other part very much.

At this time, I got entirely away from my Māoriness. I was learning something completely different, and didn't yet see how the two fitted together. Later I did. But at this time I was listening very closely to the words of my parents: 'Learn all you can about the Pākehā way of life.' So I was keen. I listened very carefully to all that was being told to me.

We also had Bible lessons in the evening. Before bed we'd gather around the big open fire in the lounge. There was a huge fireplace there, and wintertime was cold, so it was nice and warm in the lounge. Here we went over the same devotions before going to bed. The minister would ask, 'What did you understand about this today?' And then we'd share our own personal idea of what it meant to us. I know I was slow. It was all new to me, but there was no pressure on us.

Almost immediately I learnt to cook, wash and set the table Pākehā style. I know I didn't have very many clothes, but I think it was Sister Nicholls who took me down to the shop to buy a good warm jersey, something a little bit different from what I'd been used to. The emphasis was always on keeping yourself tidy, your hair clean—cleanliness was the thing. If we sat on a chair cushion, when we stood up we had to puff that cushion up again, so that anyone who came in would find the place tidy. It was all very different. And another thing, you didn't wear the other girls' things. You wore your own clothes, and each of us was given our own sort of dressing table. We each had our own comb. Well, of course, at home there was a fight over the one comb which we all shared. If I didn't get to it—and I had long hair—well, you just went without combing your hair. Not in Te Kūiti. All of this was absolutely new to me. I can't say that I adjusted quickly. I think maybe I was one of the slower ones. And your slippers. You didn't wear your slippers outside. And things were different as far as menstruation went. We were supplied with sanitary napkins. I didn't quite know what to do with them, because I was accustomed to using rags at home. I just figured it all out, I guess, by watching what the other girls were doing.

Don't get the wrong idea; it wasn't that I wasn't being loved and cared for. No, we were getting all of that. It was just the way it was being done that was unusual to me. At home, I don't know whether we brushed our teeth or not. Anyway, there was just one toothbrush there. One that we all shared, or just some of us. I don't know whether we all used it. But at Te Kūiti, you see, you kept your own clothes, brush, toothbrush and comb. We had our own towels and wash cloth. Oh yes, this was a Pākehā home of fairly high quality. We had to have baths in the bath. Of course, I missed bathing in the sea. There were two baths, I think, and toilets and all of that. Inside toilets, yes. It was quite modern. In Mōkau our toilets were outside, quite a way from the house.

It was all Māori girls at this point in my training. Most of the girls would've been brought up this way long before I was. They came from fairly good homes down near Taranaki in more urbanised areas. But I was the only one from Mōkau. I was the most country girl of the lot. I hadn't even seen a train until I came to Te Kūiti. Sometimes we used to get together and talk about how strange everything was, talk and giggle and things like that. It was all so different, and sometimes quite hard. To be absolutely honest, there were many times when I was sure I could have hopped into a bus and gone home. But I didn't. And I don't think anyone ever knew I was struggling within.

It felt like we were eating a lot more than usual. Cups of cocoa, and tea breaks with a biscuit. Plus a full breakfast, full lunch and full dinner. I thought, 'Look at my tummy'; and, of course, it meant we had to be walking and all of that sort of thing. It wasn't only how plentiful the food was, and how it was served, but how it was prepared and seasoned that was different. I think I did like it, but it was all a little bit strange to me. We had potatoes and kūmara and things like that, but it all tasted kind of off. The potatoes hadn't been planted with manure, and I hadn't ever seen cauliflower or cabbages before. In Mōkau, often if there was a group of us, Dad would put down a nice little hāngi. I missed all of that, and I missed the mussels. At home, we knew how to cook the mussels so that they weren't overdone. We seldom got mussels at Te Kūiti and when we did, they tasted different. And the milk. It was whole milk, not skim. I wasn't used to it. But we didn't have any fizzy drinks that are so much in shops today. Nothing like that. We just had to drink cold water if we wanted a drink between dining hours.

At about half past ten, it would be time for morning tea. We'd all be seated again, and there would be a cup of tea, and just maybe we'd have a single biscuit. This was the way of life, you see, a cup of tea with just one biscuit. I thought, 'Well, that's funny.'

I think it was after this break that we'd have a little bit of lawn to mow outside. We took turns mowing. We also took turns at weeding the garden. We had quite a bit of garden around, but none of that worried me. Then dinner would be served at half past twelve. Always these exact times, you see. I remember all that; it's quite clear in my mind today. There were bells, you see. At half past three another cup of tea. If we were outside, we'd have to come in and wash our hands first—everything had to be spotless. After lunch, there were more duties to do. It wasn't a sit-down way of life; it was up and going. We did as we were told. Sometimes we had to wash the windows, and the place was absolutely full of windows, so I didn't like that job very much. All these cleaning materials were there for us to use. This was different from at home. There, Mum would give us a rag or something, but we didn't have the materials to get things spotless. At Te Kūiti, there were different buckets and different tools for specific jobs.

At half past four, we had to get ready again for supper. At about five o'clock, we were to be at the table. A short prayer, bless the food, eat it, and then the dishes. Very organised. There was no machine to wash the pots, it was all of our own doing. We had to keep everything spotless.

After I got used to all of this strange way of life, I loved it, you know. After the evening meal, it would be a quiet sort of time. But we always had to be doing something with our hands. So that's when I would do a little bit of sewing. Matron was a very good dressmaker, and I learnt sewing from her. I've forgotten what we had to do first of all—something fairly simple. I think we started off making handkerchiefs or something like that. Matron would provide the material, cut it all out for us, and show us how to hem it properly.

So we were provided with whatever we needed for sewing, crocheting and knitting. I made a couple of pretty dresses that way. In those days, you could buy material here for only two shillings a yard or something like that. So off we'd go to the store. Matron, I think, went down in the car and we would meet her downtown. We'd go into the shop and she would say, 'Janey, you choose. What would you like?' But only within a certain range. I enjoyed all of that because it helped me improve my sewing. Mum had a machine but couldn't afford material.

The Church knew I had tuberculosis before I left home. They weren't concerned that I'd infect the other girls, because tuberculosis was very prevalent in those days among Māori people. I did have to have checkups, and had to be careful. But I was always very fussy in that respect. I think I kept myself a little away from other people. I think there would have also been two or three other girls there with tuberculosis at Te Kūiti.

Te Kūiti wasn't restricted. We had freedom. We got mixed up with a different circle of boys and girls and there were Bible class evenings and all that sort of thing. Sometimes we'd have special gatherings at the Methodist Church in town. Matron would have evenings when young people from the Church would come for an evening. Oh, we did lots of singing. People would play instruments like the guitar and the ukulele. The singing felt good, because it was very familiar to me. There were plenty of young people. But no special attachment or anything like that. It was all just fun. There were games we used to play.

I can remember musical chairs—such a noise, but we loved all of that. Some would play instruments, and then suddenly the music would stop, and the rest of us rushed to the nearest chair. I never won. No, I think I was always last or something. Or pushed aside by somebody else. There was plenty of roughness.

After I'd spent a year in Te Kūiti, I was told I'd be moving to Auckland.[1] I think my first thought was, 'Golly. That'll be fun, to go to Auckland.' I was ready for another adventure. In the meantime I was keeping in touch with my folks at home, so they knew exactly all the different steps that their daughter was moving up or into. I was sent on to Auckland in January or February of 1929 to a group home run by the New Zealand Education Department.[2]

Well, that opened my eyes too. At Te Kūiti, you see, we could laugh, giggle, play and make all sorts of noise. In the new place, we were quite restricted because the houses were close together. We lived in a flat, level home on level ground. We could see into the next house, practically into their bedrooms. It was a bigger house than the one in Te Kūiti, previously owned by a doctor. I remember looking around and saying, 'This is a nice home too. What a lovely home.' There were more girls, maybe around twenty or so. And these were different types of girls, too. Quite new. These were half-caste Māori girls who were grown up a bit.

This new place was called Kurahuna, and I was sent to be the head girl, I was a prefect. Here I'd begin to work more closely with the Church, and at the same time take on lots more responsibility than I'd had previously at Te Kūiti. The matron, who was widely respected among Māori people, relied on me to make sure everything was running properly. Now, I have an idea that I was given a small room to myself. The other, bigger rooms had three or four girls to each. I was getting a bit older by then, so I felt quite good about that.

There was still no thought in my mind of being afraid of anything. I think from the time I left home I was a fairly positive-thinking sort. I use the word *positive* because it wasn't in my vocabulary at that time. But I was quite sure of myself. Very confident, on the right path, and on the way to somewhere. I always had in my mind the thought that, well, maybe this isn't going to be the end for me; other doors are

Pupils at the Kurahuna Māori Girls' School, Auckland, in the early 1930s. I'm sitting at the right-hand end of the front row. Methodist Archive

going to open. I was at this place a couple of years, but I didn't worry too much about the future. I kept my mind on the thing of the day, you know, whatever I was doing at the moment.

After we'd been there a little while, it became clear there were one or two naughty girls. There were certain rules. For instance, you couldn't go out without first asking. Another one was that we had to keep in our own clothes. Things like that. Naturally, in a group of young people you have those who won't keep to the rules. Since it was my responsibility to keep order, I'd try to talk to them. If that didn't work, I'd report them to the matron, which I didn't often do unless it was something that was really beyond my control. As I look back, I can see this was good practice for running a hostel.

In Auckland, I was meeting many Pākehā people, community and church leaders alike. I also met students at the theological college, so I was mixing with all sorts of people. And I watched how to do and say things. I did have friends— boyfriends—but again, I was always careful not to get too close. I treated them all alike.

In school at Auckland in the early training years when I was about seventeen, it was quite an open house. We weren't restricted there, but still we didn't mix with the young people outside—it was always the young people within the Church. I didn't make any friends there with men outside Church circles; I knew my responsibility and stuck to my duties there. There were evenings when we entertained, and there were lots of people who came to give us lectures in deportment and entertaining. I had to take part in all that; it was part of my training to be a hostess and to receive people. My mind, I think, was taken up with all that. I was growing up, sure, but I didn't get much time to myself.

I knew one of the girls at the hostel during my time who got sort of interested in a young fellow and was going out with him, and I used to say to her, 'Well, be careful.' She was a half-caste, a very striking girl, and she said, 'I'd like to sneak out tonight and go out.' I said, 'Well, I don't know, that's throwing an extra burden on my shoulders.' And yet I didn't pimp on her. I thought she may not have been the only one to have become involved with boyfriends. And they were boyfriends from the Church, who were quite good company.

Even though I chose not to marry, I did have lots of opportunities with boys. And I loved male company, more than I did women. I loved to be with menfolk. Right throughout my life, I've always preferred friendships with men to women. I found women were gossipy. They chattered. And I found them to be judgmental, always looking to see what Heeni was wearing and that sort of thing. I didn't find that with men. I found menfolk to be a lot more solid and sensible. They always gave me that strength. I think it was because I thought deeply about things and found that men could handle this better than women. And truthfully, I was just quite comfortable with menfolk, both the young and the not quite so young. I liked the tall, well-built, intelligent fellows, especially if their bodies reflected a certain spiritual and emotional strength, and quite enjoyed the kissing and cuddling. All of my brothers were tall, strong fellows, so I wasn't quite so interested in smaller types of men, shorter than myself. I always liked dancing with taller, strong men. Although there was one young fellow for a time, I didn't make a habit of just keeping to him. I enjoyed going to the pictures with a boy, and there would be a bit of standing around the corner hugging and kissing, but there was always an instinct there about knowing how far to go. What a lot of rubbish I'm talking!

Anyway, I was being prepared for deaconess work, first at Te Kūiti and now at Kurahuna. There had been some talk among the heads of the Church about sending me on for further deaconess training in Christchurch. I suppose they were watching me back then as I moved from one place to the other, but when the application was made from Auckland for me to go to Christchurch, I was turned down at first because I was too young. I was being watched in Auckland by different committees, and medical and church people. During the year that I was turned down, I went into the home of the Reverend Seamer, who really kept an eye on me along the way. He was the one that my koro had passed me over to, and so, you see, he kept in very close contact with me all along. He used to come and visit me, but he was a very busy man. At this time, he had the Waiata Māori choir touring up and down New Zealand, so I didn't see a great deal of him. He lived in a big two-storey house in Birkenhead, and I went to his home for that year. I enjoyed that very much.

There, I helped with the housework and earned a little bit of money. The man who was in charge of looking after the reverend's home was a retired minister, you see. I knew I was being prepared for what was ahead of me. We still had Bible studies and Bible gatherings in Auckland. The deaconess there, who was in Māori work, pretty well had control of all the Auckland Māori people. She was a very famous lady, Sister Ivy Jones; you may have read about her. The gatherings she used to have. There would be crowds of young people flocking to her special evenings,

Bible studies and fun events and all that sort of thing. She was the deaconess in charge of the Auckland city area, and a JP and very widely known. The boys would gather around her, not only the Māori boys we were mixing with, but anyone who was interested in what she was doing.

At that time the Church was starting a mission in Queen Street. The minister there, C.G. Scrimgeour, was a pilot, mixed up with the love of air. He was fairly outstanding at the time, with new ideas in the Church, quite controversial and well known throughout New Zealand. He was young with a young family—a young wife and little children. He was a very bouncy sort of minister that you couldn't help but take to. And he was very interested in the elderly folk and used to gather them together; they used to come along to the Methodist Mission, and I got involved with all that.

Before I went down to Deaconess House in Christchurch, I knew what would be expected of me. I was involved with people like Sister Rita Snowden, who has written many books. She and other folks were much older than me, and they'd question me so that I'd have a pretty good sort of knowledge of the Old and the New Testaments, and also of English, psychology and all those subjects I knew I'd have to know before I left. But don't ask me about the results of the examinations I took once I got there! There were going to be lectures every day, lectures on the Old Testament, which was different for me. So, you see, the question-and-answer quiz sessions prepared me for Deaconess House.

During that year I was also having lots of fun. It wasn't a deadly sort of life, you know. People often think this about church people. I went into town quite often with friends, with boyfriends on the ferry from Birkenhead, and had lots of fun. In the back of my mind I thought, 'Now, you've got this whole year off. Enjoy it.' I had a whole year to play around. My life wasn't restricted during that time, but I knew I had to be careful. And that's when I became involved with a wider group of men and women. I'd have been about eighteen or nineteen then.

By this time, I was growing up a little bit, and though I distributed my feelings, I became interested in one particular young fellow there. He was a student at the theological college. This was a big two-storey building; it still stands there, but the road has sort of cut through that area, just over the Grafton Bridge. Yes, I became interested in one of the students there, but I knew also that he was only in his second year and that he was tied down to a four-year course. And, of course, after that he'd have to do a full year of church work before he'd be allowed to marry. I knew for myself, too, that I wanted to go to Deaconess House in Christchurch, so I didn't let myself fall desperately in love with anyone. There was another road somewhere else on which I'd be going.

The student who caught my fancy was in training as a Methodist minister, and I knew the same circumstances would be on his mind and shoulders. I'm sure he had goals that he wanted to reach. This student became the great Dr Maharāia Winiata. He went to Edinburgh, where he received his doctorate, and became a leading Māori theologian in New Zealand.[3] But we were friends, sure. We used to go out, to the pictures and walking. One day he said, 'What about coming across from Birkenhead into town?' (where he was at Trinity Training College). So I said I'd catch the ferry. Well, we met and he said we'd go to the zoo, so we walked there, which was quite a long way from Queen Street. After the zoo, we went over to the mental hospital, because the students had to take services there and he had a service that evening. We walked, and now and again we'd stop and have a cuddle and that, and then we'd walk again. But even then, there wasn't any question of any deep feelings, although I liked him very much. We ended up at the hospital at about half past six, in time for him to take the service. I knew he was clever, and he was neat and he was nice. But as the years went by, he completed his study and went to Oxford. That was after he'd married. He married a deaconess—a Pākehā deaconess. I knew his wife, too, because she was about my age, and I knew her parents when I was in Auckland. Her family went to the same church as we girls. A lovely family; the father was the organist there. When Maharāia had written to me that he'd become engaged to Frances, there was no jealousy or anything like that. I knew Frances would look after him, being a Pākehā, a neat girl. She'd help him a great deal with his work. She had a good bit more education than I did. But then I continued seeing him. There wasn't any ill feeling or anything like that.

Even after he was married, Maharāia continued the friendship with me. We were still close. Later, when I was matron of the youth hostels in Hamilton, he'd come down to pay me visits. He did wonderful things there. He'd come when I was at the hostel and help with the little magazine that we had. He'd stay at the hostel, and he'd say, 'My duties are all over now. What are you doing tonight?' And I'd say, 'Well, maybe I've got a free evening too. What about we go to the pictures?' Even after he was married, much later, when he had children. His wife, Frances, was living in Auckland, but he himself moved up and down New Zealand quite a bit. So it was a long sort of friendship, but nothing deep. He'd still want to kiss me and cuddle me, even when he was married. He'd tell me he had to prepare a talk, an address to the government, and we would talk about what he was going to say. These were nearly always free nights for me, when someone else was in charge of the hostel. I wasn't restricted, and I think I combined the two parts of my life, the social and the more serious part, my work, quite well.

I remember him going to present a lecture in Te Kūiti, and he said, 'What about you coming down with me? I'm going down there in the evening to speak to the students and then coming back.' He was staying at the hostel—in a cottage—at the time. I said I'd have to see what my programme was. He said OK, he'd be leaving at such and such a time to get down there to meet the headmaster of the school. And I went with him because I felt he was such a clever fellow, and I was learning quite a bit from him. Not only spiritual things; he wasn't only a minister, he also became a teacher and an inspector after he got his master's degree, and he travelled widely. So I felt that going with him would be beneficial to me in my work, but I was also going with him as a companion. Along the way, he'd say, 'Oh, golly, this lecture that I've got to give tonight's a bit heavy. Don't you do anything, sitting there looking at me; just you sit quietly. Oh well, let's have a kiss before we go!'

His wife is still living. But I think her family knew that Heeni had no interest in marrying him, just loved him as a mate. I was a good companion for him to travel with while he endured those heavy lectures that he was giving. There weren't many Māori people in the audiences. I was very supportive of him; I listened to him. I was a teacher for him in some ways, as he was a teacher to me. Our friendship continued right though his life, really. But he died very early. I saw him only a few hours before. He must have been not quite forty when he died of a stroke. It was discovered later that he'd worked so hard in England to get his doctorate that it had overstrained his mind. You know, he'd work day and night with very little sleep. We could all see that he was working just a little bit too hard. So one day, when he was on a marae giving an address in Māori, he collapsed. His body just gave way. By the time the doctors got through to him, I think there was nothing that could be done.

I saw him just a few hours before he went to that hui. He lived in Auckland, you see, and he came through Hamilton on his way down and called in to see me. It was very early in the morning. I think we'd just got up for breakfast and he just walked in. He said he was on his way to Tauranga and wanted to see Father Seamer, and he went in to see him and left. I think it might have been the next day that he collapsed. He didn't seem tired or overstressed, but I only saw him for a few minutes. It was business, and when he was on business, there was no 'How are you?' or that sort of thing; it was just business. To me he looked his usual self. His passing saddened me quite a bit.

4 / On to Christchurch

But you can't deny us, nor can you ignore us. You tried to destroy us, and you have failed. So whatever intellectual domestic road you undertake with us, we'll meet you on the way.

Sir Robert Mahuta

I SPENT TWO years in Auckland before I went on to Christchurch for my deaconess training. That training would prepare me for my first job.[1]

In Christchurch, we were trained to work mostly with women, you know, the women throughout the area, and the young people. We were given instructions on how to organise women's meetings and to work among children. It was the same sort of thing Sister Nicholls had done with us when she used to come visiting down our way. We also conducted Bible classes in the public schools. In those days we had permission to go to any school and organise these classes. Not today, dear. That went out years ago.

The house where I stayed in Christchurch was a very big two-storey house not far from the cathedral—just the next street over. There were squares, you know, and big open lawns, and often on a bright evening we'd have our gatherings out there, out on the lawn. Lovely times which I did enjoy; I enjoyed my time there, meeting lots of people.

It was like a big hostel, and there were about thirty girls living there each with a room of her own. Only about six were going through deaconess training; the rest would have been university students. The students were full of fun. I joined in with all of their good times. I can remember some evenings when we'd be really hungry, and although we didn't have very much money, we would see how much we had together and make a plan to get up at midnight and go down to the pie cart to get food. We'd just sneak off at night; but I only remember doing that once, because we would get into trouble if we got caught out. Later in the year, though, closer to the end of term, some of the girls would just put on their dressing gowns to go down to the street. I thought it was really fun; you know, we didn't do that sort of thing at the other school. But then, of course, I was much older; I had my twenty-first birthday down there. I'd hear the girls sneaking out because the fire escape was near my bedroom upstairs, but I closed my eyes to it because I did the same sort of thing myself! I could hear them giggling on the way back in, and I'd just turn over and hope that everything would go well with them and that they wouldn't be caught along the way. Of course, in those days it was quite safe to be going out at night in Christchurch.

In the early days at the school, I'd usually start off with breakfast and then go on my circuit round Linwood, which was appointed to me by the Methodist Deaconess

Board. The circuit took us from one area to another, visiting women at different stages of life. Mothers and children and the elderly—we saw the whole life cycle of women and their needs. We were learning how to adjust to being with adults, with children, and with those not as fortunate as ourselves. I was under the direction of a local Methodist minister, and I found him to be quite interesting. So the first few days were spent just sailing around Christchurch on a bicycle getting to know the different areas. Then we started off with district appointments. An itinerary had already been planned for me, and the minister would give me a list of people to visit. At first I was a little shy, being in a new part of New Zealand, you know. He had been there for quite a while before I arrived, so he'd know who was in need of a visit.

Typically we went on our visiting circuit in the afternoons. I'd borrowed a bicycle, and I wasn't too confident on it. Especially there, where there were hundreds of other people on bicycles. Very flat country, there. And first of all, they'd look at me and think, 'Here comes the Māori girl,' because so few Māori lived in Christchurch and seeing a Māori girl was sort of rare, an unusual sort of a person to them. But in those times I was very well received. I was always nervous visiting, but I'd find comfort in remembering the words of my koro. I would visit on behalf of the Reverend Ryan, to help him so that he could maybe do more important things working within the Church. I'd be given a list of names of those he visited and talk and give advice and moral support—anything that was needed. There were lots of families there who were poor; they liked to use the word poor, dear, people who weren't the really rich sort. I was given one or two people to see in Christchurch who were pretty well off, but most of them were of ordinary type. You know, these were already church people, and we'd talk about all sorts of things. We wouldn't necessarily stick to the purpose of our visit, although we always tried to talk about church kinds of topics. But we'd also talk about things like knitting, sewing and singing. I always felt that I was gaining from these people too, you know; gaining friendship and widening my horizons.

These were Māori women. Māori people were a good bit backward in those days, you know; so a lot of my work had to do with education and tips about how to care for the kids. First of all you had to visit the women and get their confidence, and try and organise a meeting at a set time and place—not an easy job. Sometimes it was a church building or in a private home or wherever. During the meetings, we had Bible study and some discussion on health. My training had included some health education tips. Sometimes I had to do a little bit of nursing in the home, and other times I had to discuss the women's personal health concerns.

In the afternoons, we went out visiting folks on our circuit who needed some kind of help. On the way, we went to lots of churches and lots of women's meetings, just to be there and to be ready to answer their questions. One place was called Durham Street Church. A number of the women were elderly. I think most of them were 70 and upwards, and some were having problems with walking; because I can remember some coming along with walking sticks. They were hungry and always glad to receive our food. We offered sausages and buns, and other things too. I used to enjoy going to this mission because there was a piano, and there would be lots of singing. Oh singing, yes, how I enjoyed singing. The minister's wife, who was a member of the choir, used to come along now and again, and we'd sing to these ladies.

I used to love going down to that church, but I think that was only once a week or so. We didn't do the pastoral work more than once or twice a week. On the other afternoons, I'd sometimes go down and just have a happy hour with them, a lovely, pleasant time together with them. We'd have a cup of tea and provide them with some nice biscuits and things like that. The lady in charge was wonderful, and she supplied most of the parcels. Some would have about three or four sausages or steaks or something like that; of course these things were cheap in those days. Of course this was during the Depression. Very bad poverty existed right throughout New Zealand, but my own people were lucky—they could go to the sea to gather mussels, mussels, mussels and fish, fish, fish for good meals. You know, I don't think they ever went hungry; I wasn't concerned for Mum and Dad and the family at home during those times because they had the potatoes and the kūmara, and that was our staple diet.

In Christchurch, I can remember going into one home and there was very little in the way of furniture, just a small gas heater to cook on and a pot. There was just no money around in those days. Five shillings was a lot of money, but you know, we didn't need money. We were very well cared for; we had a good bed to sleep on, food, and warm bedclothing, warm uniforms to wear and flat-heeled shoes to walk in and warm gloves and hats and scarves. But there were a lot of people around who needed clothing, and at those meetings we used to distribute things that would come from the Church. The centre there would send clothing to us to give to these poor people. The young minister used to gather in all these down-and-outs. I think they were loners, especially the men, who would just walk the streets and have nowhere to sleep. I saw a lot of men there who had nowhere to go, and hardly anything on their feet, even in winter. My heart used to go out to them; I could never imagine that sort of life because of being brought up in a home where we always had something warm to eat, even if it was only porridge. These were things that those poor people down there didn't see. I used to feel for them, very much for them, and to get over all that, I think, we used to sing. They used to enjoy singing, but they couldn't themselves sing much. We don't talk much about those days, because it was sad, seeing people like that.

When these people were sick, they'd go to the hospital there, and there was quite a well-known group of registered nurses who would go into the homes. I wasn't attached to the nurses' group, but one of the other deaconess students was appointed to that kind of work and I can remember her coming in to talk about the really sad cases that she'd come across. I just got a glimpse of it, but she was the one who was very much involved.

They sent me to the maternity home as part of my training. I remember one very young girl who had got into trouble with an unwanted pregnancy; her being so young saddened me. She was in labour, and it upset me quite a bit because she was screaming; she'd yell, and I felt that she was being left a good bit on her own. I felt that maybe the doctor and sister weren't coming in very often. I was the one who was given the gloves to rub her tum, you know, rub her when she screamed and yelled and kicked and all sorts of things. It saddened me to think she was so young, about fifteen or sixteen, and that she was having such a hard labour. I was told that evening that it was her second baby. I was glad that I only had to go to one other case after that.

I also had to go twice a week into a kindergarten. It was lovely; I just sat in a little chair with a group of young people. It was quite a big kindergarten; I think there must have been about sixty children. The lady in charge was delightful, and she was very good to me. I had to take my turn in leading the day's lessons, you know, for an hour or two, but these were just little tots, beautiful children. We said short rhymes and did simple exercises with them, kneeling in front of them or sitting in low chairs if we wanted to chat with them. We had a kind of opening exercise with a little song, and then we'd all get up and move round and round. There was nothing very complicated or heavy for the little people. Then we'd have a cup of tea and a biscuit, and they'd have their own little cups, of course. In nice weather we'd often take them for a short walk, nothing too far, there was quite an area outside with a big garden. I really enjoyed that, being with those lovely tiny people.

I was also mixing with the young people's groups in the Church, with both men and women. We'd go walking over the hills with the whole Bible class group. We'd go from Christchurch to Lyttelton over the hill, and that was an all-day walk. I can remember going to a party with a group and I got to know a lot of young fellows there, and got to like them too, and we missed the last bus home and had to walk. The matron wondered why we were so late in coming in; we didn't arrive home until the early hours of the morning.

And then we also had to take part in church services. We'd take a text from the Bible and make a service of it. I took one out in the country, and had to arrange the whole service, make a Bible reading and be responsible for the whole thing. The people there were all the usual congregation, all Pākehā; there were only one or two Māori from the north who had gone down there for holiday. I was the only one at that service; it was all part of the training. I'd have been only twenty-two, and I was really nervous. I wondered whether I'd be able to go through with it. The hymns and the prayers were no problem, but I was nervous about what I'd be talking about. There was someone there to listen and give you marks, because this was all part of the oral exams. I don't remember how many marks I was given for that, but I remember I was so glad when it was all over, and my mind didn't go back to that again because it was moving on all the time. I was nervous all along the way of my career. I knew that it was all part of the training, and always accepted whatever task I was given.

In addition to my circuit work, I attended lectures in the morning in a special room in the house that we lived in. The lecturers used to come every day from nine until twelve. We had classes in the New Testament, the Old Testament, psychology and English. English worried me a little, but there was no problem with the psychology. Because I think my old people knew quite a lot about psychology.

Most of us had a great deal of anxiety. There were one or two girls there that had no problems with that, but another girl didn't make it. She was much older and had already been engaged. She applied to the deaconess training and got through, no problem. She'd had a very good education. She was a very sporty type of girl, well built and fearless. She knew that she'd have to give four years of service after the training but she went home and met up with the man again. So they got married.

By the time I reached Deaconess House in Christchurch, I was supposed to know a lot of the Old and New Testaments, but in reality I knew very little. When we got to Deaconess House, you see, we had a different curriculum, which became lots deeper than what I'd done in previous Bible studies. The Old Testament and the way

Methodist deaconesses at a deaconess convention at Rātana Pa. near Wanganui. I'm in the back row, fourth from left, aged thirty-four, with Sister Airini Hobbs on my right. Sister Nicholls is sitting fourth from left in the front row, and Sister Ivy Jones second from left. S.M. Dixon, Elrick Studios

of life in it didn't altogether appeal to me. I had an idea about what it meant, but I couldn't relate to the depth of it that was expected of us. The other girls had lots more training than I did; and I found that I was the one lady way down on the scale because I didn't get secondary education. It was quite difficult for me, in the development of my mind at that stage, to follow and understand the esoteric meanings of the Old Testament. It was much easier for me to understand the deeper meanings of the New Testament. I was able to grasp the meaning of the Old Testament while reading about the prophets. Even today, I find the Old Testament very, very heavy reading, and I don't often go to it. I feel that, oh well, that's in the past, but they'd dwell on learning it passage by passage. One of our instructors took us through the New Testament, and he had a happy way of presenting the love of our Lord and the prophets and the disciples that I was able to follow. I used to love reading the book of Isaiah— and the Psalms, I still read those.

You know, I accepted Christianity quite readily, even though I'd been only lightly prepared by Mum saying prayers. She'd tell us, 'Don't forget—I've told you that many times, you know—don't forget to say thank you in the morning and then in the evenings.' We were only kids then but that stuck with me. To me, that's what Mum said, so I accepted it. But I also remembered the things my koro said about te runga rawa. To me, spirituality was all one thing. It wasn't divided between Māori and Christianity, it was all one to me, with my mum, my koro and the deaconess training along with the English way of life. There was no doubt or questioning of my Māori beliefs, you know. I didn't question Christianity, either. I accepted both. Yes, I don't think I deviated very much from what my mum and my koro taught me as a child.

With Sister Nicholls, when she was made an MBE (A Member of the Order of the British Empire) in Auckland in 1962.

But it all became richer, my way of thinking and my way of life. I think that perhaps it had been said to me, later when going home after a number of years, 'Oh Heeni, you've become so Pākehā.' But then I can also remember a Pākehā deaconess saying to me, 'Oh, you still cling very much to your Māori way of life. You've been away so long among the Pākehā people, but you're still so much a Māori.' And I can remember someone saying to me when I didn't have stockings on my legs, 'My goodness, you do have Pākehā legs.' And when I said why, they said, 'Why don't you get out in the sun a little more!' But even though I have a little bit of Pākehā blood there, French blood to be exact, I was very proud of my Māori. And I was told by another koro, 'Don't forget, my girl, your graciousness comes from your Māori side.' I think I've had good words spoken to me along the way, from time to time, which have helped me to keep my dignity.

But I have to admit that, when it came to learning about the religion of the Old Testament, which I didn't take book by book, it did not sink in very much. No, I didn't commit to the Old Testament in my prayers; it was always the New Testament, you know. I had heard the name of our Lord mentioned at home, yes, but it became more distinct in my mind after I left home. I'd heard His name spoken sometimes in not a very nice way. Used, you know, in almost an everyday swearing sort of way. It was probably used very little, really, in that way, but it made an impression on me, and I think I must have had a one-track sort of mind.

The beginning of the Old Testament, the Creation, was always a puzzle to me. But I loved reading about Samuel and his call. I could relate to that. I was developing my own mind at the time, and I'd read about Moses. I knew that he had been called and I knew that he didn't actually get into the Promised Land, but he saw. I knew the reason why he didn't actually get into the Promised Land where he was leading his people was because he'd sinned himself, and I was able to relate to all that. Perhaps I shouldn't put the Old Testament down, but I'm looking at it as a whole. Of course, there were lots of characters and passages here and there that I did relate to. Like David, of course, I thought he was a strong young fellow, and a coura-geous young fellow, for the things that he did. I was able to relate there, he connected to me. I think I understood how David felt; later on he was the one who was called so much. Oh dear, I'd sort of forgotten these things. You know, they did some unusual things, oh golly me. Even during Moses' time, they were talking about getting back to the simple way of life. Moses was always gathering his people together and talk-ing to them about turning from the foolish way of life, making and worshipping idols and that sort of thing. I related it to the muru hara, where the people come before their god to ask forgiveness. It was the same.

But the foundation of the New Testament fascinated me. The life of this young man, born to the Virgin Mary in a stable, fascinated me because we had something like a stable at home in Mōkau. We called it a shed. I also related to the descrip-tions of fishing in the New Testament. I used to tell a fishing story to my Sunday-school kids. This was when our Lord came along the beach and called all those there to follow Him. I was able to relate to all of that, of course, having been brought up in a seaside area. The sea, and the lakes that He calmed, all that was no problem for me to accept. And when Peter was in the boat and the ocean became very rough and their Lord was asleep, and they became anxious, and they called on Him. These things were all related to the way that I grew up. And right at the end of His life, that became very sad. And when they went to the tomb, all those womenfolk going to the tomb and seeing an imaginary person there, that was no problem for me to accept, for you know I told you about those ghosts. I was raised on stories like that.

After all those lectures and all that Bible study and all that circuit work, I left Christchurch as a deaconess. And after all that training and all those nerve-racking exams and all those speeches, I went back to Auckland, where I was given a district of my own. Here I was involved with the Māori mission work of Sister Ivy Jones. It was social work really. We had help from the students who were attending the the-ological school in Auckland.

North of Auckland, we moved along on a circuit. We went into local homes, gave short devotions, and met different kinds of folk. These were mostly Māori peo-ple. We'd visit homes where there were a lot of kiddies and young people. And I'd take them to Bible studies and Sunday school, because that was also part of our train-ing at Christchurch. These were people who weren't going to church regularly, who were living back in the country and really right away from a second, or Pākehā, way of life, mostly like my own people back in Mōkau.

So for one adventurous, fun-loving year, I did the same sort of work as Sister Nicholls. I used to think back to the time when she came into our home when I was young and when she was the only deaconess and fairly well-known throughout the area. I loved all the travelling and the visiting, just as I'm sure Sister Nicholls did when she was my age. I didn't feel burdened by heavy responsibility that year. I felt very free and enjoyed the opportunity for meeting more of my own Māori people. It broadened my horizons a good bit.

This was taken in the late 1930s or early 1940s—
probably around the time I spent in Kāwhia.

But then, *suddenly,* I was called away. My orders were to go to Kāwhia to stand in for a local minister who had become quite ill. While I was in Kāwhia, the kaumātua, who knew my whakapapa, took me under their wing. They cared for me physically, mentally and spiritually. I became one of theirs. With their aroha I absorbed the wairua of Tainui and the Kīngitanga. This was a significant time in my life, and I was strengthened and enriched for the life and work ahead of me.

PART THREE

THE HOSTELS

He kikonga whare e kitea, he kokonga
ngakau kore e kitea

The dark corners of the house may be explored,
but not the corners of the heart.

By the time Heeni was dedicated as deaconess, she had been thoroughly exposed to the best of both cultures, Māori and Pākehā. Born and raised in an aristocratic atmosphere typical of her indigenous culture and one that greatly suffered as a result of the European colonial pattern, she bridged the cultural frontier, launching her way straight into the dominant society. There she absorbed the social priorities of the Methodists, which were based on Christian compassion and kindness—lofty ideals that, theoretically at least, sit at the root of western civilization. After 15 years of thorough immersion in each culture, Heeni emerged from her deaconess training as a bicultural woman long before the concept was en vogue. Fluent in both languages and cultures, with "one foot in each well, still standing up straight," she was now ready to undertake her life's work.[1]

To many people, her bicultural achievements are extraordinary, particularly because all around the world indigenous people are not coping well in similar postcolonial circumstances. For many fourth world peoples, social problems extend from life in a consumer society whose value system runs contrary to core tribal beliefs.[2] As a tribal person, Heeni was very lucky; her elders consciously directed her with a sixth sense about a world that they knew was on the horizon, although about which they could only suppose. And, of course, she had no other option. "If your elders and family pointed you in certain directions, you could either go along with it, or you had to cut yourself off entirely. And, if you're a tribal person, you just can't do that."[3]

The hostel movement of the 1940s and 1950s represented an advocacy project for Māori young people, many from fairly prominent families, who were to benefit from a Māori home base while taking advantage of secondary and/or tertiary education available in the city. Dr. Anthony Rogers, a close personal friend of Heeni's during the hostel years, explained that the hostel was not merely a dormitory situation. More, it was a place where Māori boys and girls could live together as a cultural unit, gaining from the ways of the Pākehā from a culturally secure position. Heeni saw her new assignment not as a job or a career with all of the personal connotations and aspirations typical of Pākehātanga. Rather, her new responsibilities represented a moral duty. As a matron, she would make an important and unique contribution to her people by ensuring the sociopolitical success of the next generation of leaders.

Professor Jim Ritchie said of her position, "Heeni ultimately carved out for herself a role that wasn't pastor and wasn't social worker, you know, it was something quite unique, with Māori flavoring. She was recognized for her special quality of caring, and of course, caring is a terribly important central focus in the Māori scheme of things. Looking after kids in the hostel, she assumed the role of ultimate parent. Even back as far as 1947, I noticed that she received a lot of respect behavior. Hers was sort of like the role teachers had in aristocratic Greek families, where people were given honor because they were in charge of looking after the young."[4] Dr. Rogers elaborated, "There's something that boarding schools do. They teach you self respect, and I think she was the ideal person to do this, a perfect example to the girls in this regard."[5]

In addition to nurturing young people on the road to emotional and academic maturity, Heeni's role as matron had political ramifications. She assumed the burden of introducing the city of Hamilton's Pākehā majority to Māori culture, who until this point, knew very little about the aristocratic side of Māoridom to which she belonged. In the 1940s, for example, most Māori and Pākehā did not even share the same institutions, such as hospitals, let alone daily interaction. With minimal interpersonal contact, Hamilton residents' knowledge of Māoridom was relegated to the few Māori who wandered occasionally in from the country selling *kūmara* and potatoes. Therefore, a good deal of cultural misunderstanding existed and was exacerbated by racist beliefs on both sides that hung over from the colonial era. "Hamilton . . . was established on the site of an old Māori community called Kirikiriroa. But it was . . . on land that had been confiscated after the Waikato land wars by the very people who fought those wars. They were given land grants in return for fighting the Māori. So, it meant that Hamilton grew up not only without any Māori in it, but that the Māori were for a long time hostile to the very existence of the city itself, right up until the 1950s."[6]

Heeni was 30 when she arrived in Hamilton in 1942, at the height of World War II. With the racial climate as it was and as a young Māori woman in a new leadership role, she definitely had her political work cut out. Interestingly, it was her faith in the Pākehā people that kept her plodding along as a bridge builder across the cultural divide. Heeni believed wholeheartedly in the possibility of other people becoming bicultural, and this ideal partly represented the source of her stamina. Other resources included remembering the advice of present and past elders and her faith in God.

Princess Te Puea visited the *Rahui* Girls Hostel quite often in the beginning, lending her support and strength while Heeni became adjusted to her new role. Eventually, they developed a mentor relationship characterized by much *aroha* (love) and confidence that ultimately bloomed into a deep and lasting friendship. Dave Tumokai Panapa said of them, "Heeni was utterly devoted to Te Puea, and to Te Puea's teachings. They were kindred spirits. Heeni used to chauffeur her around,[7] and in the process she became Te Puea's confidante. Heeni was someone Te Puea could bounce ideas off of, and Te Puea (with regard to her political prominence) needed a sounding board. You need people around you that will tell you the truth. I suggest Heeni was one of those."[8]

To understand the importance of this relationship in Māori terms, and likewise, to appreciate the meaning of Te Puea's leadership to Waikato people as a whole, it is necessary to provide a short summary of her life. Te Puea's many achievements included building a cultural renaissance in the Waikato in the first half of the twentieth century. Her accomplishments lifted the Kingites from abject poverty and cultural depression resulting from the legacies of the colonial program. It was Te Puea's incessant hard work and genius for organization that established the historic Turangawaewae marae (in Ngaruawahia, 8 miles from Hamilton proper) and that provided the backdrop for Heeni's hostel work in Hamilton. Much of the following summary comes from Dr. Michael King's (1977) *Te Puea: A Biography*.

PRINCESS TE PUEA AND THE KĪNGITANGA MOVEMENT

Kīngitanga means "kingship." It is the name given to the Māori monarchist movement that had its inception in the middle nineteenth century. Initiated by an intertribal collection of *ariki* (nobility*)*, its purpose was to establish the unification of all Māori under a single leading aristocratic line. This leader would serve as a paramount chief, a respectable politician who would represent the people while they sought to terminate the forced sale of sacred lands.

By the 1850s, Māori were being attacked on all fronts—territorially, socially, and biologically. They had become politically fragmented as a result of the community damage associated with the confiscations. As tribal fragments, they were played-off against one another, outmaneuvered in negotiation, and thus easy targets for land-seeking colonists. The institutions of government, which had promised to protect their interests, were now in the hands of the land-hungry settlers. Māori surmised that modeling their leadership style on the British would provide political leverage for ameliorating rapidly declining social conditions. "Should the Māori achieve a similar unity under their own monarch, it was argued, they would be able to match European cohesion; to conserve what remained of customary law and leadership; to end the payback wars among families and tribes; to prevent the further sale of the land to Europeans with its consequent loss of livelihood and breakup of communities. These were the justifications for a Māori King raised at North Island meetings in the 1850s."[9]

Leading families met to discuss possible candidates for a leader who would act on their behalf. "The matter was subjected to the process of interminable Māori debate that some have called agreement by exhaustion. The names of the most highly regarded chiefs were canvassed at a series of meetings. Candidates were considered in the light of genealogy, current standing, and their ability to act as hosts for large and representative Māori gatherings. Finally a candidate achieved unanimity."[10] His name was Potatau:

> Those who proposed him considered [Potatau] high-ranking: he was descended from Hoturoa, captain of the Tainui canoe, whose crew provided the major antecedents of the Waikato tribes; he also had connections with other tribes and especially strong ones with *Te Arawa* (nearby tribe on the North Island). He came from a line of successful fighting chiefs. He had been an outstanding combatant himself in the days of tribal warfare and had excelled at hand-to-hand dueling. In 1845 he had become a friend of Governor George Grey and his long residence in Auckland was credited with protecting the capital from attack by Ngapuhi from the north and Hauraki from the east. He regarded himself as a friend of the Pākehā. And his territory, the Waikato, was wealthy: There was food in its rivers and lakes and vast acres of potatoes in its cultivated fields. In 1858, he was crowned by Kingmaker Tamehana with a Māori Bible at Ngaruawahia and he took the name Potatau. The elevation of Potatau was the most nationally representative gesture that Māori had made since the signing of the Treaty of Waitangi in 1840.[11]

Potatau did not live very long after he was crowned at age 80. He therefore did not have time to accomplish much in the way of the Kīngitanga agenda; however, he established the *mana* of his office. He died in June of 1860, just before the start of the land wars, and was succeeded by his son, who later became known as *Tawhiao*.

King Tawhiao had grown up in his ancestral home of *Ngaruawahia*, his *turangawaewae*, "the sacred place where he felt secure." Just 3 years after Tawhiao took office, however, he and his followers were driven out of their sanctuary by imperial troops who invaded the Waikato at the start of the Māori land wars. The imperial army defeated Tawhiao in 9 months; he and his followers then fled into the bush (forested) area, later called the *King Country*. The King Country includes a large fertile area of the Waikato, the region where Heeni was born and raised.

During his exile, many of his people's sacred places, including cemeteries and ancestral lands, were stolen. Among them was Ngaruawahia, the place where King Tawhiao's granddaughter, Te Puea, would later build a Māori renaissance. King writes,

> To punish the so-called rebels and prevent the reformation of the King Movement in Waikato, the Government confiscated one-and-a-quarter million acres of land, opening it for European settlement and agriculture. Its real objectives were the dislodging of the King movement and the acquisition of the most fertile Waikato acreage; both were achieved.[12]

A good bit of human devastation and subsequent cultural breakdown followed the land confiscations:

> Confiscation was a far greater blow than military defeat; its consequences were to ripple Waikato for the next 60 years. First, a group of tribes that had formerly been able to support themselves comfortably, and to offer hospitality liberally, were now unable even to subsist on land of their own. Secondly, the loss of sites that were traditionally significant—burial grounds, places of prayer, sites of centuries of habitation, access to the river itself—created an intense feeling of deprivation. Waikato people had lost all the places that gave them a sense of history, continuity and identity; and they had lost them to people who neither knew nor cared about the history of the land and who appeared to desecrate it as further punishment.[13]

After 20 years of soul searching, Tawhiao made an agreement with the new settler government. The king would be allowed to come safely out of exile if he agreed to open parts of King Country to the Pākehā. He reluctantly agreed. Upon signing, Tawhiao immediately went back to Ngaruawahia and wept when he discovered it was by this time a European township. Shortly thereafter, he left his sacred home again but prophesied that one day his people would enjoy a renaissance there led by one of his descendants. "This place of salvation shall not pass beyond the days of my grandchild, when we shall be reborn," he announced.

In 1894, Tawhiao's son, Mahuta, became the third Māori king. King Mahuta's first son died when he was born, so to remember his death, he gave the name Te Puea, which means "to rise to the surface," to his sister's new daughter. Te Puea was born on November 9, 1883. Although she was the niece, not the daughter of the Māori king, she would ultimately fill the leadership void left by Te Rata, Mahuta's son, and the fourth Māori king, who wound up having very little impact on the Kīngitanga agenda. "Te Rata was to be King. But as his father had recognized, he was a weak man. He had been an invalid from childhood and as an adult he suffered from rheumatism, arthritis and heart disease. He was also a shy man,[14] easily dominated. Rather than assume leadership on positions of controversy or public responsibility, as Mahuta had, even though he found it distasteful, Te Rata preferred quiet discussion about tribal history or being alone to write in his journal (he had received a primary education)."[15]

Te Puea ultimately rose to fill this leadership vacuum, first by assuming "protector" status of Te Rata and later by demonstrating her leadership. Despite a rather cavalier youth, she redirected her priorities toward the welfare of her people and the Kīngitanga movement, an agenda that now included reacquiring the stolen land.

First, she concentrated on economic development because by 1910, her people were poverty stricken and sick. Once their ancestral land had been reacquired, she focused on building a cultural infrastructure to facilitate the social solidarity required to maintain a thriving Māori culture in King Country. Te Puea then devoted the remainder of her life to building up her beloved Waikato people socially, culturally, and politically. "When she went back to her people in 1910, they had almost no land, no steady work, and no hope. In more than 40 years of relentless effort, in her own words, she made Waikato 'a people once again.'"[16]

In 1913, the Waikato people endured a devastating smallpox epidemic. This was to be the first of many times when Te Puea would demonstrate the compassionate, nurturing side of leadership.

> The small pox epidemic of 1913 had a tragic effect on Te Puea's settlement and on others along the Waikato River. With very little money or support, she organized camps to nurse those affected by what was often a fatal disease, because very few hospitals at the time would accept Māori patients. The reluctance was mutual, with most Waikato Māori fearful and suspicious of the medical profession.[17]

World War I brought the first test of Te Puea's political leadership when the New Zealand government forced Māori young men to sign up for the draft. Te Puea disagreed with the policy of forced Māori conscription for two reasons. First, many years earlier, King Tawhiao, embittered by the land wars and the devastation of the confiscations, warned his people never again to go to war: "The killing of men must stop, the destruction of land must stop. I shall bury my *patu* (club) in the earth and it shall not rise again. . . . Waikato lie down. Do not allow blood to flow from this time on."[18] Second, she could not see a rational basis for sending her young men to war to fight for land that had been stolen from them three decades before. "Taking her stand against conscription, Te Puea opened up (her village) as a refuge for men who refused to enlist. When the police party came to arrest those called up for overseas service, she led her people in a nonviolent protest. One of the young men forcibly removed by police was her future husband Tumokai Katipa."[19]

Te Puea became devoutly religious through this leadership test. During the conscription protests, the old *Pai Marire* faith (a mixture of Old Testament Scripture, appeals to ancestors and Māori Gods, and invocations to stars [reminiscent of their Polynesian sea faring past]) was resurrected among the Kingites from her own spirit. King Tawhiao introduced Pai Marire as an alternative to the Church doctrine, which had become suspect to some of the Waikatos who witnessed certain sects of missionaries that supported the settlers during the land wars. "Te Puea accepted wholly the suggestion that it was time to uplift Tawhiao's old religion. It had an obvious ability to raise and sustain morale, to recall the days of wandering in righteous exile with the old King and relate the uncertain present to a continuous history. But in addition to this, it seemed to Te Puea to be part of her own spiritual evolution and that of Waikato as a whole."[20]

Pai Marire *karakia* (prayers) were held in her village every morning and evening at 7 o'clock, rituals that she undertook until the day she died. "They made us unshakable. Those prayers incorporated Māori things that the Pākehā churches had no place for, appeals to spirits and forces they didn't know about. Every time we said them we knew our ancestors were right there with us and we were alright," said one elder interviewed by Dr. King. At first, Te Puea was suspicious of the Christian churches, but later she embraced them all. She confided in Heeni, "I want to open my arms to all religions. They are all paths to the same God."[21] Ultimately, Father Seamer became one of her closest advisors.

Among her people, Te Puea was also recognized as someone who possessed the powers of mediumship, and this was demonstrated on numerous occasions. In one such case, a liminal communion with her ancestors led to a miraculous cure. Te Puea and her doctors became convinced she was dying of tuberculosis:

> Her tuberculosis had reappeared; she had bouts with coughing and three bad hemorrhages; her heart was behaving erratically; and her weight had dropped to (98 lbs). . . . She seemed to be wasting away. Almost overnight, her hair had turned gray. Everybody believed that she was dying, as did Te Puea herself. 'I don't think I will last long, she told (a news reporter). One lung had enormous cavities, the other was infected.[22]

At one point, Te Puea collapsed in a coma-like, heavy sleep. However, after 4 hours, she suddenly awoke, and after her doctor examined her, he was amazed at what seemed to be a miraculous recovery. She later attributed her cure to the return of her uncle, King Mahuta, and his sister (her mother) while she slept. "[They] told her she was not ready to die, and shared their spiritual strength with her. She woke with the conviction that she would recover completely [having believed for the previous 12 months that she was dying]."[23]

Te Puea again displayed extraordinary compassion during the great influenza outbreak of 1918. Millions died in this epidemic worldwide. Among Māori, it was no different. Many of those who died were young people aged 20 to 40 who were in their prime and parents who looked after the young and the old. "This meant that in the aftermath, whole communities found themselves without mothers and fathers, primary wage earners and active leaders. Te Puea not only organized the nursing of the sick, but single-handedly adopted many of the orphans and elderly left behind in the wake of the death of their parents and children."[24]

After much hard work and organization, by 1919, her village was a thriving Māori community. However, it was also fast becoming unsuitable for large numbers of people who had flocked there for a host of different reasons. Overpopulation was one problem, but the Waikato River also flooded the village each year when the winter rains came. To Te Puea, it was only logical that her people should move back to the sacred area called *Ngaruawahia*. Te Puea decided to fulfill Tawhiao's prophecy—that his people would rise again, reborn from despair at his *turangawaewae*. So this became her primary goal.

From the early 1920s on, Te Puea's aims were to re-establish the *mana* and strength of the Kīngitanga, to achieve economic strength, and to build a marae at Ngaruawahia. Funds for her projects were slowly raised in a number of ways. Her people took up contracts for scrub-cutting, road-making, gum-digging. A touring concert party traveled the North Island giving performances. Not only was the tour a financial success, but it also contributed to a revival of interest in haka, and poi [traditional dance and song forms].[25]

By the late 1920s, enough money had been saved to buy back some of the stolen land at Ngaruawahia. The Tainui now had control of their own property again. "In March of 1929 the main meeting house, at the turangawaewae marae, *Mahinarangi,* was opened to an historic *hui* where 6,000 people attended. Te Puea's genius for organization and hospitality was obvious, and her reputation grew deservedly."[26]

Te Puea worked her people hard, and this brought her criticism later on—mostly for working them on Sundays. Dave Tumokai Panapa recalls the force behind her dedication: "And I can remember in the time of Te Puea, the old people gathering outside their place in the mornings and evenings for prayers. And Te Puea was saying, I work, I pray, and then I work again."[27] She led by example.

Te Puea eventually found favor with national level politicians who were sympathetic to Māori concerns. One of these was the great parliamentarian *Apirana Ngata.* Her association with him led to the reintroduction of farming for hundreds of Waikato people who were poor and struggling during the depression. The "land development scheme" was intended to provide Māori with blocks of land if they would farm it. The people were able to borrow money based on the value of certain land blocks. They then had the means to clear the land and to establish dairy cows, cattle, sheep, or crops. As their farms became profitable, the people then paid off their debts and became self-sufficient.[28] King writes,

> Māori, including Ngata and Te Puea, saw [the land schemes] as a way of enabling the Māori to retain a communal life based on Māori values; while parliamentarians viewed it far more as a way of teaching Māori to farm in a business like fashion so they would not be a drain on the public purse, and of ensuring that land was exploited for primary production as efficiently as possible.[29]

King Te Rata died in 1933; he was succeeded by the fourth Māori king, Koroki. Te Puea, however, retained her leadership post. At this time, she shifted course, turning her focus away from economic development to encouraging the Waikato people to develop their skills in arts and crafts. The way was now paved to begin reviving Māori cultural activities for the Waikato people:

> . . . [and for] the building of a house for *Koroki* [fourth Māori king] at Turangawaewae; the raising of additional meeting houses throughout the Waikato; and the construction of a fleet of canoes that would highlight the tribe's former strength as a people with a river culture, and echo the more distant Polynesian tradition of seafaring and exploration.[30]

The effects of her contributions continue today:

> An awful lot of Māori, because of where they grew up and other circumstances are not able to keep up with their cargo system, and have been disadvantaged by all of that.

But the Kīngitanga movement has been a great umbrella for the Waikato tribes. There are all sorts of smaller structures underneath it to which people can attach themselves. I notice here with my Tainui students that they are very committed to all of the rituals and festival days of the Kīngitanga, as if it were a religion itself. I mean, it's something that protects the mind, nurtures it. Very few other tribes compare in this way. A couple of tribes have big sort of supra-tribal structures which keep all the groupings together, but nothing on the scale you have here in the Waikato.[31]

By the time Heeni first came to Hamilton, Te Puea's final focus rested on getting compensation from the New Zealand government for the land confiscations 80 years previous. A settlement was finally reached in 1946 after much discussion and debate. It called for the payment of 6,000 pounds a year for 50 years and 5,000 pounds a year after that in perpetuity.

Te Puea played a leading role in these negotiations, and the offer was eventually accepted, although agreement was not unanimous. A section of Waikato held strongly to the belief that, as land was taken, only land was acceptable compensation. In Te Puea's eyes, settlement of the grievance meant that finally funds were available to continue economic development, to pay for the upkeep of Turangawaewae, and to enable her people to pursue educational goals. And it also meant official recognition of the validity of their grievance, and of the principle that unjust treatment by government should be rectified, however much time had elapsed.[32]

This was to be her final contribution to the Waikato renaissance, and with it "Te Puea gave back to the Waikato people their confidence in themselves."[33]

Te Puea's cultural renewals in Ngaruawahia provided the social foundation for Heeni's educational work in Hamilton. The idea for a girls' hostel was first raised to serve the needs of young Māori women who needed supervision while earning their school qualifications. At the time of Heeni's arrival, American servicemen were training in New Zealand, using the countryside as places to practice war games. Often, these young men would wander into various towns and townships in the North Island, like Hamilton and Ngaruawahia, to shop and play. Their presence was felt by everyone, especially young women who were attracted to their charm and good looks. Some of the Waikato elders became concerned that perhaps Māori girls might get themselves into trouble by marrying and leaving the country, or worse by getting pregnant.

So, the elders conferred with leaders in the Methodist Church, including Father Seamer, whose reputation with the Waikato people was by now above reproach. It was determined that because education was a Kīngitanga priority, especially among young country girls who did not have access to secondary education, a girls' hostel should be established.

It was here that the late Princess Te Puea, a very good friend of Father Seamer by this time, and Heeni would begin to work together as adults. Te Puea believed in the idea of the hostel from the beginning, and she and the other elders agreed that Heeni would be the best candidate for matron.

King Koroki's daughter, *Piki* (later, the present Māori queen Te Arikinui Dame Te Atairangikaahu), was a student at Heeni's hostel. Te Puea insisted, however, that the future queen of Māoridom was not to receive any kind of special treatment. She was to work as hard as possible and to learn as much as she could, but never to forget her Māori roots. "This education was for the benefit of the people, not just themselves; the one thing [Te Puea] did not want in the *Kāhui Ariki* as a result of education was a replacement of Māori communal sensitivity by a strongly individualist, competitive, money-grubbing instinct."[34]

Before Heeni could achieve a high degree of intimacy with the highest ranking Māori women in New Zealand, she had to endure certain tests discussed in her narrative:

> After the church training, Te Puea kept her eye on Heeni all the time while she grew into her new role at the hostel. Te Puea drew her into the activities at Turangawaewae marae, asking her to look after important people in social situations, partly doing kitchen and domestic things, partly supervising children . . . she became a confidante for not only Te Puea but King Koroki, and Dame Te Ata. In Māori terms this is more than just being a trusted, confidante—these people are highly tapu. When you're working closely with them, even touching them as Heeni did for Te Puea in her dying moments, you are a very special kind of person. And so a lot of their mana rubbed off on Heeni, and she is respected for that.[35]

Heeni's commitment as a bridge builder had its share of ups and downs. She, of course, felt very conscious of the image she and her students were presenting to the Pākehā public. Her hostels were located adjacent to Pākehā Hamilton residents, and it took a long time for them to become accustomed to the idea of close contact with Māori neighbors. Over the years, she had a number of complaints and criticism. There were other challenges as well, such as troubles with the law among some of her boys. These problems were made worse by Heeni's tendency to take the wrongdoings of her youth and the complaints of the Pākehā personally. Sometimes, it became so stressful that she felt the need to go off by herself to regain her peace of mind. In the words of her doctor and friend Anthony Rogers,

> Sometimes I would find her very depressed. And I realized of course what it was. It was the headlines in the papers those days about some Māori boys in trouble. There still are headlines, you know, Māori people in trouble. But I reassured her. . . . She took it personally, perhaps, to some extent. Personally and to a certain degree she assumed that it was at some level a racial failure. Well, I was the first to disabuse her of that and say that it was nothing to do with race. It was more to do with the circumstances. I would laugh it off and say, well look here, there are plenty of Pākehā that do the same and so forth![36]

Heeni's association with Dr. Rogers, who was also the medical officer for both hostels, was closer than the usual friendship. As it had been earlier in her life with Maharaia Winiata, she and Dr. Rogers became emotionally intimate.

> I always tended to gravitate to Heeni. Whenever I'd run out of conversation at receptions with anyone else, we would then sit down. One time a visitor came up and asked to be introduced to my wife. I responded and said, 'Oh no, I'm afraid. . . . I'm very sorry, this isn't my wife.' After, Heeni asked me if I was embarrassed by this. I said, 'Embarrassed, Heeni? NO! Proud. I'd be proud to have had you for my wife.' We had more philosophy, more things in common—more than I've had with any other person. But then, again, I felt that if I had married Heeni, what a waste of Heeni![37]

Dr. Rogers' mother also became fond of her. His mother had a habit of having morning tea on the verandah of the Rogers' old Victorian home on London Street, across from the boys' hostel. Heeni was a frequent visitor there, joining the rest of the family while they discussed Māori and Pākehā affairs. Dr. Rogers' mother fancied herself as an artist, a painter, liking to create still-life flowers and family portraits. She painted three charming and flattering portraits of Heeni. Each was to represent a theme in Heeni's life. The one on the cover of this book is called "The Gardener." The Pākehāness of the image speaks to the time in Heeni's life when she was learning Pākehātanga, and the gardening that goes with it. Another of the trio is titled "Integration," referring to her role as a bridge builder between the two cultures. In this picture, she looks wan and tired, typical of the times when she took problems too seriously. The last was titled "To Meet the Queen," representing the nobility theme in her life—her *whakapapa*, her association with Te Puea, and meeting the Queen Elizabeth. (In her narrative, Heeni discusses being chosen by her people to represent them during the Queen's visit to New Zealand in 1950.)

It is important to reiterate, though, that Heeni never boasted about her own nobility. People of the aristocracy do not make a habit of doing this.

> One of the characteristics of an aristocratic person in Māoridom is that you don't boast about your connections. Talking about your ancestors is something you as an aristocrat have been taught *not* to do. About the only circumstances in which somebody would do that (but never Heeni) would be if another person has accused you of not being who you are, of being a nobody. Then that's the time when you stand up and say 'Look, I've got this, this, this and this connection.' And you do this only because your birthright has been challenged. However, if it has not been challenged, which it rarely would be, then it's not an appropriate thing to do.[38]

During the hostel years, Heeni had another boyfriend named Danny Smith. Of all her male friends, she carried the most affection for him. Danny Smith was a Mohawk Indian from Toronto, a prominent New Zealand veterinarian by trade, and a frequent visitor at the royal Turangawaewae marae. He was extremely wealthy by New Zealand standards, and of course, Heeni enjoyed this. However, she was also ambivalent about it. She was unaccustomed to the grandeur of he and his family's lavish lifestyle. His sisters, who often accompanied him, also dripped with wealth. For example, Heeni remembers being struck by their unusual attitudes about clothing. One of them would often buy 60 pairs of shoes at a time, wearing each pair only once—then they would be thrown away.

At one point, Danny proposed marriage to Heeni on a cruise ship before he was to set sail for the United States, but she refused. In the end, it was because of his opulent lifestyle. Despite her rangitira status, Heeni had grown up poor from the country. She was a church person devoted to ideals, not to things. Therefore, she could not relate to it.

It would be incorrect to say Heeni opposed marriage, nor was she so busy with some kind of artificial marriage to the church that she would not have made room for it. As it turns out, Heeni did not marry for two important reasons. First, she never found the right man. "Father Seamer's only reason for why she never married wasn't that she was married to the church, which was perhaps true in a way, but that she certainly never found anyone—someone that might live up to the expectations required of such an extraordinary woman."[39] Danny Smith came close; marrying him would have meant adopting a very different lifestyle as well as having to leave her people.

The second, and more compelling, reason is that Heeni was instructed by Princess Te Puea *not* to marry—ever. It was explained to her that marriage to a Māori man meant she would have to put him first and that would require abandoning the ideals of the Kīngitanga movement to a certain degree.

Heeni was one of three visitors allowed to be with Te Puea in her dying moments in 1952. "All day on Sunday, 12 October, Te Puea lay semiconscious, her eyes closed, breathing with difficulty. Her feet, legs and back were cold. Momo (friend) rubbed them for a while in the morning and was relieved by Sister Heeni; Nobody else dared touch the old lady."[40] Heeni was one of the many people Te Puea prepared to supervene her. "It seems to me Te Puea saw Heeni as someone that was going to succeed her in a leadership role within the Kīngitanga. This was true insofar as setting the goals, articulating the vision and ideals, and upholding the mana."[41]

5 / Earning Respect

I saw her as a wonderful leader and mentor of young Māori people. Heeni got young people to come into the town of Hamilton, they lived in her hostel, and she ran that hostel like a public school, an English public school. There wasn't anything strict about it, but there was understanding. She got to know them; she encouraged them. I think she made a wonderful contribution to the community.

Dr Anthony Rogers

BY NOW, I'D spent fifteen years immersed in Pākehātanga, and I'd had exactly fifteen years in the traditional Māori way. But culturally I know I've always been more Māori. Sometimes my Pākehā blood would come across a little bit more, but I've always thought of myself as essentially Māori.

By the time I turned thirty, I'd been at the Te Kūiti School for Domestic Hygiene; I'd been in Auckland as head girl at the Kurahuna school; and I'd been initially turned down to attend Deaconess House for my training, so that was another year in Auckland spent at Father Seamer's home. Then I'd had the years in Christchurch, absolutely among Pākehā, another year in Auckland on the circuit with northern Māori people, and then my time in Kāwhia. Then, quite suddenly, I'd got a call with church orders to come to Hamilton, where I was to substitute for a minister. There was talk of a hostel, and that perhaps I'd be the matron. It was here that I'd begin to integrate my Māoriness with my Pākehā training in my own mind, and then in my world.[1]

It eventually took three to four years before I got sorted out with my own role in the Kīngitanga movement at Tūrangawaewae. I think the late Princess Te Puea was hopeful that my special training with the Church would provide a lot of potential help to her movement. My koro had told me as a young girl that I'd be a servant of the Church, but when I came to Hamilton I knew that I would also be a servant for the Kīngitanga movement. And this is when I began to see my roles coming together into one.

Around 1942, I can remember many American servicemen in New Zealand. I don't think they were British, no. Mostly it was American servicemen who came to New Zealand to train for combat. They were everywhere—the army and the air force. They were quite handsome, those young men, and very charming. They all seemed to have plenty of money, and some of the more cunning Māori girls understood this—that they had more money than the average New Zealand boyfriend did, Māori or Pākehā. For example, these boys always had plenty of chocolates, and of course this used to fascinate me. You'd see them driving around in their jeeps, looking handsome. And the girls, Māori and Pākehā alike, really got caught up in all this sort of thing. Our women were chasing them like mad.

The elders became quite concerned about all of this sort of thing. We wanted to hold on to our own, of course, here in New Zealand, especially the daughters of the leading chiefs, you know. The elders were conscious that the girls could get into trouble with these boys, that they might get pregnant or something, and that wasn't what we'd decided for our daughters. So there was plenty of kōrero at that time among church officials and Māori elders. (Remember, I'm talking about my own Tainui people here, not other tribes.)

There was a great deal of mutual concern; but the Church didn't have much money, and neither did we, and neither did Princess Te Puea, who was at the time raising money to build the now famous Tūrangawaewae marae. Money was short. I'd hate to say we were poor, but we were pretty low. So finally Father Seamer—a great man he was, really a great man—got the good idea of planning a youth hostel for these girls. The notion he had was to bring them into an appropriate city where they'd be able to attend secondary and tertiary education under Māori supervision. Some of the girls in question lived out in the country and didn't have a district high school, you see. They could only go as far as Form 1, and then they'd have to stop, as I did (though I did sit my Proficiency exam). So Father Seamer started to look around for a suitable place. Hamilton was chosen because its educational system was appropriate, and already there were some girls living in the mission house there. With Princess Te Puea's blessing, the church bought an old, two-storey building, which is still there in Bryce Street, and set it up as a hostel for Māori girls.[2]

This was to be a place for the daughters of leading families to live while they attended school. We had the two granddaughters of Rātana himself, and other leaders in the Rātana movement.[3] I had a great deal of respect for their parents and grandparents. Charming people, really. And, of course, the daughter of King Korokī also came to live with us. We affectionately called her Piki, but today she is Te Arikinui Dame Te Atairangikaahu, the present Māori queen.[4]

As I think of Te Ata and her nickname Piki, I remember an old legend from way back that made a tremendous impression on me. I think I told you about the clematis, a beautiful flower. What you see in the shops is the cultivated one, but what I'm talking about is the New Zealand native, and its Māori name, pikiarero. A beautiful flower. It's very delicate, and it climbs. Beautiful, clear-white flowers. When Piki came to us, the meaning of her name was revealed to me. I thought to myself, 'Hmmm.' My mind was beginning to look into much more of my own culture. I was away from my Pākehā training, and I was glad to come back and look further into Māori culture. And in my own mind, I thought *Piki* had a different sort of a meaning that took me back to my home in Mōkau. One year, when I was about fourteen or fifteen, we came across these beautiful flowers—some I'd never seen before. The others said, 'How are we going to get up that tree to pick those flowers?' Then we discovered that this plant had a vine, and we began to tug at the vine and noticed that it was having an effect on the flowers up there. And we broke the vine to take some home to Mum. But when we arrived all excited at having something for her, the look that my father gave us, although he didn't say a word, and the look that Mum gave us . . . I said, 'For you, Mum, for you!' but they just stood there. We'd obviously done something wrong. Dad was the first to say a few words, and he said, 'That flower is a very special flower. It is meant to beautify the bush area.' It creeps up and spreads

Back-yard view of the girls' hostel in about 1949.

itself out and continues to climb. Dad said, 'I want you to gather up all that pikiarero and take it back where you found it and lay it nicely at the trunk of the tree.' Years later I'd see it and it would always remind me of Mum and Dad and what they'd told us—never to pick it. And Te Ata reminds me of that flower.

Anyway, there were many other young people from prominent families in New Zealand who came to live with us. They attended either the Girls' High School, the Diocesan School or the technical college. I was chosen to be matron of the hostel. This saddened me a little bit, because I remembered the more mature matrons at Te Kūiti, Auckland and Christchurch, where I did my training. They'd been older people, and I felt that maybe I was too young. Really, I wasn't too happy about it in the beginning. I had to think very hard about what I'd been told by my koro—not to be afraid. I did a lot of thinking, a lot of deep thinking, and made a lot of prayers. I thought, 'Am I really up to this responsibility?' It was true that I was thirty-three years old, but I was fearful of making a mistake or failing in some way. I should emphasise that I was really scared. Here were these leading young women who were going to be coming to this place, and into my home, and I'd be fully in charge of the situation. It wasn't only that I was responsible for all of these important young women; I was also apprehensive about it knowing the conditions that would surround me, the rules. Very strict conditions, very strict conditions there, because of the status of these girls, and also because the hostel sat right in the middle of what was at the time a very conservative area.

But how could I decline? The hostel was opened in 1945. The people of Hamilton knew very little about Māoritanga, knew hardly anything about their habits, and many were not altogether that friendly to outsiders. Here I'd be coming to a city where Māori

My fine-looking girls, 1969.

people weren't seen a great deal, which meant introducing the Māori way of life, right here in the midst of this conservative place. Up until then, Pākehā people had only seen Māori people walking the street, barefoot, selling kūmara and potatoes. I think they were mainly familiar with those sort of people. So I knew we'd have to build up our reputation. I had long talks with the girls, telling them to be careful about how they conducted themselves. I had to explain to them that we were introducing a Māori way of life among strangers, who had no experience with Māori people, because none were in employment here in Hamilton. It was tremendously overwhelming at first.[5]

I knew we were being watched. There we were, right in the middle of the city. I made sure we appeared clean and in control. But naturally, young people from the country are going to be full of fun. I couldn't control all of the fun, and this became a bit of a problem later on. We had quite an area at the back of the house, and a place where the Church had put up a net so the girls could play tennis. We had a bit of a garden, and all of the girls helped with the planting and weeding. We had lovely flower gardens as well. So the girls would be outside a lot, and of course there they'd be, being noticed.

Overall, it was a fine group of girls, really. We had about twenty-seven, I think. A mob of Māori girls, really, full of life in the middle of this conservative Pākehā neighbourhood. They were all nice girls, and fine looking. I've got a photo of them. They would be away at all of these different colleges nearby from about eight thirty a.m. They'd be gone all day, and begin to come in again in the afternoon. They'd come home full of life, talking loudly and laughing and all this sort of thing. Sometimes we got complaints about the noise, but I didn't worry. They were so happy about being in life, and I wanted them to be that way. My thoughts went back to the happy days at Te Kūiti, and my own childhood.

I ran my hostel like the Pākehā one in Te Kūiti, but I also added the Māori tradition. It was, therefore, a mixture of Māori- and Pākehātanga. You have to remember that these girls had come from a very high standard of Māori homes, and I wanted them to grow naturally in both arenas. For instance, you see, we'd have devotions in Māori, and then we'd also have devotions in English. In between the two cultures, I tried to introduce our way of life there, and that's where I found it all a little bit heavy—the responsibility, I mean.

This was the reason why, while the girls were away during the day, I'd need to take a little bit of time out on my own. I would often go out: I had a car, and would drive down to Cambridge. I loved Cambridge. Where was a peaceful park there where I would do some meditation. Lots of thinking back on my own way of life. My thoughts would go back to Mōkau, where I could feel my Māoriness coming across my mind. I thought about my Māori foundations, so that I could bring them to these girls, so that they wouldn't be lost in the Pākehā world. I had to remember my early Māori training, while I walked the middle line between my Māori side and my Pākehā side. I will always, even to the day that I'll no longer be on this earth, thank the Church for my training in the Pākehā way of life. I gained so much in spiritual things, in material things, and in meeting European people up and down the land. I made so many wonderful friends. The Church helped me to do the work that I felt I was called to do, you see. But, to come back to my Tainui people, to come back here, I had to readjust a little bit, back to my own Māori way of life.

I'd go to this park when I was troubled. I thought that maybe I was too young for my position at the hostel. It was a beautiful park with many trees. I was on my own there, so I could remember Mōkau. I'd go walking around the lake. It stimulated me, because I was close to nature as it was where I was brought up at home. Among the trees at Cambridge, I could remember my own upbringing. Of course I couldn't get to the sea, not very often, because that was too far away and the roads weren't what they are today to Raglan or Kāwhia. So it was to the bush that I went to think about my Māoriness. Here, I'd move into communications with te runga rawa, the supreme one. Gently, I'd stop for a minute here and there and talk to him, just as I'm talking to you. (I didn't close my eyes as we'd been taught in our church training—I gave that up long ago.) Yes, quietly to myself, when that time sort of came. I easily cut out people walking alongside me. And I wondered about how to balance the Pākehā with the Māori. I used to ask for help from the supreme one. I'd get impressions and ideas in response, and then I'd just be still. I'd feel the strength and peace coming into my body. It was a physical sensation, absolutely.

Sometimes it was all a futile exercise and I couldn't make the connection with te runga rawa. When I was younger, I would assume this was because I hadn't been honest in some way. And I'd try and work out, well, where am I not being too honest? I had Sister Nicholls as a role model for what I was doing, but no-one else, really. And many times I'd approach te runga rawa afraid. Afraid of silly little things. Many times I'd growled at the young people; then I'd feel guilty because I'd remember that I never heard my mum or dad growl. So I would try and work it all out in my mind, work very hard in my mind, but sometimes a walk would be absolutely useless to me. I would come home even more tired than I'd been before.

But usually these meditations refreshed me, and when I returned to my girls I was more at peace. I could look at their problems from a Māori point of view, and be quite ready again to carry on with my duties. See, my health wasn't too good; and to be there with these ebullient young girls, bouncing into the house amid all the laughter and fun (which I didn't want to restrict), I had to feel refreshed and ready to make decisions.

I knew that the lady who lived down the road would be complaining about the noise of our young ones. She'd sometimes complain when the girls got out on the lawns with their tennis rackets. Of course, this wasn't a regular sort of thing, just once in a while. Anyway, about this woman, I used to think why should she be complaining about such a prominent place where girls of leading Māori families were enjoying themselves, innocently. This sort of thing did disturb my Māori mind a bit.

Oh, they played their music too, but to me it was all just fun. To me, the girls were happy and they were showing they were happy to be there. I didn't want restrictions on happiness when the girls weren't out of bounds. It all became heavy on my mind, though, when the complaints did come, which perhaps it shouldn't have. It was most difficult when they called me, accusing me of not being able to control my young people. Well, imagine twenty-seven teenage girls bouncing in, and then suddenly there was supposed to be complete peace and quiet in the area. I knew that sometimes the people were right in their complaints. If I'd been sitting there in that home or around about for years, experiencing peace and no disturbance, and then suddenly all of these girls moved in with their happy noises, well, I wonder if I would feel the same. I used to try and take these things into consideration. But these girls were living a natural way of life, and I didn't want to curb that. Not too much.

There were young people who were naughty, sure—I don't want to talk too much about them. It's only natural when there's a collection of young people with various personalities, from various backgrounds; some were from poor circumstances like my own, and others hadn't been used to any restrictions, and of course there would be some discipline problems from time to time. Sometimes my girls used to climb out the windows. I used to hear them coming down the fire escape late at night. On one occasion I had some contact with the police, because they'd been caught loitering down the street with their boyfriends or something. They were brought home by the police. It wasn't a reflection on me but, you know, I was young and I took it that way.

Some of the naughty ones are still around me. If this book doesn't come out for twenty years or so, then maybe we could go into more detail, because we'd all be away from here then. But we had a reunion last year, and there must have been about fifty of those girls who were there. They're still around, and they still come to see me.

The naughty ones were a bit more nasty at times than the boys who later came to our boys' hostel. Some of them were especially difficult when I was entertaining friends to a meal. They'd pick up their food, you know, and then they'd try to embarrass me by complaining about it very loudly. You know how girls are, a little bit secretive, and this would sort of show up in front of visitors. I remember one girl; I was entertaining visitors, and sitting at the table just next to the girls.

After grace, we sat down and she said, 'We're having the same food as we had the other night!'

I often had to be the go-between for some of the girls who pinched things like clothes, underwear and shoes from others in the hostel. And Heeni wasn't used to all of this sort of thing, because of the way I grew up. One girl would say, 'Somebody took my so and so.' And I'd reply, 'Yes, but you have another one to wear.' The girls didn't take anything from others outside the hostel, like the boys did—only from one another.

I guess the worst of it with the girls was when they stole away with their boyfriends. Sometimes it got out of control, and I had to offer forgiveness. And this was difficult. I learnt much more about forgiveness in my early Māori training, but when I was in the hostel setting, I found that it was a struggle sometimes to give it freely. But I did try. I always felt the less that was said about the doings of the naughty ones, the better these young people would recover from their actions. It would give them a better chance to mend their ways, rather than dwell on past misdeeds.

Sometimes, you know, I felt like an auntie or a mother to these girls. During happier times we were all sisters. I hopped round with them, playing tennis. I used to play with the girls a good bit. I can remember one occasion someone coming in— because the hostel was always open, anyone could come in—and I distinctly heard them say, 'Which one is Matron?'

And other times I felt like an old grandmother, or a wicked old lady maybe. I did. I had to be stern. And there were times when I had to put my foot down. Of course yelling wasn't in my nature, so I'd just quietly talk with them. It was growling, sure; maybe there would be a deeper tone in my voice when I pointed out that whatever someone had done wasn't a very nice thing to do. But that's all I needed to do. I don't think any one of them could accuse me of swearing at them.

But all of this was quite stressful at times. My doctor knew I was carrying a heavy load, and was concerned about the stress. He gave me nerve tablets to take. But I wasn't so obedient in taking those tablets. I knew my nerves were all right; there was nothing wrong with my nerves. It was just that I was so tired. What I needed most was to take a lot of rest. So I'd put the tablets aside, and the doctor would come and see me again, and he'd say, 'You better take these tablets and stay in bed a day or so.' Then he'd come back in a day and say, 'Well, how are you feeling now?'

I wasn't always honest then, and it wasn't until a while afterwards, maybe a few weeks, that I'd say, 'You know, doctor, I didn't take those tablets.'

'What?' he'd say. 'Why?'

'Because I sort of felt that all I needed was a little bit of peace and quiet, and in my walks in the Cambridge park I always felt that te runga rawa, who created my body, would know just exactly what it needed.'

Once he said to me, 'Well, I don't suppose it's any good giving a prescription.' But when I was reeling with a bad cold, or flu or some such, I'd fill those prescriptions. The doctor always used to say, 'It's that tuberculosis problem you're having.' It was the resulting cough that he gave me pills for, and I'd take those.

Another way of handling my anxiety was not so constructive. I'm naughty sometimes. If I don't want to hear something, I just cut it out from my mind. I think we all need to do that. I think all humans need to cut off now and again, and let our brains take a bit of a break too.

King Tāwhiao, who spoke of the threads of many races passing through the eye of a needle. His words were an inspiration to me as I devoted myself to the central belief of the Kīngitanga movement—that all people are one.

Princess Te Puea was a leader, a seer, and someone we revered and respected. Those of us who live in the Tainui district, which covers quite a large area really, have done our best to uphold her wisdom. Some of her instructions to us came from a prophecy made by one of the former Māori kings. This had to do with the principles of the Kīngitanga movement. One of these principles is enshrined in a whakataukī of King Tāwhiao's: 'There is but one eye of the needle through which the white, black and red threads must pass. After I am gone, hold fast to love, to the law and to the religion of Christ.'[6] All people are one, all of the different colours. I clearly remember the words of the late Princess Te Puea, who said not only to me, but to others around the marae, 'Our relationship between the Māori and Pākehā is such that we are basically one people. In the future, remember, we are to walk side by side with our Pākehā friends.' And later Te Arikinui Dame Te Atairangikaahu, the present Māori queen, said to me that my purpose in life, as well as hers, was to work for a closer relationship between our two peoples.

This was a different perspective about the Pākehā than she had originally. Early on, Princess Te Puea had been criticised for not wanting her people to become

Wearing a kiwi-feather cloak, with a family tiki handed down for over a hundred years through my mother's line. I'm barefoot so that there's nothing European about me. Te Kūiti, about 1948. Basil de Grange

educated. But by 1945, she could see that it was not only worthwhile, but absolutely necessary for carrying on with the ideals of the Kīngitanga movement. This was because earlier she was quite distressed about the Pākehā system. Oh sure, she was mad about the land confiscations and the conscription during World War One. That's because she couldn't see a way out for her people. But then you see, World War Two made her thoughts turn from her earlier years. I think she began to see that more contact was needed with the Pākehā government, with officials and business leaders and all of that sort of thing, to make a real difference. Despite all of this, I knew she drew her strength from a god that was Māori in character, so I believe she came to see that her Pai Mārire faith wasn't threatened by Pākehā education. Father Seamer and she became quite close friends, and I think he influenced her in this way also. She was a very practical person on the surface, but down deep she was a very religious person as well. She knew where her strength was coming from.

Initially, spending time with her was my one saving grace, because she offered a great deal of encouragement for me to carry on. I remember her coming into the house, and because she was well regarded by the people, even feared, I always treated her with a great deal of awe. She was a bigger, well-built lady, and very much loved by the people. She was quiet and reserved, and nobility just oozed out of her.

Sometimes she'd come in quite early in the morning just to grace us with her presence, and it would always be—for me anyway—quite an uplifting experience. She really believed in the idea of the place, because by this time she was always talking about the importance of lifting the minds of the young people to a higher realm. Sometimes we'd just have some tea and talk a little while, and then she'd be off again, as she frequently had a heavy schedule. Other times she'd call and we would go for a drive. Sometimes to Auckland, shopping. Other times, just visiting. She introduced me to strangers as her niece, and her husband Tūmōkai (Dave) was always 'Uncle Dave' to me. I remembered him from their honeymoon, when they called in and stayed for about a week, I think, with my parents and us kids. And in case you don't already know, she was married to an Englishman before she married Tūmōkai. He was an Englishman of very high standing that Father Seamer knew. She lived with him happily for a while, but then the time came when her people wanted her to come back and carry on the work of the Kīngitanga movement. Her English husband was a straightforward, Christian-thinking man who just let her go. He knew that she had a calling, and that she had to leave to pursue it. They never officially divorced. Then she married Tūmōkai in the Māori way. I can remember him being a very fine-looking, handsome man, much younger than she. Much, much younger. Their early contact with my mum and dad, and later my dedication to church work, were what brought us into alignment.

At the hostel, she came into my life again, because I was stationed here in Hamilton and doing what she thought was important work. Te Puea helped me a good deal. I was ready for her teachings. For some time my mind had been keen to learn all of the good things that Pākehā life had to offer. But now a change was occurring. When Princess Te Puea came around, I became a very good student of Māori tradition again. I was interested and wanted to learn, and so I listened a lot. I was a good listener, just as I'd been as a student in the Pākehā world. I wanted to pick up again with my own language, which, after fifteen years in the Pākehā world, wasn't too good by the time I arrived in Hamilton.

Princess Te Puea was a tremendous support for the hostel, and later on we also had a lot of stable Pākehā people who encouraged us. The mayor of Hamilton, and the Member of Parliament at the time the hostel was opened, was Dame Hilda Ross. She was a tremendous help to us. She was much older, and she soon began to visit us at the hostel. She was very good with the girls and quickly became very interested in what we were doing. She knew the mother of the Rātana girls, because the mother was also a Member of Parliament. I think Dame Hilda had obtained a good bit of knowledge about the Māori way of life this way. She also owned a big shop here in Hamilton. As time went on, the schoolteachers also became sympathetic—well, some did—toward Māori students. The teachers allowed them to speak both Māori and English. Yes. I think it took a while, though. As time went on, I think they began

'Integration', by Gwendoline Mary Augusta Rogers. I think the heaviness of my responsibilities shows in this portrait, painted when I was weary from my work as a bridge builder. Denis Rogers

to understand the status of these girls, because Pākehā in Hamilton had only been accustomed to street Māori before we came.

Dr Anthony Rogers was the physician at the girls' hostel, and later at the boys' when it was established. He became a loyal and devoted friend, very knowledgeable about things Māori. His family was very good to us, and we got tremendous support from his brother, Denis Rogers, who later became the mayor of Hamilton. Their mother was a well-known artist. She did oil paintings mostly, and painted my portrait on several different occasions. Each portrait marked a different phase in my adult life. One was titled 'Integration', which I suppose was a theme during most of my Kīngitanga, church and hostel work in Hamilton.

In my hostel work, I was bringing aspects of the Pākehā world and things Māori together into one place. One of the conditions made by the Methodist Church was that these young ladies not only receive a Pākehā education, but that they be schooled in spiritual matters as well. Several different ministers would come in. The girls would therefore have a short service once a day, and attend a longer one on Sunday morning at the Methodist church. And, of course, there was a lot of other instruction in this sort of thing, because they also had Bible studies.

But the Māori elders also insisted that the girls get an education in Māori spirituality. For this reason we did have an old gentlemen, Heemi, who lived on the premises. Reverend Heemi Rihimona, a kaumātua, was our koro. He lived in a little cottage there by our hostel, with two younger fellows who helped take care of the grounds. The girls got Māori things from him by watching the way he lived. He was a model to the young. I know they all loved him very much; I know that, because he'd talk to these girls. He was quite open and relaxed, and they'd crowd around him fairly frequently to listen to his wisdom. He was the elder of our hostel family. And our hostel family was a little tribe based on Māoritanga.

Heemi Rihimona, kaumatua at the girls' hostel, about 1946.

Later, Father Seamer lived there too, which completed the circle. He lived in the old mission house until a cottage was built for him. Then he moved into that.

All of my girls were special, but some were with me longer so we had more time to become close. I remember one who was sent over quite young, at age nine. She was a lovely half-caste Māori. Her mother was Pākehā, and dead. Her father was Māori and quite old. When he first brought her to me, I thought, just looking at him, 'This girl is young enough to be your granddaughter or something.' He was elderly, and not able to support her. When I first saw her, I thought, 'Here is a sweet little girl. She's only nine, a bit out of control with the mother gone and father not able to care for her. So, yeah, I'll take her in.' This girl didn't get into trouble with the law, but she was a good bit out of control. She needed more attention because she was so young. I had to mother that one. You know, I got very fond of her. And so did her teachers.

I was glad that I didn't know she was being abused at that young age before she came to me. This was the kind of thing that she told the other girls and that came back to me much, much later. Yes, she'd been sexually abused, and this was the reason she was sent to us. Not by the father, of course. He used to come and visit her quite often, and was most appreciative of the work we were doing for her. She called me Mum, and I really did love her. There was one unusual thing that I did find out about her. She was always wanting to be held. A very affectionate girl. And always, you know, she'd come home from school, and she'd be skipping around. Very attractive, and full of life. I was quite sad when she had to go.

She left us when she was about eighteen or nineteen to be with her dad, who was becoming really quite elderly by this time. And I was glad I'd shown a good bit of interest in her while she'd been with us. She turned out all right. Married a nice young fellow. She kept sort of coming back, keeping in touch with me. Never a word about all that she had suffered.

One of the things that kept me moving along was what I gained from being around young people all of the time. It was true that I did give a lot of myself to these young

Song and dance at the girls' hostel, 1968.

people, but I was learning all the time from them. They kept me young. They did. And all of the laughter, because this was an open sort of life that I wanted to provide them with. In the Māori way, dear. And the singing. They'd have instruments and sing and dance together in the evenings. They'd strum along on their guitar and ukulele, singing the old songs that we used to sing at home. Being with those girls was like living in a huge Māori family. Yes, I think I just naturally sort of gave myself to them.

I continued with my sewing through all of my adult life. I made my own hats, and often gave them away as gifts. I first became interested in them because we had to wear hats to be in full uniform, and I could never find a hat big enough to fit my large Māori head. I had a friend in Auckland who knew of a hatmaking course at the technical college. So I'd often just pop into the train and go up to Auckland and spend a few hours learning how to make different kinds of hats. I think I made about three or four from velour, altogether. Imagine a flat piece of heavy velour, and then we had to pull on it, shaping it, steaming it. To me it was all fun. I enjoyed all that, and also it got me away from the hostel. Even though it's work to create something with your hands, it was really relaxing for me. Many times, you know, I felt under the load. So sewing was another one of my releases.

And so was dressmaking. I took a refresher course at the technical college in Hamilton. There I met up with other women, you know. These were people whom I wouldn't otherwise come into contact with. We all became good friends. You know, our activities around the materials brought us together. 'Ah, this is the way' and 'My problem is. . . .'

The hostel girls serving up Māori hospitality during the Empire Games in 1950. I'm by the table, third from the left. Piki (now Te Arikinui Dame Te Atairangikaahu) is fifth from the left. Melbourne Herald

Zippers. I never could get them straight. You know, we had to get the zip in just the right position with no creases anywhere. Oh my Māori mind couldn't get around that one. It was my biggest problem because it had to be perfect. It had to be perfect, absolutely. So I went back and took another refresher course after a while, when the modern things were coming in. I enjoyed it immensely, but that zip was still a problem to fit into a skirt correctly. My zipper would always be crooked. Instead of lying straight and flat and natural when I tried to iron the material, well, I just about wore the material out trying to get it to sit my way.

And I made a couple of big sort of trench coats. The material was quite hard to handle. I remember one of them—I wore it for a long, long time because I made sure I got very warm material. I think the classes had two purposes, really. They gave me the chance to get away from duties from time to time, and they also enabled me to help the girls with their sewing too.

Overall, I became really involved with the hostel, and very much enjoyed what I was doing, you know. Here I was, a young deaconess, responsible for the daughters of important Māori figureheads. At one level I thought how privileged I was! Whether I was able to help them in any way, I don't know. But I did have the feeling of being honoured by having all of these very prominent young people. So there wasn't really, at that time, room to consider being a mother and a wife. No, no, no. Because I wanted to carry on with what I was doing. I didn't want to give up all of that for the responsibility of motherhood. I think maybe I felt lucky that I didn't have the responsibility of a husband and children. In fact, when I look back I can say what a privileged, yes, what a very privileged person I was. You know, to be snatched up from my country home, and then placed in all these different situations. And the

The Māori debutante ball at which I was hostess. Seated at the front are (from left to right) the Honourable Iriaka Rātana, Princess Piki, the Honourable Eruera Tirikātene and Mrs Rūti Tirikātene. I'm standing at the far left, in the dark gown.

people I was meeting. My church life, my social life and my Māori life were all one. I didn't compartmentalise these things.

At one point my girls and I were asked to receive the people who were organising and participating in the Empire Games. This was way back a long time ago. These were the first Empire Games to come to New Zealand. Princess Te Puea asked us to be responsible for one table, to have it ready for folk coming in for the luncheon. I have a picture of this event. There are all my girls right around the table. Piki is there—Princess Te Puea insisted that she performs exactly the same duties as the other girls. Her birth made no difference. She had to do all the routine work that we had to do, just as Princess Te Puea did herself. Piki was a great help to me.

Another time I was asked to chaperone a Māori girls' debutante ball. It was the second one we'd put on, and I was hostess for the evening. The girls were from all over New Zealand. Each girl had to have her own partner; usually it was a brother or a cousin that the girls chose themselves. It was a huge occasion, but the boys weren't included in this picture. Princess Piki attended this ball. The girls had to curtsey to the four of us, the two women and two men who were the hosts and hostesses of the event.

One day the late Princess Te Puea asked me to bring the girls down to the marae to help prepare the place for a big hui that was coming up. You know, tidying up the gardens, lawns and things. She suggested we have a working bee. Of course I had a tribe of girls, and I knew she wouldn't be able to arrange for anyone else to come and help on this particular Saturday. I also knew I couldn't take the girls on a weekday, because they'd be busy with school. So I agreed. Princess Te Puea knew we had all our own tools for gardening, so it was perfect. We arrived quite early in the morning with all the girls who were available. Some of them had to go off because they were in sports, but the others packed a lunch and worked the entire day. And Princess Te Puea was there with us. She worked alongside us, as usual. We called her 'the old lady', and she loved that term. So the girls got to know her in a variety of different situations.

She worked extremely hard, and toward the end of her life, one lung had entirely collapsed from tuberculosis complications, but she kept going. She knew she was dying long before she died. That's why she worked her people so hard in the final years. There was lots of criticism about her working her people every day of the week, including Sunday. A lot of that came from the Europeans around, you know, some of those deeply religious people. But I don't think those who were critical of her really knew what she was doing. She talked it over with me, and she felt that there was still tremendous work to be done to prepare that marae for the future. She was quite sure her maker would forgive her for working, working, working to get that place going properly. It wasn't for herself, but for the future generations that she worked. That marae land had been confiscated by the Pākehā, and she was responsible for getting it all back. She wanted to see that it was fully completed, in shipshape form before she passed on.

As I say, Princess Te Puea was a tremendous help to me, and eventually I became one of the people who chauffeured her.[7] I was very afraid the first time I had to drive her, which was from Ngāruawāhia to Hamilton. Driving her around I felt was an important responsibility, adding to my church work and the public responsibility I had as matron back in Hamilton. But we became friends, and it turned out to be something I thoroughly enjoyed. I remember one morning she came in to the hostel quite early, wanting to see me. She knew I hadn't been terribly well, but I explained to her that the reason I looked tired was because it was so early in the morning. And she said, 'Yes, I know that you haven't been too well. What else is the matter with you?'

'Oh,' I said, 'I don't know.'

She just stood there a moment, then said, 'I think I know what's the matter with you,' and she talked the way of the Māori so that I'd feel better. Then she said, 'Are you OK now?'

And I said, 'I'm OK.' All in Māori. And away she went.

I was better instantly. Some things I can't explain adequately to you. They're deep in Māori history. But I think what she meant was that the reason I'd been a bit ill was because I was perhaps becoming a little too, I wouldn't say close, but, you know, I used to drive her around, and we'd stop along the way and have something to eat. Maybe I'd been too intimate with the royal family. You don't get too upfront, dear. And we were getting to the point where if she admired something of mine, like a coat or something, I'd just give it to her if it fitted her nicely. So I knew I wasn't too terribly well. I had a great deal of respect for her.[8]

One time I had to drive her to Auckland, and of course I'd done this many times before. No problems there, because I knew Auckland fairly well. If she needed to see the doctor, or to do some special shopping, I usually knew the way. This time we were on our way to buy some shoes. She was in poor health then; yes, very poor health because of her tuberculosis. We'd done some shopping, and that was lovely.

My mentor and friend, the late Princess Te Puea. G.E. Ramsden Collection. Alexander Turnbull Library, G5159$^{1}/_{2}$

I very much enjoyed shopping with her, because of all the fine treatment she received. She had an account at the department store, and she was one of those who would be served in a private room upstairs. She would just sit there and try shoes on, while sales assistants came in with different ones. She picked out a couple of pairs to purchase, maybe three. Then she turned to the attendant and said, 'Now bring me another pair of shoes, something different, a younger type of shoe for Heeni.' So I got a pair of shoes that she chose for me. And I can remember these were a fairly simple pair of court shoes. They were very comfortable, and I used to wear them around a lot.

Then it was about half past five or six o'clock on our way home, so we were running into traffic. As we were approaching Grafton Bridge, which was the main highway before all the motorways came in, Princess Te Puea said to me, 'Oh stop, stop, stop!'

I said, 'We can't along here. This is where the buses stop.' She was beginning to cough, and said, 'Heeni, you must stop. I just have to stop.'

And just as I pulled over, a policeman appeared on her side, you know, and she wound the window down because she was breathing heavily. And she looked up and said, between coughs, 'Good evening, sir,' you know, to this policeman. And he looked and I think he recognised her, because she always wore that trademark white scarf. He just stood there, and I thought, 'What's going to happen now?' I didn't say a thing. But you know, that policeman stood there patiently, and she was coughing away for quite a while. And then she said, 'OK now, OK. Now we can leave.' And even though it was illegal for us to stop there, the policeman just let us go.

Yes, you know, things like that used to convince me more and more, well, that there must be something very special about her. I mean something special protecting

With Princess Te Puea, late 1930s (standing at right). Tūrangawaewae Marae Collection

her. There was another time that made me think this. I was driving Princess Te Puea and Father Seamer from Wellington back to Wanganui. We hadn't got away from Wellington until fairly late, and it was getting dark by the time we came to Otaki, and it had become foggy. Quite suddenly we came upon a barrier across the street, so I stopped. Father Seamer said, 'What have you stopped for?', and I said, 'Well, there's a sign there saying to stop.'

Suddenly a man appeared, dressed sort of like a policeman, on Father Seamer's side of the car, and noticing his collar he said, 'Good evening.' And Father Seamer said, 'Good evening, I don't know what the matter is with my driver—she's just stopped here.'

And the policeman said, 'Yes, there's a sign there indicating she should stop.'

'Well, I've got to get back to Wanganui. What's the reason? Why do we have to stop?' asked Father Seamer.

The policeman replied, 'Well, there's been a lot of work on the Manawatu Bridge, and it's ready to be opened tomorrow morning by the prime minister. But I'll break the rules and let you pass through. You'll be the first car to drive over that long bridge since construction began several months ago.' And he lifted the end of the barrier, and we passed through with no problem.

Through Princess Te Puea I was meeting people from all walks of life. She kept me quite clean and spotless in my manners and my image. I had to be presentable. Of course, I wore a deaconess uniform mostly, which was supposed to be navy, you know, plain. But I got away from strict adherence to this rule quite early in life, and made my own frocks with a bit of lace and embroidery. The other deaconesses kept very strictly to certain uniform styles, like nurses. I think I was looked upon negatively for ignoring this, but those women didn't do the kind of entertaining that I did!

One day I was called aside from the others who were serving morning tea at Tūrangawaewae, because Princess Te Puea had instructions for me: 'OK, Heeni, you are to serve Lord and Lady Mountbatten today.' Mountbatten and his wife were coming later to visit Tūrangawaewae marae. He was of course going to be a guest of the late King Korokī, the queen's father. Oh yes, he was quite a person, and his wife was very high up in that sort of area as well. So I was shocked.

'What?' I asked, taken by surprise.

'Yes, and they'll be here at half past ten to about half past eleven. Princess Te Puea will be there with you, and it will be your duty to serve her and Lord and Lady Mountbatten.'

'Oh,' I thought, 'golly me.' I told myself that I had no choice, so I'd have to do it the very best way I knew how. Of course I knew the proper etiquette for serving, but these three would be seated up there alone. I had to quickly learn the special protocol for serving high-level guests. There were certain silver pieces, and I had to stand on a certain side of them, and black coffee or white coffee, and someone else would bring the tray of food, and I'd have to walk in front of them and so on. It was all very complicated, but I was sure I could do it.

And so the time came, and I was thinking that this would also be the first time I'd served Princess Te Puea. Then suddenly I thought, 'Now which of these three do I serve first?' And I though, 'Well, the Māori custom is that you go to the man first.' So I was to serve him first, and I was all right, yes. But who would be next? I thought since Princess Te Puea was the local one, perhaps Lady Mountbatten should be second. Yes, and that was right. But it turned out that the welcome speech, and the young entertainers, who performed a very quick haka, took too much time. They were a little late in coming, and the party had to leave the marae at half past twelve. As it was, therefore, they weren't interested in the food. But they did take a sandwich. Lovely club sandwiches they were. So I got through that all right.

During this time, a close and supportive friendship developed between me and the wife of King Korokī, Te Atairangikaahu, who was Piki's mother. After King Korokī's death, the people changed Piki's name to that of her mother.

In addition to serving and helping out with guests, I also conducted Sunday-school classes on the marae. Princess Te Puea had adopted all the churchfolk who visited the marae; she embraced them all. She and Father Seamer, a deeply religious man, agreed on many spiritual things. She took a lot of strength and comfort from him, and he gained a lot of knowledge about Māori custom from her.

One day I had a group of young people on the Tūrangawaewae marae for Sunday school. Sometimes I used to have about fifty or sixty young people there, where we usually met on the veranda outside the meeting and sleeping houses. Much to my surprise, the late Princess Te Puea was there on this special Sunday. She came along and sat down with the children. Well, I was on my own that morning, and it was always difficult to hold the attention of such a very large group of young ones. I think there must have been about fifty children, and amongst them sat the late Princess Te Puea. So I thought quickly. My knees were a bit unsteady with her sitting there, so I decided to have them sing choruses. I nearly always prepared a lesson, but instead I told them a short story next, one I knew at the time and couldn't go wrong with. So away I went, and then it was finished.

Then Princess Te Puea stood up and said in Māori, 'You listen.' She wanted to give the children a lesson of her own. First, she praised them for being so well behaved (they behaved nicely because she was sitting there). Then she said, 'This is what I'd like to tell you children. As you move around from Sunday school to Sunday school, from pā to pā, I want you to remember something that my dad told me long ago.' (And of course I knew her dad very well, and used to call him Koro. He was Dame Te Ata's grandfather. I thought the world of him.) 'I remember when I was a little girl like you, my dad would call to me and say, "I want you to come here so I can tell you a story". Well, I must have only been about twelve at the time, and he'd say, "If you were in a room all by yourself, when neither I nor your mum were around, and you happened to notice that on the table there was a bowl of fruit, you might be tempted to look around and say to yourself, 'Golly, I'd like to steal one of those nice rosy looking apples; I'd like to pinch one of those.'" . . . ' And then Te Puea stopped suddenly. Heavy pause. Everything was quiet. 'My dad went on to say, "Remember, you're never alone even though you might feel you're all by yourself in that room. You're never by yourself. I'm not there, your mum Tiahuia isn't there, but there's always someone else, someone high above who is there."' Te Puea was referring, of course, to te runga rawa, the highest being, the supreme one.

This story of hers really stuck in my mind. I think it was very beautiful, and it made an impression on me because of the connection with my own mum and dad. I thought this was something very important to get across to the young people of that time, because some serious Māori youth problems were just getting started. There had been some children before this occasion who had been very difficult to control. A number of them had already begun stealing.

I worked pretty hard at relating to children of all types. There were times when I was also patted on the back, which helped a good bit. Elders would sometimes say, 'My word, you have got a personality that gets across to them!' Maybe I worked on all of that too, but it used to tire me absolutely. Sometimes I'd come home from that kind of work with a pain in my throat. Not from yelling—it was part of our training not to yell. We were instructed in a bit of psychology, and we weren't to yell. But I've had throat problems a long time; I don't know exactly why. I was just always glad when my break came along during Sunday school.

My brother Paddy—Patrick Michael O'Halloran Taylor—served in World War Two. Two years before he arrived home, Princess Te Puea called and said to me, 'Your brother is going to come home, but he's going to arrive wounded. He will still come home though.' It didn't upset me or anything. I think I just believed what she said. You have to remember that at this time there was lots of news coming over that so-and-so had been wounded, and so-and-so had been killed, so we were quite prepared for it. I was in Auckland visiting when suddenly an urgent message came, and I knew it was about Paddy. My brother must have given my name as next of kin. When I held the telegram I thought, 'How am I going to open this?' It was from the air centre in London.

It read: 'Your brother has been wounded.' I remember my mum and dad and Princess Te Puea discussing how it would be when he came home from the war. There were certain Māori rituals he'd have to go through. Before he went away, Princess Te Puea called and gave me a message to give to my dad about what to do with my brother. You know, like take him down to the river, and this sort of thing. So I had to listen very hard to what the instructions were that she gave me, and then I travelled down on my own and gave this message to my mum and dad. So, naturally, we waited for Paddy to come home, and there were many anxious moments until we got word, much later, that the war was over and he'd be coming home. But he was to stay on in England a bit first, because he had fallen in love with an English lady. He sent word back that he was going to marry her, and that he'd be coming ahead of her soon. She was to follow later.

But she never did come, dear. I think it caused him a good bit of pain, on top of the fact that he'd been shot and his wounds were not healing well at all. He'd been a gunner, and on a particular evening the plane he was flying was hit over Germany. He was shot through the leg, and the pilot, who was a Māori from Dunedin, got them back to England and rushed him into hospital there. And I remember Paddy telling me that he lay unconscious for a couple of days or so. When he came to, he started to look out for his mates, but couldn't find them by enquiring with the nurses. And then, after a day or so, he guessed that his plane had been shot down on another mission, and his mates had been killed. That's exactly what had happened; and their bodies were never recovered. His best friend was the squadron leader, and he died as well. Their mission had been the transfer of troops onto battleships out on the ocean somewhere.

Before this happened, I had a letter from Paddy. I think there were seventy-something Māori boys in his group, but nearly three-quarters of them didn't come home. This was quite hard on him, and I don't think he realised at the time what losing friends on the battlefield would be like. I still sort of feel today that the best of our Māori men were lost in the war. They signed up quickly because, you know, the thrill of going to another country, going away, and the new experience of it all, but most of them didn't realise they wouldn't be coming home. So we have a whole generation of men who missed their steadying influence on Māori life. Had they not gone overseas, I think they'd have been here to help our young lads. I can think of a number of them who were fine, well-educated people who, when they died, left a hole here at home.

Paddy was lucky. When he arrived home, he told Mum that he'd rather the family didn't ask too many questions about what had happened overseas. It was so painful for him to talk. I could see his point of view, and never asked him. He offered what I've just told you. I sometimes think about that lady he fell in love with. He not only came back with a lame leg, but also a wounded heart. She didn't even write to him. And after he left England, he never heard from her again. But then, of course,

With the late Princess Te Puea (left) and Princess Terito of Rarotonga (centre)
in Auckland a few months after the 1947 Pacific islands tour.

anything could have happened. Anything could have happened to her. We'll never know for sure.

Much later he became friendly with another woman and they lived together. Her husband had died and she was left with grown-up children. It was a good arrangement, because they'd been friends for a long time. But she soon died from cancer. A year later, so did my brother. With him it was cancer of the bones. Neither of his wounds ever did heal. Every now and again his leg would break, and finally it caught cancer.

In 1947, Princess Te Puea, Piki and myself set off on a Pacific tour. It was a new experience for me, a flight away from my home in New Zealand. We first flew to Noumea, where we spent one night on our way to Fiji. We spent the night, and woke up to some fairly rotten weather, really. We took off into this storm, and the plane was bumping up and down, absolutely. We wondered what was happening. First of all the copilot came through and said, 'Belt up!' This was a private plane, with a group of about twenty-five people or so. And then the word came that we were flying through severe turbulence. And I thought, 'Oh golly me,' but I wasn't afraid. No, I wasn't afraid at all. I can honestly say I wasn't. Suddenly, we were warned about a drop, but fortunately we were all belted in. It gave us a good jolt. Princess Te Puea was sitting just in front of us, and suddenly she turned around and looked at me, pointing to the wings of the plane. I was sitting near the window, and I could see the wings, and also this rainbow. It wasn't too far away from the plane. Princess Te Puea was sitting there with her husband, and they just sat and watched. I don't think she signalled to any of the others, just to me. And then I looked out and took in this beautiful rainbow. I knew that we were completely and totally safe at this point. A rainbow always means fear not.

I was chosen by my people and the Department of Māori Affairs to represent the Māori people when the young Queen Elizabeth came through New Zealand in 1954, shortly after her coronation. I remember my brother Paddy had explained his impressions of England and the royal family, the aristocracy and all. He said, 'New Zealand is only a wee little thing, you know. In the history of the world, we've done nothing. In World War Two the English were fighting for tradition, castles and the ideals of aristocracy.' And, of course, this fascinated me. And then suddenly, when I was chosen to represent my people, I felt I understood more about who the Queen was, and what she stood for, what the royal family was all about. Before this time, I just knew of them in the magazines.

After the news had properly sunk in that I'd be going, I thought I couldn't wear an old deaconess uniform to this very important dinner affair. I thought it over, and decided to go to a proper dressmaker. There were these two ladies who were very prominent dressmakers. We met and they said, 'Ah, we'll dress you up!'

They took me into town, but there was nothing exciting in Hamilton. So we went to Auckland and found the right fabric, and these ladies didn't just buy a bit of it, they ended up purchasing the whole roll. 'The church will have to do something to put toward this, but we'll worry about it later.' The reason they bought the whole roll was because they were preparing gowns for five other women who would also be attending the dinner. So they knew there would be others who would be out looking for material, and they wanted to ensure that no-one else might show up with a gown made of my material. And it was lovely. It was brocade, a fairly heavy fabric, so you didn't need to wear layers underneath. It was an off-gold colour, somewhere between cream and gold. Lovely, and absolutely beautiful with long black hair. I never did see the material for the other ladies' gowns. The dressmakers thought it wouldn't be right because, as they said, 'You wouldn't like us to show your gown to them, would you?' Of course not. Better that we didn't know in advance.

I had to buy a proper foundation too. These ladies came with me, the two of them, and I didn't appreciate all of the fuss. For them, of course, it was fun, but it wasn't so much for me. Because, you know, I had these two ladies and the sales assistants helping me try on all of these bras and girdles. You know, the whole thing, the slip, all of it. And shoes. I had to buy shoes and they were very difficult to find, because I have such wide feet. And it was a very costly business. I never did ask the church to pay for it. It took me months to pay it all off.

This continued for I don't know how long while we got the gown fitted. The skirt had to have a cord along the back of the hemline to tighten me up. I didn't want to show my chest at all, but the dressmakers wouldn't have it. 'We're going to make it low,' they said.

'Not too low, not too low in the front there,' I said. 'I'd like to wear my tiki, so that'll be just right. It'll just hide my cleavage.'

And at the last two fittings they were quite stern with me. 'Heeni, you must hold your tummy in. Stand steady now. Curtsey to us.' Many times I had to do that.

I looked at what the other ladies wore, and many of their gowns were much more elaborate. Some were all sort of puffed up. That was the style in those days. Many

'To Meet the Queen', by Gwendoline Mary Augusta Rogers, painted to commemorate my meeting Queen Elizabeth. Denis Rogers

of them wore glittery things around their necks, but I was comfortable with my tiki, and that's all. I thought, 'I'm glad I'm wearing what I am wearing.' Simple and elegant, yes, that's what I thought.

They arranged for me to have a Māori escort. He was a very tall, respected Māori. Fairly prominent. His father was a minister in the Methodist Church, which is why I guess they chose him. It was about seven o'clock, and after I'd got dressed, I waited for my taxi. There were no private cars. It all felt to me a little bit like a fairy tale. It did, dear. Yes, because the streets of Hamilton were lined with this motorcade. I've never seen so many people or so many police around New Zealand. And the army. They stood behind the police, who were lined up on both sides of the street. And the lights inside the taxi were all on so everyone could see who was who, and what was what. And the crowds were cheering, you know. At first I thought, 'Oh, golly me,' you know. But then I sort of entered into the spirit of it all. We were told to sit fairly close to the windows so that the crowd could see us. We'd been given all of the protocol in advance, how to wave and smile. It was all beautiful.

We all had to be lined up inside the Embassy Hotel, twenty minutes or so before the royal car was to arrive. Then we were to curtsey. I'd had to wear my shoes for a few days in advance, so that I wouldn't slip when I curtsied to Queen Elizabeth and her husband, the Duke of Edinburgh.

I did actually meet Queen Elizabeth. I shook her hand, and I thought she was beautiful. Her gown was off-blue, and stunning. In those days she was quite young, and so natural. I thought she was really down to earth. She didn't wear her crown, and wasn't off-putting at all. We were close to the main table, and could hear and see almost all of what was going on. The duke made everybody feel at home, because after grace he began to play with the silverware and tell jokes.

The meal was beautiful. I enjoyed myself thoroughly. And I'll never forget dessert. It was summertime and we had strawberries and ice cream. I still have the menu card for the evening. I felt like it was all a bit unnatural, and yet I was really excited to be participating. I felt very humble about it all. It was a privilege to have been chosen. And, of course, I remember my debutante girls curtseying to me.

As her time came closer to the end, I think Te Puea became concerned about what would happen after her death. I think she was thinking about leadership two generations from then. She was also trying to train different people, but people, being what they are, are naturally only people. Some would go along with her ideas, others would not. But the majority really did have a lot of affection for her. But she was worried about the future, what was going to happen, because she knew there wasn't a male. King Korokī didn't have a son. Robert Mahuta was very much in the picture, but then a lot of the people were never with Robert, and he was much, much younger. I think he was still in school when she died.

I told her doctor around the time that she passed on, that she was quite cold, physically. And this was of some concern to her. There were several people who used to, you know, sit quite close to her, and some would sleep next to her. She was always in her own blanket, though. You know the old Māori custom. You never share your blanket or your mate with anybody else. On two occasions I had to sleep next to her. Te Puea had lots of people in her orbit. But only a few would tell her the truth. And I think she trusted me this way. I wanted to keep her warm. We were friends.

I was with Princess Te Puea before she passed on. I was rubbing her back, and her feet, and then about midnight I noticed she was sleeping. All of the folk said that I could go home, which I did. As I arrived at my house, a ruru, or morepork, called. I was told the next day that she passed on fifteen minutes or so after I left. I wasn't surprised, because I could feel the coldness of the body and of the feet.[9]

6 / My Lovely Boys

From the time I first met Heeni in 1947, I have always noticed she got a lot of respect. I experienced Heeni at first as being clearly a very warm, nurturing, caring person who had assumed major responsibilities because of her role in the Church. Not necessarily in the orthodoxy of the Church, you see; but she ultimately carved out for herself a special role which wasn't quite pastor and wasn't social worker. You know, it was something quite 'other' with Māori flavouring.

Professor James Ritchie

ABOUT 1951, I moved to the boys' hostel. Those were very happy years. I enjoyed being with the boys very much. Now that the girls' hostel was established, Princess Te Puea had seen to it that I was to move on to a new venture. Somebody else would be taking my place with the girls, I was to be matron of the boys' hostel. Māori boys would live in the new hostel in Hamilton while they attended the polytech.

I had a group of about forty boys from different tribes throughout the North Island. I found them lots more cooperative than the girls. I discovered they would help me with whatever I was doing, but unlike the girls, suddenly they would be off doing something else. And it seemed they were always hungry. Of course, they were paying for their training—a lot of them were attending the tech taking carpentry courses or radio work, while their parents were paying a certain amount toward their board. It wasn't a free place. All these young people were paying something toward their board. I was also contributing something to my board. When I became a deaconess, I had to pay through serving, promising to serve so many years. For me, it wasn't actually money that passed over, it was service.

I'd try to do what I could to help my boys, so that when they went back to their own people they could take something they'd gained from our hostel. One thing I helped them with was teaching them to be more confident among the Pākehā. I can remember on various occasions the boys coming home from the polytech feeling a little upset. They came to me saying, 'Oh, those Pākehā boys in our group up at the tech sort of sit in one corner of the room and just look at us. We just keep to ourselves, and this sort of separation bothers us a little bit.' And I can distinctly remember saying to my boys, 'Well, I think it's up to you to make the break. Why don't you go across the room and go over to them and chat with them the way you chat among yourselves? Because maybe they're wondering about you since you're a different colour. Maybe they're a little uncomfortable. And you're looking at them in the same way, and like them you're wondering what's going on in their minds too. It may take a little while, but I feel that if you do, you'll be successful and bring a closer relationship between our two young people. And when you're among Pākehā

As I appeared in a newspaper article about my hostel work in the early 1950s. Edward W. Bock

people, you pull yourselves together and conduct yourselves in the way and in the manner that they do in their culture.' I often spoke that way to my young men.

I think the adjustment had been easier for me because of the way I'd been brought up. Remember, we had such an open way about our home, and visited freely back and forth with our closest neighbours, who were Pākehā. And my mum and dad encouraged the children next door to think of them as their mum and dad, and their mum became Mum Ferguson to me. It was quite natural for us all to be just one people. As I grew up, I somehow felt that maybe I was brought into the world for a special sort of purpose. And perhaps this open situation with Pākehā in my early years prepared me for building an important bridge between our two cultures—by helping young people I was put into contact with those who were learning the Pākehā way of life.

I always think how lucky I was to be born into that situation, and I'll be grateful for this all my life. I remember on the night of my dedication to the Church that I paid tribute to my home, to my mum and dad for the kind of atmosphere that I was brought up in, for the freedom of movement among Pākehā folk. I suppose I was special. I was lucky and fortunate to be born into that family and to have such a wonderful caring mum and dad.

The boys might have had some problems with the other boys, but they had absolutely no problem mixing with different kinds of girls. Honestly, you should have seen it. There at the hostel, around about a quarter to five when the boys would be coming home, all these girls would be standing all around outside waiting for them to come home—Māori, Pākehā, Chinese and Indian girls. These girls knew they couldn't come in, but there they were, standing around outside. I had many boys there, handsome boys all, and of course they were guys the girls would be attracted to because they were all going to the technical college and were bright and charming. They knew that here were boys who were going to make something of themselves. In the evenings they'd call. We had only one phone for forty boys, with an extension in my room for calls at night; and it became such a problem that I had to talk it over with the boys. I told them I'd arrange for a special line just for their use, which they would have to pay for, so that my line could be free. We arranged that fairly quickly. And they rang round the clock.

The boys were all from fairly prominent families, with two years at secondary school behind them before they were eligible to come to Hamilton and live at the hostel. I remember one boy who was very tall, a half-caste Māori, and very handsome. He was one of the first to come to me, and ended up staying for nine years. He was one of the ones that was chased quite a bit by these girls. One time, as we were having the evening meal, the phone rang in the dining room and it was for him. He whispered to me, 'Is it a girl, is it a girl?' And I said, 'Yes, it's a girl.' And then he said, 'Just tell her I'm not here!' And I said, 'OK, OK.' They were really fun; they kept me laughing, alive and young.

I can remember another young fellow who was a real Māori—he had no other blood and was well built and a fine-looking young man and very easy to get along with. He said to me, 'Those blimmin''—sometimes they didn't mind the language they used—'those blimmin' young girls up at the tech wear such short skirts, you know, they seem to like to bend over whenever we're around and you can almost see their blimmin' behinds!' He wasn't attracted to this kind of behaviour, and I can see his point of view.

A typical day had many ups and downs, but mostly there were happy times. Life was not dull. The hostel had its moments that kept me moving along with the young ones. That was life, and I was seeing that it was fun to be with these young people,

Residents at the boys' hostel, Hamilton, about 1970. I'm sitting fifth from the right in the second row back. On my right is Mr Michael Connelly from the Department of Māori Affairs.

and I always remembered what a privilege it was for me. I learnt a lot from them, because they didn't hesitate to come to me and open their hearts.

Yes, I found that the boys were more open than the girls had been. They didn't hide anything from me. Even those who had already been drinking continued to drink at the hostel; and although there was a rule that they were permitted to drink out, they weren't allowed to bring drink onto the property there. I remember having a chat with one fellow who wasn't with the Methodist Church. He was a meat inspector who had done his training and got a job here while he was waiting to sit for an exam for his second degree. He said, 'Matron, I find it rather difficult coming here—your church rules are difficult to take. Growing up at home among my family, drinking at the table was quite a common thing, and it was allowed that I could take part with them in their drinking. And coming here to this hostel, this Methodist hostel which I'm grateful to be at, I find it difficult to swallow that drink isn't permitted here on the premises.' I said, 'No, not on the premises here, but what you do away from here is your own business.' He said, 'Oh, very well, but I still find it difficult to swallow.' I guess I knew that he was bringing it in anyway, but I closed my eyes to lots of things. He was a gentlemanly boy and he'd take part in all the activities of the hostel and was a tremendous help to me. I knew there were members of my staff that weren't too happy about me closing my eyes, but sometimes I had to put my foot down and say, 'It is I who happens to be the matron here, and what I feel within myself to be the most important priority is to help these young fellows get through their studies.' I could see ahead in my own mind, and I knew that this boy could be dismissed for his drinking, and that didn't agree with my way of thinking. I knew he had a good future ahead of him, and I'd rather see that the boys got through their training, which would help them in their future life long after they'd grown out of drinking.

After the evening meal, we'd have activities in the recreational hall that the Church built on the premises. Here, the boys would play table tennis or entertain their friends. It was quite a large area in there, and the hall became their property as soon as they came in after the evening meal. And I'd always make time to have a private chat in my own lounge there, if a boy wanted to talk to me, which they did do.

There was another boy who was a heavy drinker already at about seventeen or eighteen. That was the age they were coming to us. He wasn't as gentlemanly, no, a little more aggressive in his style. He'd often come home so drunk, making a lot of noise and this sort of thing. This would upset me, because here we were right in the middle of the city with people living all around. But the rules weren't that tight; we couldn't tie them all down and say, 'No, no no.' Unlike the other boys, this one didn't come and talk to me, and I felt he was one of the ones I tried hardest to get to, but we never did quite connect. There seemed to be a barrier there that I just couldn't get across. And when he left I felt very sad. Not very long after that, he got caught up in the army and was sent off to Singapore. It must have been just a few days after he arrived in Singapore that he went swimming with a group of Māori lads who were also over there. He had an accident while diving. He must have struck his head on the bottom of the pool, and became paralysed from the neck down. His auntie was living here in Hamilton, and she told me about the incident soon after it happened. He was moved back to an Auckland hospital, and they didn't seem to think there would be any hope for this young fellow. I made up my mind that I'd go to the hospital to see him, and although it wasn't visiting hours, I was allowed to go in. I told him he'd been on my mind, and he said in a very low sort of voice, 'I don't think there's anything that can be done for me. I injured all that part of the head, and it's affected my brain.' He was grateful that I'd come to see him, and his last words to me were, 'Come and see me again.' But I didn't get back to see him again, because he died shortly thereafter. When I heard the news, I felt within myself that I was quite at peace. I'd been to see him to make some connection with him again. It turned out that I didn't really get through to him at the hostel as I would've liked, but I think he was about the only boy that I felt that way about.

On the outside of my life, it looked like I was the matron of a hostel, the organiser, the supervisor, the person who made sure that everything ran correctly. But I believe my true role was to be a friend to these young people, to see what they needed in order to help them along their way of life. They were all different personalities, of course, so I had to make some adjustments. Yet I knew in the process of growing and helping them along that my strength lay, as a role model, to help them see what they could do for their iwi, for their people. And I think my true purpose was helping to mould and shape future leaders, to help our people. I felt that when opportunities came along to have these quiet private chats with my young people, they were seeking something more deeply. And then I'd open up about my own feelings, providing them with what wisdom and advice that I could, based on Māori tradition and my own experience.

But as I say, I had fun with them too, and was privileged to be included in some of their outings. Sometimes they'd form a rugby match, and say, 'Come on, come along. We're all playing at rugby in the park.' And they'd hurry me, of course; they didn't realise that I had other things to attend to before I could become free and available to go with them. They'd say, 'Hurry up. We'll leave you behind if you don't hurry up and get ready.' But I knew they'd wait, and when I was ready we'd go and enjoy all the fun.

I'd also go to the movies, sometimes with the boys and sometimes with the woman who was working as our cook. I was very fond of going to all the films that came along. We'd go to see films like *The Sound of Music*. This was the most gorgeous film, with the songs and the mountains and all the children. We'd see the afternoon show during the day so that we could be back to make the evening meal. So you see, it wasn't a dull sort of life that I led, because I entered into all the fun that the young people had.

The boys used to play rugby with some of the Mormon boys. I was always flexible with other denominations. The Mormons were just becoming established in Hamilton, and building their temple here. One of the main principles with the Mormon Church was to prepare for the future. No smoking, of course, and no drinking. I thought that was good. Socialising with the Mormons was better sometimes than with the Māori, who would just get their pay and spend it down at the pub and away goes most of the pay. But with the Mormons, you see, they had to budget; they had to put quite a bit aside. I knew that they had to give one tenth of what they were getting to the Church. I got to know them during that early stage while they were building the temple and breaking the ground. A lot of people from the north would come down here and help to till the land and prepare everything. There were a lot of Māori people working with Mormon church leaders. Māori people loved their church very much. So I got to know them. They were always very fond of singing, and they were training young people, not only with singing, but they incorporated everything to do with Māori culture. They had a local singing group which was taken overseas. I used to go up there with friends quite a bit and listen to them. They had a lady conductor who was in control of the choir. Sometimes I went with my own young people to listen and enjoy all that. They had some lovely voices and the singing was beautiful. I used to have quite a group of Mormon singers come to my hostel, especially when they were entertaining a group from Tahiti or Hawaii or one of those places. I'd entertain them at the hostel, so in exchange, they'd entertain me in the evenings. This was quite a solid relationship. I also enjoyed going to the Catholic church, especially to their midnight services. I went because of the singing and the young people. Their church was just full of young people.

From early in childhood, my whole life seems to have been organised around singing. At the boys' hostel it was no different. The boys also organised a group of singers, who would entertain us in the evenings in their recreation hall, which was apart from the main building. It was a huge hall, where we could easily entertain a couple of hundred people. It had its own toilets and kitchen, a proper kitchen where they could set up their own supper. There were some lovely voices. They had their own group of people who would look after their programme, and sometimes they'd submit the final programme to me for approval, but I'd say, 'Well, it's your evening, you're running it, so go ahead.' There were no restrictions in the recreational hall—they had absolute freedom there. They could do whatever they wanted to do. They'd arrange their evenings and invite their girlfriends to come along and take part. There were lots of fun evenings and always plenty of singing. It was make your own music, make your own dance, make your own songs. It was also a way of keeping the boys away from the streets and giving them the

Song and dance at the boy's hostel, early 1960s.

opportunity to entertain on their own Tūrangawaewae. They had their own haka, and there would be groups of the haka. They'd sometimes invite friends from the tech, and it was all very mixed, Māori and Pākehā. The songs would be in both Māori and Pākehā. It was a delight to me to hear them sing their songs. And you know, I gained a tremendous love.

The boys also organised lectures in the hall given by important people in the area. One time, they invited the superintendant of police to come and talk about things according to the law. You must remember that there were lots of very good boys among my boys, excellent boys. There were also one or two who were naughty and were beginning to get into minor trouble with the police. I don't know how they worked this one out, but they decided that they'd like to invite the superintendent of police, Ian Hamilton, to come and spend an evening with them, so that they could ask questions and that sort of thing. They wanted it to be a private evening. When they came to me and asked what I thought of their idea, I said, 'Well, if you've made all these arrangements already, go ahead. God be with you, and I think it's a very good move.' I always tried to encourage them.

They wanted me to arrange supper for the superintendent after the programme in my private dining room. And I thought, 'Oh, this is a good idea. I'll get to meet him too.' That was arranged, and so the head boy brought them along to me in my private suite and introduced him, and I took to him almost immediately and found him to be most interesting. He told me just a very brief account of the meeting with the boys and how thrilled he was to have the opportunity of meeting them. He didn't tell me about all the questions they fired at him. We had a lovely dinner, and he enjoyed a special chocolate cake for him, and I felt that was the beginning of a good relationship between myself and the police.

I did have some problems with the naughty ones. There was one fellow, a big tall guy from right here in Hamilton. He came home late one night, and because he was a big stump of a boy, you could hear him walking—thump, thump, thump. And he was talking very loudly, so I thought, maybe this guy's drunk. And I thought, 'Oh golly me, here it is after midnight and he's being too loud.' Remember, I was always conscious of the image we were presenting to the neighbourhood. It would only mean more talk about these Māori people, how rough they were and making life uncomfortable for those on the outside, if the boys behaved in such a way that caused people to complain. So I went down in my heavy dressing gown, and ran right into him. He was coming out of his room again, and he stood over me, because he was much taller than I am, and bigger, of course. I said, 'What are you doing?', and I yelled then. 'What are you doing making all this noise at this time of the night? Have you no sympathy for our next-door neighbours?' He stood quite still when I spoke, and that made me nervous. I wasn't scared of him, but I could smell the drink on him and knew that he was absolutely drunk. So I said, 'Stop this bloody noise now or I'll give you a hiding. That's your room, that's your bed there. Now I'm going to stand here and see that you get there, even if I have to undress you! Get into your bed and go to sleep, now! And don't get up again until morning, when you've calmed down.' And he did stay there, which greatly surprised me. He could have easily grabbed me and thrown me out, because I was quite close to him.

Not long after this incident, he came to me after he'd just received his pay cheque and wanted to pay up all the money that he owed. He was owing quite a lot in his board, unknown to me. I told him he knew very well that I wasn't the one to take the money for board, but I'd make an exception today (because I still smelt a bit of the drink on him). He had a motorbike and was going home for the weekend. He wanted to leave all the money with us that he owed. Of course, he didn't owe me any money personally. All the boys who borrowed from me always gave the money back again. I was never out of pocket. And I was always happy if I had money to give them, so that they wouldn't be tempted to pinch down the street, or steal among themselves. And so I said, 'Well, be careful. Are you going straight home now?'

He said that he was, and I said, 'Well, be careful. Are you all right?'

He said, 'Yes, Sister, I'm all right.'

So I said, 'Goodbye, dear.'

So away he went, and that very evening I got a call from the hospital wanting to speak with the matron. They said, 'Bad news, bad news. A young fellow was picked up on the road. His bike had gone over on a corner and he was found in the ditch, dead. So do you think you could come up and identify the body?' I didn't know what to say. That was one of the moments in life when I was simply at a loss for words. I couldn't go. The woman who had been with me as sub-matron that year, Sister Mary Sealey, ended up offering to go in my place. I remind her every now and again that I'll never forget her doing that for me, because I wouldn't have known what to do. I don't think I would have been able to drive myself up there.

I often think that it was very interesting that he cleared up all his debt right before he died, as though he were clearing his way. I knew before he came that he was a very heavy drinker. He was much older than these other boys. I tried to help him and would tell him, 'The drink isn't doing you any good.'

'I can't help it,' he'd say. 'I go down there to see my mates and then on payday they say "Come on, let's have a drink." And then I have one and I don't know when to stop.'

Like at the girls' hostel, I sometimes felt that life was very heavy, and that I had to get away to think by myself. Many times I was tired from the burden of carrying on what I was doing. At these times, I'd reflect on my belief in God, which was perhaps even deeper than either my Christian or Māori religious feelings. But I was able to gain strength from my Māori teachings, and also gain a great deal of strength from above. And in those times, I'd go away to be with myself where I could get the spiritual nourishment that I needed to gain back my peace of mind. I'd think, well, what could I do to keep these kids from doing the kinds of things they were doing, things like drinking or going down the street and breaking into places?

Most of this sort of thing happened at night-time. They'd be running out, you see, while I'd be thinking, 'Oh well, they're all in bed now.' But they wouldn't be in bed, and in the morning I'd find that some kids had been down the street and had broken into shops—the sorts of things that are happening today, but not to the same degree. I think if I were doing the same sort of thing today, that I'd have dropped out of it all. Back then, it was just sort of beginning. And always, well, the police would be around my way visiting in the morning. And that used to scare me, absolutely frighten me, to think that the police would come and that the people around the neighbourhood would know. Our image was vulnerable. The hostel was a wide-open place, you know, no gates anywhere. The boys could run out from any point of the hostel; it was meant to be a wide-open place for the public and for the boys so that the young people coming in would feel that they could come and go as they pleased. There were rules, but they were not strict. Well, the police would come and tell me what had happened and we'd have to do something. These things were just beginning to happen in Hamilton then.

There was one occasion when a policeman came; he was a very young fellow and I was thinking, 'Oh golly me, you can't be very much older than my boys.' I think this case was a little bit more serious, and he was trying to force this one boy to admit he had done whatever it was. Anyway, I saw him go out with my boy, out onto the front lawn there, and I saw him shaking my boy, and I thought, 'What is he on about?' I think he was trying to persuade him to own up to what he'd done, but the boys weren't always responsible for the illegal things that went on. And I thought to myself, 'Oh, I wonder whether the boys are being subjected to questions that would puzzle them,' and that in the end they'd be forced to say yes. None of my boys were ever taken away; I think they were always sort of helped along and given another chance. But forcing them to admit guilt didn't stop until I was brave enough once to say to the young police who came around, 'Why do you always have to come here?' And they said, 'Well, it's the law that we question a lot of young people living together.' But I'd stick up for my boys. I'd try to find out myself, quietly, from the other boys, if they were responsible for what had happened. In some cases, I found out much, much later on that they weren't always telling the truth even to me. But in one case, I knew a boy hadn't done what he was being accused of and I stuck up for him with the police. And the man from the station said, 'Don't fear, Matron, we'll take your word for it.' And I was so pleased to hear that from the police, that they'd take my word. I appreciated that very much, but I knew also that things were beginning to get really tough. It was the beginning of a certain Māori restlessness throughout the country. Because there were lots of other things coming in—drugs, for instance. And drinking. Boys were coming

The boys' hostel, Te Rāhui Tāne, River Road. The hostel was originally in London Street, and when it was relocated in 1963 the archway was moved and erected at this new site in memory of the late Princess Te Puea. The inscription on the archway reads: 'She loves her people.' Waikato Times

into the hostel already steeped in alcohol and drugs, so I was relieved to know that my time was just about up, and that sometime in the future I'd no longer have to be dealing with things like that.

Sometimes I'd feel that I just had to get away. It wasn't only because my boys were such a worry, always getting into trouble; I was also under a lot of criticism from the special Pākehā tutors, who got involved with complaining to the Māori Affairs Department. They were probing into what was going on at the hostel, and they didn't understand the type of boys who were coming in from country places where the people hardly had anything at all. Some of the boys would also complain about not having sufficient food. As I say, they were always hungry. Not all, there were just certain ones. And that worried me for quite a long, long while. And I thought, my goodness me, these boys had come from country places and weren't used to having a great deal of food like they were getting at the hostel. They'd get a good breakfast, and then they'd be away all day at school, and get back home again maybe half an hour or so before the evening meal. For breakfast they'd get porridge, toast, honey and cheese and butter and things like that. It was the same sort of thing that I got in my training days. Then they could make their own lunches; the bread would be there, and the butter and fillings would be provided. Then for dinner there would be a choice of meat, and always with Māori people

With two of my lovely boys, late 1960s or early 1970s. Kenley Studios

you put bread on the table, and we'd always get a sweet. They could get a second helping if they wanted to.

So whoever was doing the criticising, they just didn't understand. I talked about it with my kaumātua, and they said, 'No problem, just carry on with what you're doing.' Now that Te Puea was gone, I went to Dame Te Ata's mother quite a bit for advice. There were many kuia at the Tūrangawaewae marae at this time, and they all encouraged me.

But the criticism was still heavy on my mind. I'd go off for a walk during the day, just to get away and have a bit of rest before the boys all came home. When you're trying to do the best that you can do, it hurts when you get criticised, and there were times when I didn't know what else to do. I knew that, and sometimes when I got stirred up, I'd tell them, 'I'm the matron here. You fellows can say what you like, but I'm the matron.'

As I look back, I remember there were other criticisms that made no sense. Sometimes I'd hear criticism about the length of the boys' hair. Boys were just beginning to wear their hair long, and I can remember some of the parents saying to me, 'Why don't you see that they get a haircut?' I said, 'Well, that's for you to talk to your son about. He wouldn't take any notice of me.' That was the problem. And we had lots of problems, problems with girls, even with their girlfriends becoming pregnant.

But I also had my allies among the boys. There were boys that were a tremendous help by sticking up for me. I found that they comforted me sometimes, as well as me comforting them. One of the boys comes around to see me still, bringing all of his kids with him. And he'll say to them, 'Come say hello to your nana.' At that stage you become a nana. He used to be a real support to me, and would say, 'Those boys, don't you take any notice of those boys. Leave it to me.' And they used to be afraid of him, because he was big.

I tried not to let these things worry me too much because I realised I needed to watch my health. All through my life I had to be careful of a weakness in my chest. All along, my doctor would send me up to the hospital to have a check-up for that

Pirimai ('Come close to me').

chest problem. Yes, it seems I've always had tuberculosis, for many years. Even when I was at the hostel, very rarely did I go out in the evenings with low-necked evening wear. Oh, I suppose about once a year or so I'd go to a special occasion where I'd wear a low-cut evening gown. But even going out to dinner, I always had to wear a scarf or something around my neck or my voice would go, like it has sometimes during our long talks. Many times the doctor said, 'Look here, if you don't take care of that voice it'll go and it'll never come back to you again.' And that used to scare me for a day or so, and then I'd sort of forget about it.

Princess Te Puea had adopted a hundred orphans whose parents died in the great influenza epidemic.[1] When these children grew up, she had them all helping her in different ways. That's how I met Danny Smith, who was part American Indian—Mohawk I think—from Toronto, Canada. He'd been a friend of one of her orphans. Danny was a veterinarian who looked after the animals on Te Puea's farm. He was a half-caste, with a fair complexion, sharp features and thick black hair. She'd make sure that he got word to come to her functions, and gradually, you see, we got to know each other. He was quite a regular visitor there at the Tūrangawaewae marae. By that time, I'd been doing my share of things at Tūrangawaewae, helping to serve the tables, serve afternoon tea and things like that.

Danny, being a vet you see, was interested in animals, and that interested me because at that time I had a little doggy, Pirimai. He was a tiny little doggy, so small that he fitted into my pocket when I first picked him up from a lady breeder. *Pirimai* means 'Come close to me'. He was a thoroughbred special Sydney silky. He was a very smart little dog; he wouldn't bark at all the boys, but if someone else came into the yard, he'd growl, and I'd know immediately that there was a stranger coming onto the premises. He was with me for sixteen years. It was Danny who attended him first.

I'd known Danny quite a while before that, and of course I knew he was quite an outstanding veterinary doctor, and I knew he'd be able to give me information. So later, at Tūrangawaewae, I told him about Pirimai, you know, and he said to bring him over to where he lived, where all his gear was. So I took Pirimai over to Danny's home, and yes, Pirimai fell in love with Danny.

One of the things that Danny did tell me, right from the beginning, was not to take Pirimai with me when I was going out on my visits, in my work. Because once I began to do that, he'd be the first to get into the car. So I didn't take him with me. But he'd always know when I was going off, and he'd become sad and run under a chair, you know, and sit there and not let me see his face. But he was marvellous. Pirimai reminded me of all the animals on my place back home, and I was able to sit and talk with Danny about this.

So I got to know Danny, and he'd come visiting. He used to come over to the hostel, and was quite an interesting person. I also met his sisters, who were coming over to see their only brother. He'd come from Putāruru when he was over this way and take me to the pictures, or he'd take me out for meals. That got my mind away from the heavy tasks and responsibilities that were facing me at the boys' hostel. And I think Danny had to get away from things too, so he'd come into the hostel. He had a huge American car, a Cadillac, so we'd drive around in style. He was at Putāruru for quite some time, but eventually felt he had to go back to Canada to do a little bit more work to help his own people. He was quite a leader.

One day when I came home to the hostel, I happened to walk in while Danny was chatting with Reverend Seamer, and realised that Danny was giving money to the hostel for the work that we were doing. Because he had quite a lot of money, he was giving quite freely to us. Not very long after the queen's visit in 1953, his sisters came over. They wanted to stay in Hamilton, so he booked them into a special suite, the very one that the queen had stayed in. So he came around to see me and said his sisters were coming over and that they'd been booked into the queen's suite. And they'd like me to come along and have the evening meal with them. It was beautiful. You should have seen this suite that the sisters were booked into. He'd just ring a bell and help would come up, whatever you wanted, drinks or anything like that, to be served there in the room. Yes, they had money.[2]

That wasn't the only time they came: the sisters came quite often to see their brother. They were beautiful looking ladies; both of them doctors in America. They'd arrive by plane at Auckland. To show you how much money they had—they had a man friend with them, too—they'd hire a taxi the moment they arrived and travel right through New Zealand in it with the meter running. Yes, sometimes for months at a time. And one of these sisters said that she had to go shopping for shoes; she said, 'I have to buy about sixty pairs of shoes.' She said she needn't come back again to buy shoes; she could wear one pair and then throw them out! And the things they wore. Oh, golly me. That hat, the gloves and the material. And plenty of jewellery. I've never forgotten that.

The girls used to send me things. They'd send me a cheque and say, 'Just buy whatever you want. Danny will give you anything.' I knew that, but I didn't want to play on that. I guess, in a way, the money kept me away from him. Being in church work, and coming from a poor home, the difference always presented itself before me.

With Danny Smith (second from left) and his sisters and their friends in front of Tūrangawaewae marae in the late 1950s.

But I did love the clothes. I always liked nice clothes, and because of the work I was in I knew I had to be presentable. It was far more difficult for a Māori to move around among Pākehā people in New Zealand at that time. You had to be absolutely spotless, and I loved that. As long as I had enough money to buy nice things, I was happy.

I wasn't terribly interested in travelling overseas. I don't know why. But Danny did ask me to think about going overseas. He was going on holiday back to his family. When his sisters were leaving New Zealand, they had to go up to Auckland to catch the boat. Danny got in touch with me and said, 'Well, the girls are catching the boat toward evening. What about coming up with us to say cheerio to them?' I thought, 'Oh well, that'll be an experience, to go to the boat,' so I didn't look any further ahead. I'd sailed up and down from Wellington to Christchurch by ferry, but that was a much, much smaller boat. So away we went. We had an early meal, and Danny asked me if I'd ever been on an ocean-going liner. When I said no, the sisters said, 'I wonder if they'd let us on early so that Heeni can have a look at the boat and the cabins where we'll be staying?' We went early, and were permitted to get on, he as the brother and I as the brother's friend. So away we went, and the sisters went to sit in the lounge and said to Danny, 'You go and show Heeni around the ship.' He asked one of the attendants if we'd be able to go through the boat to show me around, and they said yes, but they'd have to be attending to the passengers getting on, so just have a quick look. Well, I was quite energetic in those days, but I was still hanging onto Danny's hand. Danny was hanging onto me too, and away we went. We went right through the boat and down to the cabins where they were going to be staying. And they were just lovely big rooms. I think they even had private bathrooms. I know they travelled in style. I know that. Then Danny said to me, just before we got back to where the sisters were. 'Why don't you come with me one day. We'll go by sea back to my country.' I was stumped; I don't know whether I said anything at all. Because I knew that I'd have to give up my work here to marry him. I didn't think it would be appropriate. I think the thought of my people came into my mind, although he was very well known and liked and respected, and very much loved, very much loved by my people.

It wasn't very long after that, I think, when the call became more urgent for him to go back home. I saw quite a lot of him before he left, because he kept coming to the hostel. I can remember him kissing me before, but one time it as a more lingering kiss and I didn't feel quite so comfortable. Then I think he grabbed me. I think at that stage I thought, 'Maybe—no, not him.' It was a feeling. He grabbed me and kissed me on the lips and I felt this feeling creep up my back which made me, not immediately veer away from him, but slowly sort of draw away from him. After that I got a feeling of fear. I thought this was not to be, because his work would've taken him around here, there and everywhere. I thought, if children came along, what would I do over there? I didn't want to have children away from my people. I thought about all these things; although I did have quite a deep feeling for him.

I don't know if it was because of this incident or afterward when I read somewhere that the Mohawk Indians had a brutal streak, but I'd got that funny feeling up my back, and I just knew I couldn't be with him. When the Māori get a feeling, beware. Several times he'd pleaded with me to just go on holiday; he'd be going back to the States for a week or a fortnight, and I got very tempted once or twice, very tempted. But there was always this question of money. That would have been a new kind of life for me again. I thought, oh, this would be the kind of life I'd have. I couldn't get away from the idea. I knew he was giving money to other causes here in New Zealand. The church people that I'd been with hadn't been of that class, you know; they didn't have money to throw around. We were all servants, sort of. We're talking lots of money here, which really scared me a little bit, having been brought up a poor little country girl.

And then, there were the words of Te Puea. I didn't tell you earlier, dear, but before she died, she gave her last wishes for me. She said, 'Do not ever turn your back on the Kīngitanga.' At the time it didn't worry me quite so much. I just thought, 'Well, I don't think that would be something that I'd ever do. But she also followed up with a second instruction. Of course she was in critical health at the time, and she said, 'The other thing I'm going to tell you is my wish that you not marry.' Well, that made me sit up. I said, 'Why?' Very few people in those days would have answered back, but I'd become close to her because she knew that my mother and father had told me I was to be a servant of King Korokī. So I did answer back, I did. 'Why, why, why?' And she said again, 'My feeling is that I would rather you not marry.' I was still a young woman, quite young. Her wish saddened me. Then she explained, 'If you were to marry, then your husband will become the head one, and no-one will know where he will take you. Once you marry, you will no longer be your own boss, and will have to do what your own husband says, and he could take you away.' I could see immediately: her wish that I not marry followed from her first instruction that I not turn my back on the Kīngitanga. I thought to myself, quite right I suppose. At that moment I was aware of my love for her. Even though she knew I was fond of men, that I enjoyed their company more than I did women, she could see into my future. Te Puea saw long ago some of the things I'd be doing with regard to the Kīngitanga. For example, the amazing things that have happened since my retirement, and the things like a closer link with Robert Mahuta, and Dame Te Ata, Tūrangawaewae marae and the whole community. These would not have happened had I married. Te Puea was right, and in Māori terms she was quite a visionary.

Danny eventually moved back to the United States, where his family, most of whom were physicians, lived. There he was doing things for his own people, because they were in need of guidance. Later, he came out for another visit with his two sisters. It was during this visit, here in Hamilton, that the older sister took me aside and said to me, 'Why don't you marry Danny? I know he's very fond of you. Why don't you marry him?' I didn't know what to say. She said Danny would take me overseas and show me the world. But Danny was very wealthy, and I was a bit intimidated by all of this. It was because we were poor here, you know. Princess Te Puea and all of her people had to work extremely hard to raise enough money to build the Tūrangawaewae marae. We were always fundraising. And to see all of that money— well. There were days when I thought, 'Yes, wouldn't it be lovely.' But then I'd think, 'What would I do with it?' All these thoughts did go through my mind a good bit. But the money didn't interest me. I don't know why. Perhaps it was because of the vast differences between loving a Māori man and Danny being Indian, although he didn't look Indian. I could have married him, but to do that would have meant that I wouldn't be able to be near my people. And I had an idea that maybe Danny was concerned too about taking me away from what I was doing with the Church and this sort of thing. He didn't pressure me.

People knew he was coming to the hostel to see me. On one occasion, the late Princess Te Puea's husband said to me, 'I think you would be giving up a tremendous lot, you know, to back away from your own people.' Oh, I listened to all that they said, because I was weighing it up in my own mind. But ultimately, the decision not to marry him was made by circumstance. It just sort of naturally fizzled out. But often my mind would go back and I'd think about it, and wonder what would've happened had I married him. And yet to move away from my own people into a strange foreign country. Well, I think it would have been a tremendous shock for me. But he was the one person that I got to know really well, and really had affection for, aroha. Yes, you see, I also got a glimpse into that type of world of the rich, the very rich. Sometimes I feel a bit sad about it. I haven't thought about it all in a long while. You've got me reminiscing. No, I think I did the right thing. It's just that the right thing isn't always the happiest thing, at least at the time.

Later, I heard that he'd married. In his house at Putāruru, he had a couple who were working as housekeepers for him, and the wife died. He was interested in a friend of theirs who had lost her husband. She was a good bit older than Danny, from Auckland. She was a lady who always needed him, and he was a very loving, caring sort of fellow. Always wanting to do things for people. The husband of the original housekeeper went off somewhere with another lady after a while, so this lady came to look after Danny. He came over to see me one time towards the end of his time here. 'I'm going over to England, selling up here,' he said. He had wonderful training, his English and his manners were just perfect. And he said this other lady was going with him. I said, 'That is nice, Danny, that is nice,' and he said they'd come over to see me before they went off.

Then the time came when I'd retired, after I'd started doing museum work, and I suddenly got a telephone call. This would've been a few years after they'd left. He'd written a letter to me once, and I think the sister had written once. But suddenly I got this telephone call saying, 'Heeni!', and I recognised the voice immediately and said, 'Danny!'

'Yes,' he said, 'that's me.'

I said, 'Where are you?'

And he said, 'Here in Hamilton.'

'Oh no,' I said.

'Yes,' he said, 'I have been ringing around and I've discovered that you're at the museum. Then I got your telephone number. Can I come around to see you?'

I said, 'Oh, sure! Come around now. We've just had our evening meal.'

He said he'd made enquiries and thought he knew just where I was. And he came around with his new friend.

Although Danny had aged, and had to be in his sixties at that time, he was very differently dressed. He'd changed. Here I was, always used to meeting him in a suit. I got a bit of a shock, always being used to seeing this nice young fellow in well set-up sort of New Zealand clothes. But to see him when I opened the door—his hair was long and his face was quite a bit more sharp, and his colour had become a little bit darker, more red. He had Indian things on, beads and things—he looked quite different. Yes, an Indian gown he was wearing. I guess he'd found his roots again. But he didn't hesitate to hug me and give me a kiss while she was there; he didn't hesitate and neither did I. I think the aroha still came uppermost, because I'd learnt a lot from him, as I did from Maha [Maharāia Winiata], only in a different way. He was a lover of animals, and a lover of nature, and that all appealed to a part of me.

Danny did all the talking, and I think they must have stayed with me until very late that evening. He said he was moving off tomorrow and flying back home. I said, 'Oh, Danny.' He said, 'Maybe one day I'll come back this way again.' That was eighteen years ago.

I don't have any regrets, but after all, I am a natural being and I have missed having a child of my own. All of the deaconesses I trained with were ultimately married happily. Mostly to business people, as I remember. But I was quite different from their way of thinking. Some were just more interested in the money. They did their service, and then settled down and had children. I just wanted to continue with my work. But when I see the other young people who have been with me, boys and girls, and they come here with their little ones, I look at their babies and naturally feel a bit of a twinge. Their little fingers always fascinate me. The perfectness of their tiny, little fingers. I always look at their fingers and toes—how perfect they are, you know. It always amazes me. But I became more involved in what I was doing, and didn't let my mind dwell on that. You can't recall or turn back the years that have gone by, and so I've always been one to live for today. Yesterday has gone and you can't do anything about that. So you just move on and learn from the past. I think my life has been mostly not to cry over what you didn't do. When the opportunity you had has gone by, you can't recall it, you can't erase it, you can't do a thing about it. You just continue on along the way of life today, and lead as full a life as you can and don't think about tomorrow until it comes. All these people haven't come my way, and I haven't come their way, for no purpose. What's that a great philosopher said? 'Not all your tears, not all, can erase or take away what has gone before.'[3]

You know the Reverend Seamer lived to a great age, and he was absolutely loved by the Waikato people. I suppose he's been gone now for about forty years. He was very close to Te Puea and involved intimately with what we were doing. He died at the boys' hostel on London Street. He didn't want to go into a home. I think he was around eighty-six years old. His only daughter wanted to put him into a Methodist rest home in Auckland, but he didn't want that. He wanted to stay among his Māori people. Sister Airini Hobbs, a Methodist deaconess and a friend of many years, and I looked after him in the final days. We had two doctors coming in regularly, and we knew pretty well, because Father Seamer had told us, that he was going to die. And I was to make the arrangements. He wanted his body cremated, and I was to arrange for the undertaker to come. On this certain morning, he knew; his mind was clear, although he was in a lot of pain, and he said, 'Well, I've come to the last step, but my Lord said to me, "Not yet, Seamer, not yet. Go back."' He said to us, 'I'm only living on borrowed time, you know.' Then he turned to me, just me, and said, 'Next week now, I want you to ring the undertaker. I want my body cremated almost immediately.' We were constantly with him, and on the night of the next week that he'd indicated, I said to Sister Hobbs, 'You take a rest and I'll sit up and stay with him.' I'd see him raising his hands and then bringing them down again; he was meditating until the final moments. It came to about twelve o'clock, and I could see that he was going to be passing in a very short while, because I could see the movement becoming slower. I knew that he was going to die. I was sitting there, watching the eyes, and watching the body. Then there was no life in the body—just very quiet, very peaceful. I could hear him saying, very softly, from down deep in the throat where the voice was coming from. 'I'm all right. Go and have a bit of a rest.' Those might have been his last words. And I was wide awake until early morning. There was no movement in the body, and I straightened out his arms for him. I thought to myself, 'If this is death, who should be afraid of death?' I could see his colour changing; you know, he was very pale, being Australian, and I thought to myself, 'No, I'm not afraid of death.' The Lord had taken him very gracefully. And I called Sister Hobbs, and she went to ring the doctor.

Before Father Seamer's death, I was still here in Hamilton when I suddenly got a ring to say, 'I think Dad's passing away. Mum's very much with him. Do you think you could come immediately?' I didn't let anything stand in my way. I knew the hostel would carry on just the same, so I got a few things together and went on down.

By the time I arrived in Mōkau, Dad was gone. And his body—Mum had dressed him in his suit, but his body was still warm. This was getting toward evening, and they had his body laid out on his mattress with pillows and all. And I said to my mum, 'Tonight I'm going to sleep next to my dad.' Not so much in tears, as I'd shed my tears before I went down, but I felt quite at peace. I knew that Dad had been a hard-working man, and I knew that his body was getting tired. So I felt very little in the way of grief; I just thought, well, he's going to be with his Lord. Sure, I had a good weep, but I felt he was freed from all his pain, from his exhaustion, and I felt that he was gifted with a good, full life. I stayed there quite a while after my dad's death. And then when my mum became ill, I went down and brought her up to stay with me at the hostel. Mum lived on quite a number of years. She was eighty-something too. After the passing of my mum and dad, I kept very much up here in Hamilton. I went back home only once a year or so.

I sometimes feel my mum and dad are around. Sometimes when I'm not feeling terribly good, well, I'll get a feeling. This would be a Māori feeling, which I keep separate. If I've kept my eyes too much on the earthly, for too long in this world, then I'll remember to say to myself, Dad always did tell me to lift my thoughts up. I get feelings that come from a higher place. These are intuitive thoughts and impressions that are connected with this idea of lifting. In the evening I sometimes stand straight here in my home, and lift my thoughts. I lift up my mouth to the hills to take my eyes off the earthly and onto something higher. When I get up to the hills, I begin to think, what's higher then, what's beyond those hills?

Mum and Dad, they believed in their Lord. But they were also as God created them Māori, and He gave them that Māori tradition. Just as He created other people and gave them certain powers, I thought that I was very lucky. I'm very lucky that He created me the daughter of my mum, and of my dad, and that I was brought up in a very humble home—but rich in Māori tradition.

When I was about forty, I kept telling my doctor that there was something wrong with my eye. I was always rubbing it, and it was worrying me quite a bit. So he looked at it, but said he couldn't see anything there. He said, 'Come back and I'll see you again next week.' So I went back to him, and he said, 'Yes, now I can see you're having a problem with that eye.' He immediately sent me to a specialist. But the specialist was so busy, he couldn't see me for at least three months. He instructed me not to rub my eyes, but I said I couldn't help it, there was something about it that worried me. 'Well, try not to rub your eye,' he said. And I did try.

Within that three-month wait, there were an unusual number of tangi. Well, at a tangi, of course, you weep, you know. The tears just come and you hear the other women weeping, and this makes you cry some more. You just want to weep with them. So I did a lot of weeping in that three months. Then finally my appointment came, and off I went to see the specialist. I hadn't been to see him before. So he looked at me and said, 'You had a blood clot in your eye, but don't be alarmed. Have you been weeping a lot?'

I said, 'Yes, doctor. I've been going to tangi and I've been weeping.'

The specialist said, 'That has saved your eye, because all that blood has been washed away. Even if you'd come to me when your doctor phoned me, I wouldn't have been able to do anything for you.' He did more of an examination, and then said, 'You're forty-something?'

I said, 'Yes.'

He explained that there was now a cataract beginning to grow in my eye. And he said that once a cataract has begun to grow in one eye, the other eye will come to feel sorry for it, and it will begin growing one as well. But not to worry. He gave me drops. The nurse scheduled another appointment. 'Now I'll have to see you quite often,' he said. I did see him quite often for eighteen years. So I got to know this man fairly well. Of course, I took to him immediately. He was a lovely, handsome doctor. I used to say to myself, 'I think I could easily fall in love with him.' And he used to get so close when he got his tools and looked into my eyes. He was very handsome. I always used to make sure that my mouth was fresh. I really liked him, I really did. But of course, his wife was the office manager. I used to pay the nurse instead.

There was another specialist that I saw when I was going through—oh, what's that Pākehā word?—menopause. Menopause, that's it. I was in my early forties. I was having a bit of a problem with it. I was having flooding, losing an awful lot, plus I was anaemic. The first two days of the month were very hard. I couldn't do my work. Not every month, because it was never regular. Much pain. And in those days there were no wonder drugs for bad periods. It left me pretty well incapacitated. Round about this time, my doctor ordered me to eat raw steak, red meat. 'She's got to live on that,' he said. My doctor thought I was too young yet for menopause. In those days, there wasn't the same medical knowledge in the world that we have today. So life was a bit hard.

He suggested that I see a specialist who worked in Auckland. This doctor became almost like a father to me. He was very well known throughout New Zealand. So much so that the government listened to what he had to say with regard to Māori problems. Early in the morning, I had an examination under anesthesia. He did a thorough examination—there were no problems at all. Everything was quite clear. But the drugs took a long time to wear off. Toward the evening, I was still under the influence. I was in bed when the woman I was staying with came in, and I said, 'There's somebody under my bed!' And she said, 'Are you sure?' And I said, 'Yes, I know there's somebody under my bed! There's a man under my bed!' What do you think of that?

I remember when I realised I was starting to go through my menopause and came face to face with the fact that I would never have children. I think I knew before the time came, because I couldn't ever forget entirely what my mum had said. She'd told me that after I'd passed the age of thirty, certain problems in that area would crop up. I had a fairly difficult time, although I didn't have to go off work, as I did for six months with the other problem with my chest. I just had to carry on. And I was lucky, you see, with my doctor. He kept a very close watch on me. My symptoms were mainly tiredness, and he said, 'Well, of course you're tired; you're carrying a heavy

At the boys' hostel in the late 1960s or early 1970s. On my left is James Tu Whenua, my adopted son.

At James' wedding, in the early 1970s.

load. You must put your feet up.' And he tells me I should rest up, have a nap in the afternoon. I always liked to leave my resting hours until night-time. But he said, 'You must put your feet up during the day. When your young people are away, you've got the house all to yourself.' I had young people to do the cooking and the cleaning and that sort of thing, so there was no need for me to do anything, really. And I used to get migraine headaches. Just now and again I'd get very sickly and have migraine headaches, and he'd say to me, 'Don't shut yourself up; I'll give you something to take.' But I was never very keen on medicine. He said, 'Well, go for a walk.' I said, 'Oh, I'm too tired to go for a walk. You just go for a walk!' And he'd laugh.

My doctor was marvellous. He was marvellous to me during that time, because he'd say to me, 'Now, you'll probably have a problem with sleeping,' to which I said, 'Yes, I can't sleep.'

So he said, 'Well, you'll probably have strange thoughts in your mind.'

'Strange thoughts?' I said, 'Like what?'

'Ah, well, like running away and leaving this place. Something like that. You'll have strange thoughts coming into your mind.' He went on to say, 'Now, should you get thoughts like that in your mind—and if they come they'll have a habit of coming at night-time when you're in your room and you're by yourself, and you'll tell me that you twist and turn and can't sleep—once those peculiar thoughts come into your mind, you give me a call, even if it's the middle of the night.'

And I thought to myself, 'Well, Heeni, you've got to handle those thoughts your-self, because there's no way you're going to call him to the middle of the night!' I knew he was a very busy doctor and I knew he had a lot of people he was caring for, and I wouldn't dare. My doctor didn't even charge me there. There's a sort of bond, I think, between doctors and anyone in church work.

He was right. I did have strange thoughts, and they were always about running away. I'd never had those thoughts before, and it's a funny thing, but later on when I talked with another friend who had also gone through this period, she said, 'Well, I was always running away too, but my running away was to do away with myself.' And I said my running away was to run away from what I was doing. 'Well,' she said, 'it could have led to that, but you must have been stronger-minded.'

I can't say that I had a bad time, but there were sleepless nights and thoughts, and sometimes I felt I was being overpowered by something, as though there were something heavy on me. But I didn't give way to the pressure, and after I got through that, which really didn't take very long, I was OK. Except that I became a good bit more tired. I used to think back to what my mum would say: she told me that all these things are natural and women will have to accept them as natural and not to fight. I never did fight against anything like that, but I was strong-minded. She always said to keep yourself clean, keep yourself warm and move around. Don't just sit still or lie around. That was one thing my mum used to say: 'Don't lie around too much, that's no good, because when you're lying around these things will build up in your mind. And if you can, get out; get involved with people or do something a bit dif-ferent.' And I've remembered that all my life.

PART FOUR

FROM MATRON TO MATRIARCH

Mā muri ka tika, ai a mua.

If everything behind the scenes is done correctly,
all will be well on the marae.

Respected for many long years of service to both the Tainui people and the Hamilton community, Heeni had become a pillar of the Waikato. By the 1970s, after 20 years as matron of Māori youth hostels, however, it was time for her to retire. Heeni's physician suggested she give up work gradually, so a part-time job was organized at the Hamilton Museum. She was to be "Keeper of the Tainui Waka," which had been restored under Te Puea's administration after it lay hidden in a swamp for many years. Te Arikinui Dame Te Atairangikaahu later donated it to the museum and to the Hamilton community as a gesture of good will. Symbolically, it was a graceful passage from one level of cultural service to another; the association with the museum would mark her transition from matron to matriarch.

In the prime of her life, Heeni had been responsible for caring for the heart and soul of the Māori people—their sons and daughters. In retirement, she would be doing the same, but with a more abstract focus. The Tainui waka represents the original canoe on which Captain Hotorua brought Heeni's people to Aotearoa. Looking after such a culturally significant symbol of the Waikato tribes' renaissance magnified Heeni's mana and moved her into a matriarchal role. "Primarily Heeni is a mother figure to us in a very large sense. Our people guarded her."[1] In turn, Heeni guarded the beloved young ones, and later the precious Tainui waka.

Her service in this regard is also related to the place of her birth and, by kin extension, to her ancestral marae. In Mokau, her relatives and ancestors had the responsibility for guarding the anchor for the actual Tainui waka. Now, in her later life, it would be she who secured the grandest symbol of the canoe itself. "The anchor stands for the Tainui canoe lay near Heeni's ancestral marae, near where she grew up in Mokau. That anchor came right along with the Tainui canoe. It is so big; it really takes two people to lift. Heeni's people took care of that anchor and it had exactly the same symbolic significance as it would have for us. It is the anchor. Anchor of the canoe, anchor of the people. It's terribly important to their religion."[2] Heeni's relatives had protected the canoe's anchor at the time of her birth. When she retired and became protector of the canoe, Heeni had completed a spiritual circuit of her life.

After 8 years or so, Heeni left the museum and assumed her role as full-time supporter and nurturer of the Kīngitanga movement. The Kīngitanga movement encourages bicultural ideals—intercultural education, respect for mutual traditions, and the sharing of institutions in culturally appropriate ways. "Commitment is a word that I would use to describe her role in the Kīngitanga—by attending the coronations on a regular basis, by attendance also at various hui, dinners, and tangi. Moreover, quite often, even when her health has been a bit poor, she has made it a point to be there, and to be supportive. And not only physically, but if I may mention also, committed from a financial aspect. At a variety of levels. As an advisor. Yes. It's a holistic approach, a total commitment to everything."[3] Another of her commitments has been to serve as a trusted friend and counselor to those who visit her home regularly in search of compassionate counsel.

Heeni's retirement narrative is more contemporary than the preceding ones. In it, she provides reflections on today's issues, in Māori terms, and on her own role as servant to the Kīngitanga. To understand these meditations, it is important to provide background to the sociological condition of New Zealand.

The following section highlights indices of socioeconomic stress for Māori. Sovereignty disputes relative to the Treaty of Waitangi are linked to socioeconomic stress because the resultant problems have impeded economic self-determination. Heeni's people are an exception. Despite these barriers, the Tainui have made significant advances toward economic self-determination. I have also outlined their progress in the following section because their achievements and the Kīngitanga are as extraordinary as Heeni herself.

LEGACIES OF FOURTH WORLD STATUS

The Māori are one of many fourth world peoples. James Ritchie suggests that fourth world peoples are those who live on or near their original homeland, culturally and economically submerged within a wider dominant society whose government is increasingly transnational in its economic activities. Consequently, fourth world peoples are those whose cultural traditions are in jeopardy while they struggle to overcome a disproportionate number of social problems to achieve economic self-determination. The test question for determining fourth world status is the following: How does the dominant racial/ethnic group (usually Anglo) in a country (with a history of colonization) compare with the subordinate ethnicities in terms of the traditional socioeconomic stress markers? For example, disporportionate unemployment rates, education levels, income levels, government support payments, average number of persons per household, tenure of dwelling, and types of occupation. Most often, the answer is that the indigenous are the indigents, considerably worse off than the colonizers. Māoridom is no exception.

At the beginning of the 21st century, fourth world status translates into the following challenges for Māoridom: (1) disproportionately high rates of unemployment and underemployment; (2) historical losses of timber, fishing, and other economic resources; (3) disproportionately higher rates of "ethnostress,"[4] including depression, alcohol, suicide, violent and accidental death; and (4) child welfare problems.

On the other hand, it would be unfair to paint a desperate picture of Māoridom as a place where everyone is impoverished and suffering. There are many that have not fallen through the cracks. The Kīngitanga movement in the Waikato and the Ratana movement elsewhere, with their emphasis on social solidarity and education, have contributed greatly to the mobility of Māori young people. Nevertheless, there are those who suffer from the legacies of colonialism, such as those in urban areas and in ghetto situations. The film *Once Were Warriors* accurately depicts the social condition of these families who are broken, dysfunctional, and underemployed. Rural Māori, who rely on inadequate government support payment for survival, are also vulnerable. Often, they must supplement their diet with traditional subsistence activities such as collecting oysters, scallops, and mussels. In this day and age, traditional subsistence can be dangerous.

For example, in 1993, an algal bloom made desperate situations go from bad to worse. The New Zealand government had implemented a shellfish ban because a toxic algal bloom made people sick after they consumed some that had been poisoned. Shortly thereafter, the Waikato Times reported:

> Some Māori are eating toxic shellfish, Northern Māori Minister of Policy Bruce Gregory says: 'Many were on the "starvation line" and until now had managed to

survive on shellfish.' Their plight will only be relived by major attempts to clean up our coastal waters. [However], in the meantime these desperate people will continue to starve or succumb to sickness or possible death through eating shellfish. Health Department figures show that 105 people have become sick.[5]

The following statistics from the 1991 New Zealand census paint part of the contemporary socioeconomic picture in New Zealand. Compared with the more recent 1996 census, the socioeconomic trends are similar. Disparities between Māori and non-Māori have remained the same.

DISTRIBUTION OF NEW ZEALAND ETHNIC GROUPS

Figure 1 shows the distribution of race and ethnicity for New Zealand. The 1991 national census report counted a total of 3.3 million people now living in the island country, a full 1 million of whom reside in Auckland, compared with 800,000 who live in all of the cities and towns combined in the South Island. Figure 1 shows 80% of New Zealanders claim European ancestry (mostly British and Scotch/Irish). The bulk of the remaining 20% are Māori, who represent 14% of the total New Zealand population. Samoans make up 2%, and the rest are divided among Chinese, Indian, and other Pacific Islanders. To put it in American terms, the ethnic distribution of Māori to Pākehā in New Zealand compares roughly to the ratio of African-Americans to Anglos in the southeastern United States.

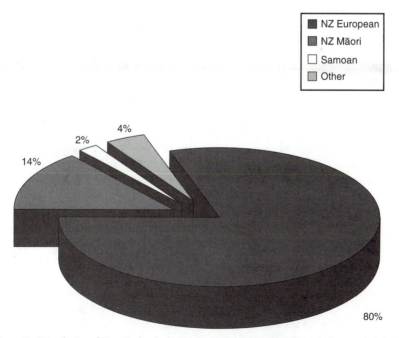

Figure 1. Distribution of New Zealand ethnic groups (New Zealand total population equals 3,375,903 individuals). (Source: 1991 Census Report. Wellington, NZ: Department of Statistics.)

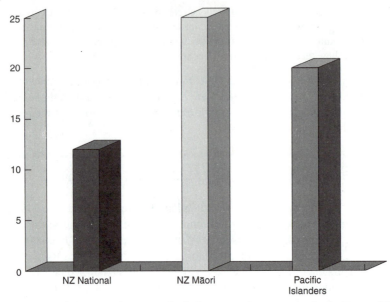

Figure 2. Unemployment rate by New Zealand ethnic group. (Source: 1991 Census Report. Wellington, NZ: Department of Statistics.)

UNEMPLOYMENT RATES BY NEW ZEALAND ETHNIC GROUP

Figure 2 shows the various unemployment rates by race/ethnic status in New Zealand. The unemployment rates for Māori and Pacific Islanders are disproportionately higher than the national rate. Māori unemployment is the highest of all. The New Zealand national rate stands at 11%, whereas the Māori and Pacific Islanders come in at 24% and 20%, respectively. Elevated unemployment rates are a major contributor to poverty, and these are correlated with lower educational attainment levels.

EDUCATION LEVELS BY NEW ZEALAND ETHNIC GROUP

Because education is usually regarded as a ticket to a stable economic future in technological societies, it is understandable why Māori and Pacific Islanders are falling behind. These groups share asymmetrically lower educational attainment levels and are most vulnerable to not becoming and remaining gainfully employed, reinforcing a cycle of poverty most intense for these ethnic categories.

New Zealand breaks down their census report on education in terms of two categories: secondary school qualifications and tertiary ones. Figure 3 shows the various levels of primary and secondary school qualifications earned by New Zealanders. Almost two-thirds of all New Zealand Māori have no school certification, meaning they do not have the equivalent of a high school degree. The same is true for more than half of the Pacific Islanders. However, New Zealand also has a high number (46%) of Pākehā who have no school certification. In this regard, New Zealand falls well behind its Western counterparts.

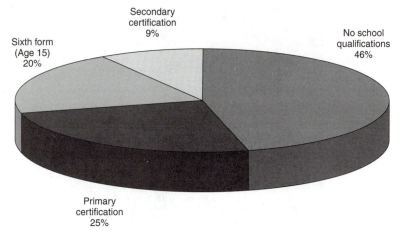

Figure 3. Educational achievement levels over age 15 for New Zealand Europeans. (Source: 1991 Census Report. Wellington, NZ: Department of Statistics.)

In New Zealand, one can go back to school as an adult to receive compensatory training to prepare for tertiary education if desired. This would be comparable to a GED (General Education Degree) in the United States.

Figure 4 shows the percentages of the population who have tertiary education. Among European New Zealanders, 30% have some kind of tertiary degree, whereas only 17% of Māori and, likewise, 11% of Pacific Islanders can say the same.

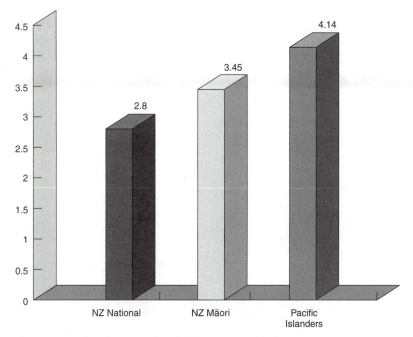

Figure 4. Average number of persons per household by New Zealand ethnic group. (Source: 1991 Census Report. Wellington, NZ: Department of Statistics.)

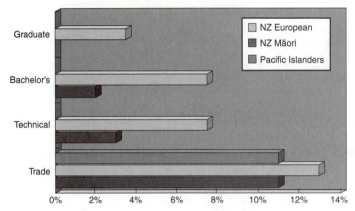

Figure 5. Types of tertiary qualification by New Zealand ethnic group. (Source: 1991 Census Report. Wellington, NZ: Department of Statistics.)

Figure 5 shows types of tertiary education, including trade, technical, bachelor's, and graduate degrees. The highest represented category for all New Zealand ethnic groups is a trade degree, such as carpentry, masonry, or machinist. Only 14% of New Zealand Europeans have either a technical or bachelor's degree, as do 5% of Māori and fewer than 1% of Pacific Islanders. Only 3% of New Zealand Europeans have a graduate degree, and fewer than 1% of both Māori and Pacific Islanders can say the same.

Many older Pākehā perceive the downfall of the "apprentice system" as one of the contributing factors to high unemployment rates over the last decade. Previously in New Zealand, trades such as carpentry, masonry, joinery, electrical, painting, and plastery could be learned through apprenticeships offered to high school students. "Students would be hired from school that did not know anything about the building trade. Employers would pay training costs without a lot of output from the apprentice."[6] The neophyte would then learn the trade while he or she continued with his or her academic instruction. In this way, employers kept down the cost

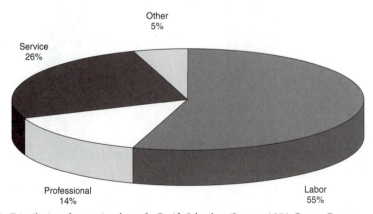

Figure 6. Distribution of occupational type for Pacific Islanders. (Source: 1991 Census Report. Wellington, NZ: Department of Statistics.)

of building with the help of hard-working young students who received valuable on-the-job training. Today, many students go to technical school to learn a trade instead of taking apprenticeships.

DISTRIBUTION OF OCCUPATIONAL TYPES

Education levels are directly correlated with occupational types. Figure 6 shows the distribution of occupation by New Zealand ethnic group. For all ethnic categories, laborer has the highest representation. Māori and Pacific Islanders make up the bulk of this employment category at 50% and 55%, respectively. Only 40% of New Zealand Europeans call themselves laborers. Types of occupation are directly correlated with income levels.

NUMBER OF PERSONS PER AVERAGE HOUSING UNIT

Generally speaking, the wealthier people enjoy more living space (square feet) per individual. Figure 7 shows the percentages of New Zealand households containing

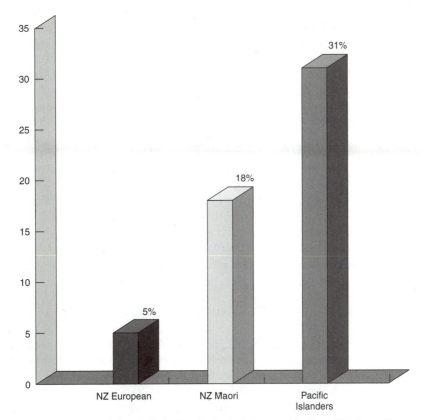

Figure 7. One or more family households by New Zealand ethnic group. (Source: 1991 Census Report. Wellington, NZ: Department of Statistics.)

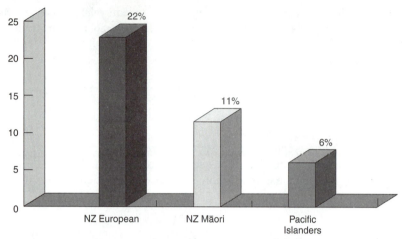

Figure 8. One-person households by New Zealand ethnic group. (Source: 1991 Census Report. Wellington, NZ: Department of Statistics.)

one or more families by ethnic group. Only 5% of New Zealand European households have more than one family living under one roof, whereas 18% of Māori and 31% of Pacific Islanders contain multiple families in single-family dwellings.

By contrast, Figure 8 shows only 6% of Pacific Islanders and 11% of Māori live in one-person households. These figures compare with 22% of New Zealand Europeans who live alone.

Health problems linked to overcrowding include a weakened immune system brought on by poverty and a poor diet, as well as a susceptibility to communicable diseases brought on by intimate exchanges with potential carriers. Two class-based, communicable diseases disproportionately affecting the Māori are "glue ear" and meningococcus. Glue ear can be traced back to British ghettos where poor children suffered from runny, infectious ear problems. Meningococcus has been on the increase in New Zealand for the last several years, as it has been in the United States, and is linked to overcrowding and substandard housing. From 1991 to early 1993, the number of confirmed cases tripled in New Zealand. It is commonly recognized that Māori also suffer disproportionately from chronic diseases, such as cancer, diabetes, and heart disease. These illnesses are linked in part to lack of information about the importance of a healthy diet and exercise.

TENURE OF DWELLING

Figure 9 shows tenure of dwelling by New Zealand ethnic group. Equal numbers of New Zealand European, Māori, and Pacific Islanders own their own homes with a mortgage. However, only 8% of Pacific Islanders and 15% of Māori own their own home without a mortgage, compared with the New Zealand national rate of 34%. Similarly, 57% and 37% of Māori and Pacific Islanders, respectively, rent their domicile, compared with the lower New Zealand national rate of 23%.

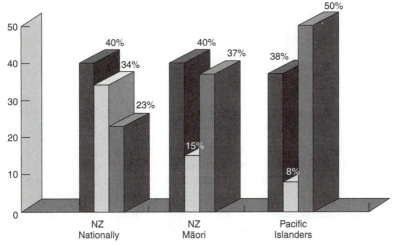

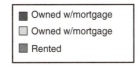

Figure 9. Tenure of dwelling by New Zealand ethnic group. (Source: 1991 Census Report. Wellington, NZ: Department of Statistics.)

CRIME RATES

Although Māori make up only 14% of the entire New Zealand population, nearly half the number of adult men and women in prison who responded to a justice department survey in 1992 were Māori according to the New Zealand Press Association.[7]

Many Pākehā perceive the Māori crime problem as being linked to some kind of racial failure. On the contrary, crime problems derive from a living context characterized by unemployment, poverty, and health problems that stem from low educational attainment. For example, the 1993 prison statistics surveys showed that many offenders, including Māori, could not read or write.

COMMENTS

Professor James Ritchie has suggested that biculturalism, based on sound economic development strategies, is the answer to fourth world problems on the cusp of the twenty-first century. He notes that the various fourth world renaissances, such as the political emergences of Native American groups and the New Zealand Māori, have brought about the development of two intertwined political objectives, which are based entirely on indigenous questions of sovereignty and political viability in a fourth world context: (1) to penetrate the bastions of power and become politically audible and visible, and (2) to capture or repossess traditional resources upon which to base some measure of economic self-determination.

Ritchie argues that in order for indigenous groups to retain their cultural heritage for generations to come, they must become viable trading partners in the modern economy, earn revenue, and then reinvest the income back into social institutions that are controlled by tribal organizations. Cultural heritage is thus protected by a release from fiscal dependency on the federal government and outsider interference. He argues that indigenous people must undertake these activities while at the same time withstanding internal challenges from indigenous adversaries—factionalism, as well as external challenges that may come from other political entities, corporations, lobbying groups, or public protest.[10] The following discussion tests his criteria among Māori.

1. To Become Politically Audible and Visible

In the 1990s, Māori tribes are increasingly seeking, to varying degrees, political and economic self-determination—or, more specifically, sovereign control over their own economic, social, and spiritual resources. However, this political intention often results in conflict. It divides people along traditionally disparate lines depending on their European and/or indigenous notions of sovereignty. For example, there has been a historical clash between tribal expectations of sovereignty, which in theory is guaranteed by treaty, and European-derived ones as a practical matter. To Māori, sovereignty means the legitimate exercise of power and authority by the people themselves—sometimes in partnership with other national entities, sometimes not. They want to direct their own authentic courses of political action, separate and apart from any kind of dependency status. The national government, on the other hand, tends to view this question in a more qualified manner, regardless of previous agreements that otherwise may recognize sovereignty. Even during liberal periods of federal policy, Māori groups have been handicapped by the paternalism that characterizes their relationship with the colonizing body politic.

In New Zealand, these disputes have arisen because of the incongruence between the Māori and English versions of the Treaty of Waitangi in which significant discrepancies exist between the words used for *governorship* and *sovereignty*.

As discussed in the previous part, The Treaty of Waitangi was an agreement between Māori chiefs and the British Crown. From the Māori perspective, the treaty ceded *governorship* of their lands to the Crown, but Māori retained *sovereignty*. In return, the Māori were to obtain full rights as British citizens, which included health, education, and welfare. However, the colonial interpretation of the Treaty of Waitangi was different from the Māori version. From the colonists' perspective, the Māori ceded sovereignty to the Crown; Māori were not to be treated as equal British citizens and were thus barred from certain public institutions, denied full political rights, and forced to endure a steady stream of land alienation. Moreover, the treaty was never ratified into law. Thus, unlike in the United States, the treaty has never been a politically viable basis for considering criteria that relate to contemporary Māori land claims. The treaty is also an enduring symbol for Māori protest.[11] The focus of such protest has been to advocate the protection of rights as conferred in the treaty as well as to develop partnership relationships with the Crown.

There are at least two controversial discrepancies, which have had the effect of impeding the Māori political process. These are obstacles that will likely remain until Parliament deals squarely with the following points. The first contention pivots on the word used to connote who exactly retains absolute authority in New Zealand. In this case, "the moral validity of the Treaty hangs on the translation of the word sovereignty."[12] The English version (DOC.1) reads as follows:

[The Māori will] cede to her majesty the Queen of England absolutely and without reservation all the rights and powers of sovereignty, which the said confederation of individual Chiefs respectively exercise or possess, or may be supposed to exercise or possess over their respective territories as the sole sovereigns thereof.[13]

The English version uses the word *sovereignty*, whereas the Māori version uses the word *governorship*. By contrast, the Māori version (DOC.2), when it is translated back into English, reads as follows:

[The Māori will] cede without reservation to the Queen of England forever the governorship of all their lands.[14]

The word *governorship,* or *kawanatanga*, was substituted incorrectly by the missionary Henry Williams for the more accurate translation of sovereignty—*mana whenua* (sovereignty over the land) or else rangatiritanga.[15] To make matters more ambiguous, *kawanatanga* is not even a pure Māori word; it is "missionary Māori" derived from biblical notions of the governor status of Pontius Pilate, the Roman governor in the Bible. "It intended to imply authority in an abstract rather than a concrete sense."[16] This meant governorship was a new concept for the Māori, which only added to the confusion.

To the Māori, kawanatanga meant ceding rulership on behalf of the sovereign. "That the treaty did not appear to [cede] anything substantial to the Crown from the Māori viewpoint is encapsulated in a comment by [one of the attendant Chiefs]: 'The shadow of the land (the governance) goes to Queen Victoria, but the substance (sovereignty) remains with us.'"[17]

From the Māori standpoint, this article (with its cession of kawanatanga) gave the Queen the right to govern the country, ultimately to be replaced by the constitutional government of New Zealand, but all the same, governorship, not sovereignty. "The Māori might well have assumed, therefore, that their sovereign rights were actually being confirmed in return for a limited concession of power in kawanatanga."[18]

The second discrepancy also arises out of the question of sovereignty. The first part of the second article of the Treaty of Waitangi in the English version (DOC.1) reads as follows:

[The Māori are entitled to] the full, exclusive and undisturbed possession of their lands and estates, forests and fisheries, and other properties which they may collectively or individually possess.[19]

The Māori version (DOC.2) reads as follows:

[The Māori are entitled to] the full Chieftainship (Rangatiritangi) of their homes and all their treasured possessions.[20]

Although the latter version of the text leaves out estates, forests, and fisheries, it does use the word *rangatiritangi,* meaning mana or sovereignty over *tonga katoa,* which can be translated as "all our treasured possessions" or "everything which we value." This, of course, included more than fisheries, lands, and other food sources. It also included things more abstract, such as language, spirituality, health practices, and so on. "From the Māori viewpoint, the guarantee of rangatiritanga of their lands is equivalent to the guarantee of their sovereignty."[21] Hence, they viewed their cultural universe as protected under the sovereign control of the people themselves.

The English version clearly provided more sovereignty to the Crown and secured less for the Māori. However, over a century of colonial legislation and official policy following the treaty period, the provisions of sovereignty and equal protection as British subjects were outrightly ignored or undermined by subsequent legislation. The land wars, the land confiscations that followed, and later amalgamation policy were all violations of the Treaty of Waitangi from the Māori point of view.

Therefore, Māori attempts to become politically audible and visible have been severely impeded by these illegal activities, contributing to the submersion of Māoritanga and the socioeconomic conditions that have thus resulted.

Figure 10 shows the opposing interpretations of the essential meaning of the Treaty of Waitangi. The colonial interpretation of the treaty resulted in Māoritanga being trapped within Pākehā-dominated institutions from the 1850s until the Māori renaissance of the 1980s. The Māori understanding of treaty provisions is very much in line with Ritchie's notion of biculturalism. They saw the Treaty of Waitangi as establishing two sovereign nations, such that each culture was independent and free to offer partnership of various kinds to the other if desired.

This interpretation gulf has been made worse by the fact that the treaty has never been ratified. Therefore, the courts do not protect it. Until recently, Māori have had no legal recourse when seeking to rectify their situations; therefore, the treaty has been unenforceable and vulnerable to the cyclical nature of changing political climates.

For now, the government is receiving recommendations from the Waitangi Tribunal, which hears Māori claims according to the provisions of the Treaty of Waitangi. The Waitangi Tribunal was established in 1975 as a result of the Treaty of Waitangi Act. It was a liberal measure intended to restore indigenous political authority—a reactionary move by Parliament, preceded by vehement indigenous protest in the 1960s and 1970s. Its purpose is to "make recommendations on claims relating to the practical application of the principles of the treaty and, for that purpose, to determine its meaning and effect and whether certain matters are inconsistent with those principles."[22]

However, until the act was recently amended, the tribunal had no authority whatsoever to consider land confiscation before 1975, which protected the government from reviewing the transgressions of the 1860s, when millions of acres were stolen by new settlers. When it was finally amended in 1985, the tribunal could begin hearing claims referring back to 1840.[23]

Although the tribunal is certainly a step in the right direction, Māori interests will continue to be vulnerable until ratification. When the political tides change

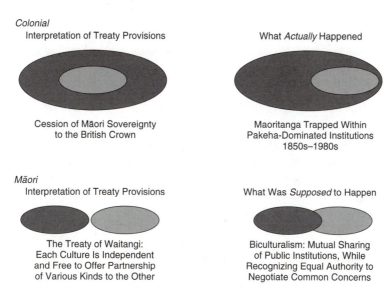

Figure 10. Colonial interpretation of treaty provisions. (Bernard Dennehy, 1993.)

again, as they most likely will, the tribunal's recommendations may never get past the committee stage, putting Māori interests again on the back burner.

Non-Māori opposition to Māori demands that the treaty be honored and the land be returned have created increasingly high racial tensions into the 1990s. Non-Māori find the Māori sovereignty issues unsettling and try to pin them down to something more solid and controllable.[24] The consensus among non-Māori is that sovereignty is a local concern. Hugh Fletcher, chief executive officer for Fletcher Challenge Limited, put it this way:

> One thing the Māori DID give up in the *Treaty of Waitangi* was sovereignty—in a national and international sense. However, [they] did not give up local authority—and Māori sovereignty should be seen as a local issue. I personally think they do themselves a lot of damage in running the more extreme sovereignty arguments. There is no chance that Māori are going to get a separate parliament that is going to have any authority over New Zealand. I don't think they have the sympathy of the public—nor will they ever get it.[25]

Steven Young, a Wellington civil engineering consultant of Chinese ancestry, said,

> A vague document like the *Treaty of Waitangi* can say whatever one wishes to make of it. What matters is the weight of numbers and relative strength and who has access to the organs of power. No doubt if Māori were 90 percent of the population, the Treaty would be interpreted in a way which was very favorable to the Māori.[26]

In Māori circles, sovereignty issues are used to assert pride, identity, and independence. Sandra Lee, Māori minister of Parliament for Auckland Central, commented, "It's an indisputable fact. Māori are a sovereign indigenous people. We are a nation of people. This is our *turangawaewae* (resting place). Irrespective [sic?] of who holds power at any given time and their political morals, they cannot negate the facts."[27] Robert Mahuta, principal negotiator for the Tainui Trust Board in the historic Waikato *raupatu* settlement, said, "You may have had our lands, but you never had our *rangatiratanga*. No way do you have the power nor the capacity to 'restore' it. It survived, as did the Kīngitanga, in spite of what the Crown did."[28]

2. To Capture and Repossess Traditional Resources

The Waikato tribes are not waiting for the government to ratify the treaty. The Tainui, in particular, have taken their own unique direction with the New Zealand government—beginning with the establishment of the Kīngitanga, saying no to conscription, the cultural renaissance that followed, and holding on to their communal way of life despite all of the considerable odds stacked against them.[28] "The odd thing is that if you look at the Kīngitanga as a whole, it is stronger now than it was 80 or 90 or 100 years ago. It's made more accommodations to the majority culture in terms of administrative structure and technology, but it is now more solid than ever."[29]

The Tainui have worked very hard at becoming economically self-determinate under the leadership of Robert Mahuta and with the intellectual support of the Māori Studies and Research Center at the University of Waikato in Hamilton. Mahuta has written extensively on the subject of tribal development and methods for breaking out of economic dependency. He suggests indigenous people tend to choose one of two strategies for negotiating issues of sovereignty with their dominant government.

Whereas scholars tend to see a capitalistic model as making for a stronger defense, native activists view it as assimilative and therefore inappropriate. They argue that economic self-determination must be separated from traditional sovereignty or indigeneity. To accept and use a corporate model that will guarantee wealth may enhance the economic security of the people, but is thought among some to be a "sell-out." They are critical of economic self-determination schemes that downplay the cultural side of the argument. They worry that the desire for wealth in the present may come back to haunt generations of native people in the future, whose traditions will be threatened by European models for the exercise of power.

Mahuta asserts that by taking a reactive stance, tribal intellectuals are cultural nationalists who make a strong argument about the need to retain such things as language and religion. The arguments come from urban Māori whose parents simply stopped speaking Māori in the 1940s and 1950s, particularly when they had moved away from rural situations. The adult children are caught between two worlds, secure in neither. Thus, recovering the language fits a sense of security in the absence of basic cultural messages. "And that's the anxiety I think that the modern second or third generation urbanized Māori are having. They want to get back on the set of rails, the continuous learning and security which comes from receiving those absolutely basic cultural beliefs and standards."[30] Their arguments are characterized by militancy with an anti-Pākehā bias and are most always coming from a position of dependency.

In contrast, the economic nationalists propose that indigenous social problems result from the loss of "cultural capital"; in their view, this can be ameliorated by linking sovereignty and self-determination to the capitalist system. Indigenous governments, using a corporate model, are empowered to funnel revenue back into the social infrastructure, which then creates cultural capital. Cultural capital can be used to create culturally relevant programs and institutions to facilitate a better-educated, employed, and healthy populace. In these instances, economic nationalism comes first, and cultural nationalism comes second. "The main thing about a capitalist system," says Bob Mahuta, "is that you have to have capital to produce the profit in order to be able to utilize it (culturally)."[9]

By taking a proactive stance, the tribe thinks of itself as a national entity in a transnational economy. It, therefore, becomes its own corporation, finding the means necessary to become financially solvent and thus economically self-determinate. "That's how I see our people as being in those two camps. And I pride myself as being part of the latter. Now we have made the tribe a corporation, forcing the government to deal with us as such."[31] The Tainui have been successful in winning concessions from the New Zealand government for land confiscated after the land wars. In two such deals, the government recently handed over old military bases called *Te Rapa* (stern of a canoe) and *Hopuhopu* (an adze carried by chiefs of high rank and distinction). The tribe uses these bases as an infrastructure to facilitate the economic activities of the tribal corporation.

For example, Te Rapa contains many old military buildings that have now been converted to storage areas. The space inside is rented by the square meter to local Hamilton businesses that would prefer to have extra stock on hand rather than ordering more merchandise and risking losing business by waiting for delivery from Auckland. At both Te Rapa and Hopuhopu, the Tainui have converted old military barracks into hotel accommodations. The tribe hosts conventions offering Polynesian hospitality, competing with local hotels. The money earned from these ventures is reinvested back into the corporation and then spent according to the agenda of the Kīngitanga movement. For example, the tribe was able to hand out 10 educational scholarships totaling $100,000 in 1992.[32]

More recently, the Waikato *Raupatu* settlement claim has fostered the capturing and repossession of traditional resources, both cultural and human. The Tainui won an initial settlement claim from the New Zealand government in 1995 that comes after more than 80 years of building a relationship with the New Zealand government and a decade of hard negotiations and political dealings. According to Mahuta, "We wanted to [re-]establish an economic base, to develop our own economic programs, to expand that base, to enhance employment opportunities for our people, and to play a much more significant role in the development of this country."[33]

The settlement package is valued at 170 million New Zealand dollars in cash and land parcels. This includes a large parcel of formerly owned properties in the city of Hamilton. The Tainui is the first Māori tribe to win such a settlement, which is in line with Article II of the Treaty of Waitangi. Land once thought stolen and gone forever is now back in the hands of the tribe.

The settlement monies are meant to ameliorate disproportionately higher unemployment and lower incomes by allowing for the (re)capturing of human resources as well. The Tainui intend to ameliorate these conditions by providing skilled and unskilled jobs to Māori people in any of a number of businesses, operations, and institutions paid for with revenue earned from the settlement.

Breaking the cycle of dependency requires the commitment of many people over several generations, as we have seen. Very few indigenous groups have accomplished this in the face of such overwhelming odds—invasions, wars, stolen land, assimilation policies, and cultural submersion.

No one can predict the future for indigenous people as they continue to seek sovereignty from the nation states within which they are submerged, but I believe a strong argument can be made that the Tainui have responded successfully to challenges as they go along—just as their Polynesian ancestors have done for more than 3,000 years. The Tainui are in a very real sense international people. "This culture is able to transform itself and be renewed all the time, and there are sayings handed down which become proverbs. Proverbs are bridges really, between the past and the present. What the proverbs tell us is that it doesn't really matter how much things change, we will always be the same."[36]

7 / Reflections

When we see Sister Heeni there, returned to Māoridom, she sits in that house and keeps it warm. Part of her mahi, her job, is to keep us warm; and we know that things are all right by her presence there. We would certainly miss the day when she wasn't there. She's like a part of the furniture, something old and something treasured. Not old in a decrepit sense, but like a living taonga, a treasure, an irreplaceable treasure.

Dave Tūmōkai Pānapa

I WAS RELIEVED when the law changed and gave women workers the chance to retire at age sixty. I sent word to the head of the department in Auckland that my sixtieth birthday was coming up and that I wanted to retire at the end of the year. I told my doctor about it, and he said, 'Well, the first thing you have to do is look for a part-time job.' I said, 'No fear, doctor, but first I want to rest and sleep for months!'

He used to be quite stern with me, and said, 'I know you, Heeni. You'll sleep for a week, and then you'll get up and you'll wonder what am I going to do? Begin to look for a part-time job now.'

At this time, I got a very nice letter back from Auckland thanking me for devoting my life to church work. They accepted my resignation for the end of the year. And when Dame Te Ata came to see me she said, 'I'm very pleased about your retirement, because you've lived such a hectic, difficult way of life.' She said, 'Enjoy, come down, come off now, and enjoy the rest. You've still got a good few years ahead of you. Enjoy the rest of those years.' And I thought, 'Well now, that's lovely.'

But I actually got a part-time job at the museum before I even left the hostel, at the insistence of my doctor. That would've been in 1974, I became the attendant of the museum, the old museum in London Street. A funny thing—the Farmers' Trading Company bought the old boys' hostel in London Street from us, and moved the museum in there. So I was again working in London Street. It was into the new museum that they'd gifted the waka, the canoe, to the new city of Hamilton. This was Te Winika. And Te Arikinui Dame Te Atairangikaahu had gifted it to the city of Hamilton, as a symbol of unity between things Māori and Pākehā. So I became the keeper of the waka, you might say. So my work at the museum was another level of care for my people. I really enjoyed my duties there. It was such a totally different way of life from what I'd been living.

I stayed with the museum about seven years, and then I found it was time to retire from my working life altogether. After I retired, a friend of mine who was a member of the boys' hostel committee said, 'Why don't we go on an overseas tour, Heeni?' Her husband had died; she was alone. I'd known her for a number of years,

Shaking hands with a former board member of the boys' hostel on my retirement.

At my retirement from the hostels at the Methodist Centre in London Street with Te Arikinui Dame Te Atairangikaahu and Terotohiko Jones in 1974.

HEENI WHAREMARU in the Waikato Art Museum beside Te Winika, the Waikato canoe.

Heeni's moving on

A familiar face left Waikato Art Museum on Friday. Museum attendant Heeni Wharemaru sat in the gallery for the last time, answering inquiries from visitors and chatting to them.

She took the part-time job about eight years ago, soon after the art museum moved to its London St, Hamilton.

She said it was a marked change from her previous youth work with the Methodist Church, but offered her the same contact with people that she had always enjoyed.

Mrs Wharemaru is a member of the Waikato-Maniapoto tribes and is also involved in arranging functions at Turangawaewae and other marae.

The art museum job was her first involvement with any gallery or museum, other than as a casual visitor. She said she'd learnt a lot during her time there and looked forward to the day the art museum moved to its new building, to be built in Grantham St.

Mrs Wharemaru plans to continue her church and marae work.

In 1981 I retired from my post at the Waikato Museum, where I'd been Keeper of Te Winika. Waikato Times

so I said, 'Oh yes, what a good idea! How much is it going to cost us?' She worked it all out. We'd be away for three months or so, I think—after all, this was a world tour! But for some reason or another, my brother Paddy suddenly arrived and asked if he could stay with me for a night. I told him he could stay as long as he liked. He was on his own this time—his wife Mary didn't come with him. So I talked to him about the trip I was planning, and he said, 'Why, you foolish woman! You're paying rent here where you're staying now, and that money's going down the drain, and now you're talking about going over to the United Kingdom and the United States! I think you're very foolish. How much money is it going to cost you?' I said about three thousand dollars. 'Oh, you're mad!' he said. For some reason or other, he didn't seem to want me to go. So that's when I began to look around for a place to buy instead. That's when I found this house. I'm most grateful to my brother, because you know I wouldn't have been able to pay for this place if I'd taken that trip. That's how I got it, and he paid a good bit of it for me. I wouldn't have had that cash, but then I would have had the experience.

Another time, one of my close friends here asked me what I going to do now that I was retired. I hadn't told her about what Te Puea had said, about not marrying and not turning my back on the Kīngitanga; I just replied, 'Well, I don't know. Why?' She'd been with me down home. I think it was five years after I'd retired, and Te Puea was gone, Dame Te Ata's mum and dad had passed on, and I was feeling quite free.

And so was this friend of mine. You see, her children had grown up, and she said, 'What if we moved from here and went and lived in New Plymouth? I love that place!' I said, 'Well, maybe. I'll get in touch with some of the members of my family living down that way.' Not very long after, my brother turned up again to see how I was doing. I said 'Well, Paddy, I've retired and I've been thinking of going to New Plymouth.' And you know what he said to me? Exactly what Te Puea had said. The first thing he said to me was, 'Oh, after all these years you've been so close to the Kīngitanga, are you going to turn your back on it?' Well, oh dear, my head turned round. I thought, 'Oh God,' and dropped the idea immediately.

But it's very nice here—just look at that view. And not very long after that, Paddy and Mary came up and stayed with me for a few days, and he said, 'I see you've still got the same old black-and-white TV.'

I said, 'Oh well, how can I afford a new one after paying for this house?'

'Oh,' he said, 'you trade that one in and I'll give you so much for the new one.'

I loved my brother. I loved all my brothers, but this one was a good bit younger, and I think I loved him lots more.

I've always thanked my Lord for leading me into this way of life. My faith in my Lord is something that is really real to me. And it's been a long life; you know, I'm eighty-four years old and still involved with things there at Tūrangawaewae. I've been so blessed to have very high-calibre people around me from the very beginning—people who are around me still and have supported my role. I've always felt so privileged.

I'm confident about the direction of the Kīngitanga movement. The late Princess Te Puea was very firm in her idea that we are one people in closeness to our maker. He created all people, and so we are one, whatever colour. And that's all coming through. Because our marae down here is named after King Tāwhiao's saying that many different colours of people will be threaded through the eye of the needle at the Tūrangawaewae marae. The late Princess Te Puea used to say to us that Pākehā and Māori are one: 'At the moment we're travelling along in our canoe, our waka, and they're travelling along in their own waka. We're moving toward one destiny, in the same ocean. And as we get closer, try to take from the Pākehā waka the very good things that they have in it. And you try to live such a life that they can see the good that's in our waka. And travel along that way.' The truth of her word seems to be coming to me over the years. And looking at life today, among my people and the Pākehā people, there seems to be a closer coming-together. There'll be passages along that way which will be turbulent, but in the end we'll come through. And this is not to be looked at as a frightening thing, but as a beautiful one.

I think that the present queen has done a lot to bring people together in a peaceful way. She's a very peaceful lady. The meaning of her nickname, Piki, reflects her strength. As the years have moved, I've kept this in my mind. She's one of the most influential women here in New Zealand, and I can see her influence spreading, as though she were a flower with the vitality to climb and the strength to carry on.

The idea that the King movement and the Rātana movement can coexist is well institutionalised now. There might be pockets of ill feelings up and down the country,

The 50th anniversary of the girls' hostel. Dame Te Ata is seated second from the left; I'm sitting far right.

but I'd say on the whole that we've come a long, long way from the disputes of the past—a long, long way.

I think Te Puea saw that I'd be needed in certain areas. Just quite recently one of our Methodist lady ministers requested of Te Arikinui Dame Te Atairangikaahu that she be able to write her master's degree at Waikato University, and asked if she could base her thesis on the Kīngitanga. When Dame Te Ata called about it, I got a bit of a shock. I've told you I do get feelings, you know. Te Ata said the minister was going to come around and see me. She said, 'She's coming to see you, and if you, Heeni, feel that she's all right, then it will be all right, but if you feel that she's not the one . . .' (Immediately I knew she was not the one.) 'Well, it's over to you.' First of all, I said to myself, I'm a servant of the Kīngitanga, and second of all, Te Puea raised me a bit higher. She told me to deal with situations with my whole body, and sometimes I get this sort of feeling where answers are already coming into my head. And so I put the phone down. I was so pleased that Dame Te Ata had got in touch with me. Immediately after I put the phone down, it began to ring again. And I thought to myself, 'This will be this lady ringing me,' so I didn't answer it. I went to have a drink. Our water—you know what they say about the Waikato River and its healing properties. So I went to my tap to drink a little bit of water and throw a little on my head and on my face. And the phone was still ringing, so I answered it and heard, 'Auntie Heeni, you're at home.'

She talked a little and then said, 'Auntie Heeni, I'd like to come over and see you.' I knew exactly what was going to be coming up. She said, 'It's something very important. Do you think I could come over and see you this evening?' The time was getting on, you know, and I said, 'I think I've got someone coming along this evening.' I wanted some time, you know, because I could sense the urgency. She did come, yes, the following morning. I knew that she'd begin by getting me—this is Māori protocol—and then she'd have a little prayer, and then she'd settle down and begin to tell me what it was all about. She stood up during this—this was the proper protocol. I thanked her for the greeting, for her short prayer, all in Māori. Then she explained it all to me very fully. Then I had a question to ask her before we went on. 'I want to ask you, have you talked this over with your people? Tell me your mind. Is it something that you really want to do in your heart?' She hesitated and hung her head. It wasn't the Kīngitanga but the poukai[1] she was interested in, and you can't separate the two. It wasn't right.

There are other times when I've got feelings feelings in my head. I can remember at the beginning of my work at the boys' hostel, answers or impressions about certain situations would just sort of come to me. Sometimes at night, but not always. Sometimes I'd get them when I was just moving around doing my daily routine. For example, sometimes when I'm in a crowd, I feel that I'm not in a crowd, but by myself, and I can withdraw, and then I can come back and say, 'Oh,' and then I'll have the answer to some problem. Sometimes it'll be a stupid little problem, like where I might find a special pair of earrings I've been looking to buy. Other times, it'll be something more serious—about how to handle a personality problem at work, or something of that sort.

There have been several other things I've had to do for Te Arikinui Dame Te Atairangikaahu over the years, which I couldn't have done if I'd chosen to marry. Several times I've had to represent her when she was having her kids. I'd often go down there and stand in for her.

There were other things, too, which are deeply Māori. When Dame Te Ata had to have surgery, she had to go to the hospital at Waikato. I went up to see her because of my concern, and she was still groggy from the operation. There were other people in the room, but she didn't want me to leave. I sat next to her while she held my hand. And then she said to me, 'Before you leave this hospital, I want you to go to the next room and find Robert Mahuta's wife, Raiha. She will explain to you exactly what has happened to me. She'll explain all that to you so that your mind will be clear.' To a Māori, you see, the body is very tapu. Te Ata wanted me to know what part of her body had been removed. And for me to hear from Raiha, that's significant. Not to hear it from anyone else but from her own very close family member, who was to be with her for all the days in the hospital. Raiha, who had years of training mostly for body massage and in nursing, had a room right next to Te Ata's room. But when I went into that room, I couldn't find her anywhere. I thought, 'Well, I can't leave the hospital'—I'd been commanded not to leave until I found her. So I went around the ward, and I inquired of the nurses as to where she was. I said that it was imperative that I see her before I leave. And I went to her room and sat and waited an hour or longer until she returned. And she said to me, 'Heeni, have you been with Te Ata all this time? Or have you been waiting for me?' 'Yes,' I replied. I told her that Te Ata had said not to leave the hospital until I'd seen her. So she explained to me exactly what had happened from the moment she came into the hospital. I was relieved to hear from Raiha. She knew the significance of Te Ata's request. Te Ata had also told me, 'I don't want you to worry too much over me. My faith in my Lord is firm.' I'd known for quite some time that she was growing up in her faith. So that didn't come to me as a surprise, but I was very happy to know that. My tribute to her will never be adequate.

There's still a lot of learning to be done between the Pākehā and Māori worlds, but I feel that the majority of folk are adjusting. There are radicals, of course, both Māori and Pākehā, but I think the majority of Māori thinking is pretty healthy. You don't hear about that, though. Instead, you always hear about these strange Māori. Yes, extreme. But I don't take a great deal of notice of them, because I think their days will pass very quickly; whereas the solid ones, I think, will continue to come through.

We Māori have come a long way, but there are still some problems—and there will probably always be problems. If Princess Te Puea were alive today, I don't know what she would think of her people. Who is happy with our people today? I don't know whether she'd feel her dreams and teachings had been learnt or not.

You would've read just recently where the air force base has been returned to the Tainui, and the Hopuhopu military camp also. Those areas were originally Tainui property before they were taken in the land confiscations. And now the Raupatu settlement. I think the return of these has strengthened us. We're on very good terms with the Pākehā because they can see now that some of the 'injustice' (I think is the word that you use) that was done years ago is gradually being healed. So, I think we here will just continue to go along in a peaceful way of life, as we have done over the years. The land is gradually being returned, yes, pieces of land that were taken away from our people.

But Te Puea, I think, would be worried, perhaps, about how we are going to manage the return of the land. Are we sufficiently capable of learning to cope with what's coming back, and coming back so quickly? Like Hopuhopu and Te Rapa. And not too long ago I was told that another piece of land, just at the back of the Te Puea estate, was also being returned. I don't think she ever talked to me about the return of the land, so I really don't know what she'd think. My main talk with her was always the development of the Tūrangawaewae marae. She worked so hard to raise the standard of our area. And I think she would be very happy with what has happened there. It's a beautiful place now.

But it has its problems too, many problems. Young-people problems, mostly. But that's not an isolated case, that's all over. And this is such a concern, because the present generation's leadership wants to look down and see emerging leaders. And it's hard to find, among the youth, leaders who will be able to fill these vacancies. We're not giving them the opportunity to reach their proper potential. The other problem is that we lost a lot of potential leaders in World War Two, in the Māori Battalion. We lost a lot of brilliant young people. There's already talk of the language beginning to die out, that it won't be able to endure much longer. We need leaders who'll make it a priority, leaders who can speak fluent Māori. But you know, there's a great saying among my folk: 'When a leader falls, there's always another one that will rise and take his place.'

I may as well tell you that there may be criticism about choosing you to write my story. Many people think that perhaps they should have chosen a Māori to come and see me. But whoever thought that would really have very little knowledge of me.

So they'll be watching you, wondering what is this American lady saying about our Heeni now? They'll all be watching. I'm thinking not only of the book and of myself, but also thinking of you in the future and of protecting you. I've already taken you into the heart of the past, where not too many people have gone, so there'll be a lot of people that'll be jealous. But they cannot question the fact of my talking to you. No-one here or anywhere around New Zealand would question the fact of Heeni talking. What I've told you over these months, I would never, never have thought of saying if we'd chosen someone Māori to come and see me. All the same, they're going to wonder why Heeni chose an American girl when she could have chosen someone here in New Zealand. But that doesn't bother met at all, because I feel so very proud that you're almost a part of me.

I would like my story to be written in such a way that the young ones today can get something from it—both Māori and Pākehā. I look upon the young ones today that are getting in so much trouble as lost, because of the mixture of blood and the little care they've received at home. To me these naughty ones are sort of a 'lost tribe'. They've had very little help from their home and very little education. They don't know whether they're really Māori or, when they go to the other world, European. Well, they're neither one nor the other. These ones are a bit of a problem to us today.[2]

Much of my life has been about bridging the two worlds—the Pākehā and the Māori worlds. So many people struggle with that, but it's never been a problem for me, absolutely no problem. When I'm with Māori people at a tangi or a hui, I'm Māori with them. Absolutely Māori with them. I speak Māori and do all the things that they do. Weep with them over the dead, sit beside the bed. I'm Māori when I'm with them. When I'm with people of other races, I remember my Pākehā training,

Meeting and working with Pākehā. Welcoming the governor general Sir David Beattie, during his first visit to the Waikato Museum in about 1980. Campbell Smith, the museum's art director, is on the right.

and yet I also remember I'm Māori. My graciousness, as I've said before, comes from my Māori side. I'm sorry to have to say that. But I try to be very gracious in the Pākehā context, and I dress like a Pākehā. When I go to a tangi, I wear the type of clothes that we Māori wear, all black. Because a tangi is something very real and deeply rooted in Māori culture. But when I go to a Pākehā gathering, I dress according to that gathering. And that's what these young people today need to do, to strike a balance between their two worlds.

Of course, it is important for us to hang onto our traditions. For instance, we don't sell our traditional Māori carvings, but we do give them as gifts to prominent people who come among us in our own tribe—we do give a special piece of carving. But very seldom greenstone. We feel that the greenstone is a part of ourselves, like the carving, pieces of ourselves that belong to the iwi. This is the feeling of my own people, the Tainui. It's almost like giving your body, yourself, away. We're careful where we draw the line. But to overseas visitors we do give small gifts of Māori carving.

My phone seems to ring all the time these days. People just ringing me up and telling me things, or inviting me places, a lot of which I have to turn down. And lots of calls about advice. Today I've got this boy coming to see me; he wants to bring his lady friend along so that I can meet her. He's one of the young fellows I met through my museum connection, and he's been coming to see me quite a bit for advice about the Treaty. I don't know why they come to see me; I can't really give them any advice. But they do keep coming—even some of the boys that were with me at the hostel. And I like it because they offer to drive me out to do my shopping or to pick up things for me.

But this one wants me to meet his young lady and to quietly just look her over and give him my first impression, you know. I think I can say, after all these years with my type of work, I can get an accurate impression immediately after I meet a person. This is the sort of thing that my boys used to spring on me, and continue to do today, saying, 'This one's special. Can I bring her around?' And then afterwards, you see, he'll come over to see me again. There won't be any talk about her or anything, just a pleasant visit over a cup of tea. But later he'll say, 'Well, what did you think of her?' And I'll tell him that's up to him, but, of course, I'll be completely honest. If she's going to be too Pākehā in her style or something, I'll simply say to him, 'Well, you'll have to change your ways.' But I never talk about particular problems to anyone else. When this boy comes, it'll just be something between him and myself, nobody else.

I think the traditional way between men and women is better than the way things are today, better than changing partners all the time. And nowadays everyone wants to be the boss. I always think that if a man is strong in his principles, if he's walking on a strong foundation, that is good. If he has knowledge of his beginnings, that will give him an incentive to stand firm—not to bash his wife around or anything like you see today, but to be a strong leader. There are hundreds of good Māori people today that have been brought up like I've been brought up, but you don't hear about them.

I have seen problems with the mixed marriages and relationships that my people have been involved with. I've seen problems where a Māori boy would not be up to the standard of the Pākehā young lady, and the reverse, and so I've said quite often, 'You'll have to pull yourself together, my boy.' Say the young lady was very educated, then I'd try to persuade the boy to go back to university. I'd sometimes even offer to help a little with that, financially, because I always want to see my young people go forward. And if possible I'd do without things that I don't need, really, because I get very well cared for here and I've got all I need. If I see someone's potential, then I try to help.

They also come to me asking advice about sex. Can you imagine? Me? The natural way of life among the old people, when they went to their to hui and they were all sleeping up in the meeting house, was that you slept on your own rug or on your own mat. You didn't dare, even if you were courting, to go off with your boyfriend. If you did, you'd get a jolly good hiding. This was very important, to keep yourself tapu until the time that the tribe consecrated the union. In the meantime, you kept yourself clean.

One Pākehā lady came to see me, complaining that her husband wanted to have sex too often. Honestly, she was so sick and tired from it. I don't know quite what to say when they come to me asking these questions about their husbands, boyfriends and sex. I just listen, and sometimes that's what they've come for anyway, just to have someone to listen to them.

And sometimes they'll come just to visit. I had some wonderful boys, you know. And even the naughty ones, the ones who were causing the problems, they've grown up to be lovely fellows. One or two of the really naughty ones went into fairly prominent positions in the social welfare department, into the law. One of my first boys is down at Wellington, with the police. And another one is in Australia doing some wonderful work there among the Aborigines. A lot of my boys married into European families, and sometimes they'd bring their young babies along to meet me. One of my girls married a European and they live in Australia and have two children there. My own niece married a European. My little niece went to live in England for a while. I do believe that it is good for young people to go and see other parts of the world, because once they've reached a certain age, they'll want to come home to their roots. And they'll come home with the experience of the world on them. Lots of our young people are over in London. But when they reach a certain age, say about twenty or thirty, the Māori blood seems to become more important. It brings them back to where they belong, and of course, along comes the family too. I see them on the marae trying to catch up where they left off. It's lovely to see the Pākehā little ones here.

A year or two ago, a Hamilton city council member called me up. Margaret Evans, the mayor, had the idea of honouring people who have been known to play a part here in the city of Hamilton. So they phoned me, and the lady said, 'We want to have a talk with you.' Then she explained the purpose of her call, and I said, 'Oh, no thank you, no thank you.' And the lady said, 'I'll ring you again.' She did ring again, but I still declined. And then one of my deaconess friends, a member of the city council, got in touch with me and she said, 'What's this I hear about you, Heeni, not accepting the city council's invitation?'

I said, 'Well, Nadine, you know jolly well that I'm past all that. I don't care to be recognised.'

The ceremony for which I don't have a speech prepared. I was included in a group honoured by the mayor of Hamilton for contributions to the local community, in about 1990.

'Oh well,' she said, 'you aren't going to let me down.'

And I said, 'What do you mean?'

And she said, 'Well, I'm putting your name forward, and I'm not the only one. One of the Māori girls is also going to be recommending you. So you can't let me down, old girl.'

I said, 'Oh well, I'll think about it anyway.' And then I thought, 'Oh golly me, I bet I get a call from the mayor's office.' Which I did do. They mentioned to me that there would be twenty or so of us who would be honoured for our contribution to education in Hamilton. And I said, 'Do we have to make speeches?'

'No,' she said, 'because the meeting has to go quickly since the mayor has got another meeting following that one.'

'No speeches?' I said.

'No.'

'OK then, I will.'

During the ceremony, I was about the last one down the list, and the first one made a speech! And I thought to myself, 'Oh golly me, I've been tricked!' And each one that was called up made a speech! 'Oh no,' I thought, 'what to do?' I did feel nervous, I did, that evening. I wished the floor would open up and I'd sink down. I've felt that many times, many times right up until my retirement. 'Well,' I thought, and looked around; I could see around me, you know. I could see a few Māori people there, but the hall was mostly full of Pākehā people. So quickly I listened, you know, and thought, 'Oh no, you'll have to make a speech, girl. You'd better calm yourself down.' And I've got a knack, you know, right from a long way back, of turning myself off and not hearing what's going on around me. So I just sat there and made up a speech. It might have been about a quarter of an hour, no longer than that.

My old doctor was there, and he rang me afterwards. He said, 'Oh Heeni, your speech was the best speech that was made there that evening.' Because while I was thinking what to say, my thoughts had gone back to the times, you know, when we first came to Hamilton. I think I remember saying, 'You know, my mind goes back to the time when very few Māori people walked the streets of Hamilton.' I think I opened it that way. And then I commented on what a lovely place Hamilton is, you know, when the sun's shining. And I also mentioned what a great part in my life Dr Rogers had played at both the girls' and boys' hostels. Of course, I didn't say Hamilton was a conservative city when we came. I didn't say that we'd been sort of looked on not with joy and happiness the very first year we were there.

During retirement, I spend much of my time reflecting on my life and just relaxing. I often have talks with my God, even today. In Te Kūiti, we were told to kneel to pray, but I've given up that idea of kneeling long ago. When I left Te Kūiti and went to Auckland, it was always kneeling. When I went to the training in Christchurch, we were always told to kneel. When I finished all that, I gave up this idea of kneeling. Even with my most serious problems, I don't kneel. I often just come out here in my garden and just talk to my God. I used to think about what my koro said. I know He will just listen to me at any time. There's no need for me to kneel before Him. I

With nephew Boysie and his wife, Googie, behind my family home in Mōkau, 1993.

thought, 'Well, Heeni can talk to the supreme one at any time'. And it also gave me the idea quite early after my training to keep that line of communication open, not to wait until you're on your knees, but to keep that communication line open always.

I don't think about death very much. Quite a lot of people have the belief that there's some sort of life after death, but I don't dwell on that point a great deal. I always remember my koro saying not to worry about that, it's not for me to worry about it. That's what he meant when he said, 'Fear not.' I suppose that in death we find out that we are part of a much bigger world. But in the meantime, live out the life you've been called to in this world, and don't worry too much about the next one. If you fulfill the purpose for which you are sent into this world, you are preparing yourself for the next one.

I'm glad I'm not rich. I'm lucky and haven't got money that will take my thoughts away from what's important. I especially feel this way when I'm hearing about a family that hasn't much food. It's always food that gets me. When I sit down and say grace before I eat, I remember those who don't have half of what I have on my plate. I think maybe the rich miss out, for I think that a person who is religious and had money wouldn't want to spend it on himself—he'd want to spread it out and help the needy. It's only recently that I've been able to give anything of a financial nature to the marae. Before that we had to work, work, work. We had to build up that marae. We had to do baking and sell to make money. And having visitors—the government would send visitors around to us. And we had to do fundraising all the time. It's only just recently that I've been able to give a little bit. I used to get tired because I'd be called down there to help in the garden, help cleaning, help scrubbing down those carvings. That's one thing not many people know, I suppose: whenever there's a hui on we've got to get out and prepare to scrub those paintings. Everything has to be spotless. And that's on all marae. But now, maybe we won't have to work so hard. I remember I'd come home dead tired, because I'd also have my hostel work. Of course, I don't do that heavy work now. There are always other ones coming along that carry on. They go down and set up those tables and so many knives and forks. I had training in all that.

There have been such wonderful experiences throughout my life, it's a growing sort of thing all the time in my mind. I haven't yet got to the point where I've stopped growing. But those three things that my koro said—don't forget to look above, don't be afraid, and be honest—have always stayed with me. You see, we were brought up that if you aren't honest, all that will get back to you later on in life. So we were always to be careful. This was another thing that Princess Te Puea said: always be careful what you say, about what comes out of your mouth, because you can't take it back again and swallow it. Always think first what you're going to say. So your mana comes from being honest in all things—leadership through honesty and integrity. I've always remembered the things my koro said, and I can't say that I've ever ceased from thinking that way.

At my home in Hamilton, August 1994.

I'm lucky to have had the wisdom of Māori elders and church people right through my life. I remember what one of Eva Rickard's uncles said about life. He was an early missionary around this area. 'And remember when you are happy, give thanks. When you are sad, remember that the Word says: "You are my people and I am your God." (Or the other way around, to put it in Māori terms.) Give thanks also in severe sadness, or in the taking of a loved one. And hang onto these words that whatever comes your way, remember always: we do belong, all people.' He would say not only the Māori people. He was also one of those that believed that we are basically one.

We have a family burial ground—it's round the bridge up on a hill in Mōkau. It's a beautiful cemetery looking out toward the sea—a beautiful sea. They're together, Mum and Dad. Mum was buried on top of my dad. My sister died last year, the eldest of my sisters, and she's buried there. But I don't think you can continue to put the family one on top of the other. I don't think we can put anyone on top of Mum.

I still think that maybe my Lord has something for me to do before I'm called away from this earth. I feel that my time has not yet come, that maybe there's still something that I have to fulfill. I still feel that way. I haven't closed my mind to my purpose of being here on earth. It would be foolish to do that while I'm still alive.

Notes

Introduction

1. King, M., 1977, *Te Puea: A Biography.* Hodder and Stoughton, Auckland.
   Te Puea was a mentor for many Tainui women, including Heeni. She was a person with whom Heeni became intimately involved while she was building a cultural renaissance in the Waikato.
2. The Rātana faith began with the vision of Tahupōtiki Wiremu Rātana, from a famous Methodist family although not a member of the Church.
   This Movement first developed as a Religious Movement centred in Divine Healing. ...Underneath all Maori restlessness lay their unhappiness about land, and their dissatisfaction with the handling of the Treaty of Waitangi by successive Colonial Governments. Many Maoris had also read much of the Old Testament as a reflection of the experiences of the Maori Race, and there had been those who had used this to expound a doctrine of the Maoris being 'The Lost Ten Tribes of the House of Israel'. From this there naturally rose a steady expectation of a Messianic deliverer...
   Laurenson, G., 1973, *Te Hahi Weteriana: Three Half Centuries of the Methodist Maori Missions 1822–1972,* p. 216. Proceedings of the Wesley Historical Society of New Zealand, 27(1 and 2).
3. Though not a universal Māori belief, some groups subscribe to the idea of a supreme being who rules over secondary, departmental gods who are the personification of various natural phenomena. (It is not known for sure whether or not this represents a pre-European belief system, but it is included here for the purpose of elaboration.) Io, the Supreme Being, stands alone, unknown to the majority of people except the first order of priests and superior families. Below Io are gods such as Papa (Earth) and Rangi (Sky), who can be placated by means of ritual offerings. Together this pantheon creates order and design out of chaos; without the gods life would be destructive and polluted.
4. Fry, R., 1987, *Out of the Silence: Methodist Women of Aotearoa 1822–1985,* p. 106. Methodist Publishing, Christchurch.
5. From a personal interview with the late Dave Tūmōkai Pānapa, May 1993.
6. Laurenson, op. cit., p. 173.
7. Ibid., p. 173.
8. Personal interview, 1993.
9. Fry, op. cit., p. 60.
10. Ibid., p. 99.
11. Ibid., pp. 104–5.
12. From a personal interview with Michael King, 1993.
13. From a personal interview with Dr Anthony Rogers, August 1993.
14. Personal interview, 1993.
15. Personal interview, 1993.
16. From a personal interview with Professor James Ritchie, Māori Studies and Research Centre, University of Waikato, August 1993.
17. Personal interview, 1993.
18. Personal interview, 1993.
19. Personal interview, 1993.
20. Personal interview, 1993.
21. From a personal interview with Sir Robert Mahuta, Director of the Māori Studies and Research Centre, University of Waikato, August 1993.
22. Personal interview, 1993.

Part One

1. The Tainui are a confederation of four subtribes (Raukawa, Hauraka, Waikato, Maniapoto) in the central North Island.
2. Te Puea was a mentor for many Tainui women, including Heeni. See King, M. 1977. *Te Puea: A Biography.* Auckland: Hodder and Stoughton.
3. From the emic perspective, the European intrusion as just another stimulus for adaptation, something the Polynesians were well accustomed to after a 7,000-year stint of navigating the great Pacific Ocean.
4. Sahlins, Marshall. 1958. *Social Stratification in Polynesia.* American Ethnological Society Monograph. Seattle: University of Washington Press.

5. Firth, Raymond. "Encounters with Tikopia over Sixty Years." *Oceania* 60:241-249.

6. Goldman, Irving. 1970. *Ancient Polynesian Society*. Chicago: University of Chicago Press.

7. Postarrival stories tell of korotangi becoming petrified and turned to stone as it is currently. Korotangi is now held in the Waikato museum on public display.

8. Recent studies source the origins of the New Zealand kūmara to South America.

9. Siers, J. 1967. *The Maori People*. London: Seven Seas Publishing Party, LTD, p. 4.

10. Puketapu-Hetet, E. 1989. *Maori Weaving*. Auckland: Pitman. From Patterson, J. 1992. *Exploring Maori Values*. Palmerston North: Dunmore Press, p. 94.

11. Siers, p. 10.

12. Siers, p. 7.

13. In this way, tapu is a major religious concept that gives order to the Māori world.

14. Historically referred to a dwelling place or name belonging to a whaanau or hapū.

15. Walker, R. 1987. *Nga Tau Tohetohe: Years of Anger*. Auckland: Penguin Books, pp. 28-29.

16. Siers, p. 6.

17. Laurenson, G. 1973. *Te Hahi Weteriana: Three Half Centuries of the Methodist Maori Missions 1822-1972*. Proceedings of the Wesley Historical Society of New Zealand, 27 (1 and 2). p. 173.

18. Laurenson, op. cit., p. 173.

19. Laurenson, op. cit., p. 173.

20. Laurenson, op. cit., p. 173.

21. From a personal interview with the late Dave Tumokai Panapa, May 1993.

22. Siers, p. 9.

23. Howard, A., and Kirkpatrick, J. 1970. "Traditional and Modern Adoption Patterns in Hawaii." In *Adoption in Eastern Oceania*, ed. Caroll, V. Honolulu: University of Hawaii Press, Honolulu, pp. 21-51.

24. Howard and Kirkpatrick, op. cit., p. 75.

25. Howard and Kirkpatrick, op. cit., p. 75.

26. Howard and Kirkpatrick, op. cit., p. 75.

27. Terrell, J. 1994. "Anthropology and Adoption." *American Anthropologist* 96(1):155-160.

28. Patterson, J. 1992. *Exploring Maori Values*. Pamerston North: Dunmore Press, p. 88.

29. J. and J. Ritchie. *Violence in New Zealand*. Wellington: Allen and Unwin.

30. Siers, p. 7.

31. Jackson, M. 1988. "The Maori and the Criminal Justice System: A New Zealand Perspective, He Whaipanga Hou, Part 2 Department of Justice, Wellington, from Patterson, op. cit., p. 81.

32. J. and J. Ritchie. *Violence in New Zealand*. Wellington: Allen and Unwin, p. 110.

33. Personal interview with the late Dave Tumokai Panapa, May 1993.

34. J. and J. Ritchie, op. cit., 113-114.

35. J. and J. Ritchie, op. cit., p. 114.

36. Siers, op. cit., p. 8.

37. Siers, 1967, op. cit., p. 79.

38. Goldman, op. cit., p. 37.

39. Personal interview with Dave Tumokai Panapa, May 1993.

40. Personal interview with Dave Tumokai Panapa, May 1993.

41. Barlow, op. cit., p. 174.

42. Walker, R. 1987. *Nga Tau Tohetohe: Years of Anger*. Auckland: Penguin Books, pp. 136-137.

43. Although not a universal Māori belief, some groups subscribe to the idea that a supreme being rules over secondary, departmental gods who are the personification of various natural phenomena. (It is not know for sure whether this represents a pre-European belief system, but it is included here for the purposes of explication. Io, the Supreme Being, stands alone, unknown to the majority of people except the first order of priests and superior families. Below Io are gods such as Papa (Earth) and Rangi (Sky), who can be placated by means of ritual offerings. Together this pantheon creates order and design out of chaos: without the gods, life would be destructive and polluted.

44. Barlow, C. 1991. *Tikanga Whakaaro: Key Concepts in Maori Culture*. Auckland: Oxford University Press, pp. 11-12.

45. Patterson, op. cit., p. 145.

46. Fry, Ruth. 1987. *Out of the Silence: Methodist Women of Aotearoa 1822-1985*. Methodist Publishing, Christchurch, p. 106.

47. Laurenson, G. 1973. *Te Hahi Weteriana: Three Half Centuries of the Methodist Maori Missions 1822-1972*. Proceedings of the Wesley Historical Society of New Zealand, 27(1 and 2), p. 216.

48. Personal interview with the late Dave Tumokai Panapa, May 1993.
49. Siers, op. cit., p. 10.
50. Siers, op. cit., p. 10.
51. Siers, op. cit., p. 17.
52. Siers, op. cit., p. 20.
53. Siers, op. cit., p. 20.
54. Conversation with Nanaia Mahuta, March 1999.
55. Siers, op. cit., p. 22.
56. Siers, op. cit., p. 24.
57. Siers, op. cit., p. 25.

Chapter 1

1. The protocol for properly handling the umbilical cord is what most differentiates a common from an aristocratic birth:

    The cutting of the cord was usually achieved with a sharp piece of flint and the cut was smeared with oil pressed from seeds of the titaki tree. The area was then dressed with the inner bark of the lacewood tree soaked in titoki oil. The dried cord, after being separated from the navel, was placed in a cleft of a rock, in a tree or buried on a boundary, a method common throughout Polynesia.

    Siers, J., 1967, *The Maori People*, p. 9. Sevenseas Publishing Ltd, London.

2. Because of the economic impact of colonisation, Heeni's birth, on the surface, was much like a commoner's birth (except for the treatment of the umbilical cord). Commoners were born with little ceremony in a rough sort of shelter. In all of Māori society, blood associated with menstruation and childbirth was generally considered tapu, so it was necessary to isolate the expectant mother from the rest of the village. The mother's mother and other related women, as well as her husband, would help. Before colonisation, childbirth among the aristocracy was much more elaborate. A special house was built where female attendants waited on the expectant mother.

3. Females in an aristocratic line were raised as puhi and given in marriage to someone of similar status. Often such daughters were kept virginal and strictly guarded, with the ultimate aim of a political marriage. In the higher echelons of Māori society, marriage was often a political instrument, and a girl's parents made the decision as to whom she would marry.

4. Chiefly status was so ascribed because he could trace his ancestry all the way back to a leader on the canoe that brought the iwi's ancestors to New Zealand. A chief was considered tapu. His special status ensured he would be treated with the utmost respect. This deference extended to his hair, to his eating utensils, and sometimes to the ground on which he walked.

5. Traditionally, adoption was practiced all over Polynesia. On some islands, 30–70 percent of households were involved with child adoption in one way or another. According to Polynesian anthropologies, adoption serves at least three purposes: it redistributes child wealth so that all families benefit, i.e., it equalises major differences in family size; it helps satisfy the labour needs of those family economies with otherwise few or no children to draw upon; and it is a strategic means for maintaining cooperative relationships between groups such that a network of interdependency is built and maintained. See Howard, A., et al., 1970, 'Traditional and Modern Adoption Patterns in Hawaii' in Carroll, V., (ed.), *Adoption in Eastern Oceania*, pp. 21–51. University of Hawaii Press, Honolulu.

6. In Heeni's family's case, the purpose of adoption was to strengthen intertribal bonds. A child would be given to another subtribe or iwi to acquire the bloodlines of the aristocracy across iwi boundaries, and marae would remain deeply connected. So important was this process that an adoption would most likely be decided before the child concerned was even conceived. The depth of the importance of the process becomes more clear when one considers the etymology of the word *iwi*. Literally, it means 'bone'. An adopted child keeps the bloodline intact; the bones of the tribe bind all of the people together.

    There was that relationship among the tribe...not blood relationship, but bone relationship. When a person died and they buried him, in twelve months they cleaned him and took the bone, and they looked after the bones.

    Personal interview with Dave Tūmōkai Pānapa, 1993.

7. Heeni's koro was a tohunga, a religious expert who was directly concerned with spiritual matters. Tohunga among the senior class were fully trained doctors, military leaders, craftsmen and/or agricultural experts. They knew ventriloquism, hypnotism and telepathy. When healing, they used a combination of herbs and rituals to bring about a cure.

8. Institutionalised warfare is a hallmark of Polynesian and Māori culture. Traditionally, war could be provoked by insult, adultery or revenge. Or it could be brought on by trade disputes or battles for territory. For example, if the resources in one area became depleted, a village there would have to rely on alternative resources nearby which may have been the exclusive territory of another village. This would provoke attacks. An attack would bring the demand for utu, or retribution, which would eventually lead to war.

    Māori also practised cannibalism. After a battle, the victors used the slain for food. Traditionally, cannibalism had both practical and symbolic purposes. First, it satisfied hunger for meat protein, which was extremely scarce before the arrival of Europeans. Second, it served a psychological purpose by reducing enemies to the lowly status of food and, so it was believed, transferring the mana of the vanquished to the victor.

9. On all Polynesian islands except Aotearoa, tapa cloth traditionally served as fabric for making clothes, kits and mats. The material for tapa cloth is obtained from the oti plant, but this could not survive in the colder regions of New Zealand. Māori therefore had to seek a substitute, and found it in flax, which flourishes throughout the country. After special preparation, flax was woven. Kiwi feathers and, later, dog hair were added to cloaks for additional warmth. The late Rangimarie Hetet was one of the finest traditional weavers in New Zealand. Her clothes are on display at the Kirkirima (Hamilton) Museum.

10. To mix food and body accouterments is tapu in Māori society. *Tapu* has more than one meaning:
    The term has two quite distinct usages, one active, the other passive. As an active quality, tapu suggests a contained potency of some thing, place or person. In its passive usage, it means forbidden or dangerous...
    Shore, B., 1985, *Polynesian Worldview: A Synthesis*. Unpublished manuscript.
    To mix food and body elements represents the forbidden and dangerous aspect—the act is something that could contaminate the essential parity of each. Tapu is essential to traditional Māori life because it gives order to the world.

11. *Weaving is more than just a product of manual skills. From the simple rourou food basket to the prestigious kahu kiwi, weaving is endorsed with the very essence of the spiritual values of Maori people. The ancient Polynesian belief is that the artist is a vehicle through whom the gods create. Art is sacred and interrelated with the concepts of mauri, mana and tapu.*
    Puketapu-Hetet, E., 1989, *Maori Weaving*, Pitman, Auckland. From Patterson, J., 1992. *Exploring Mūa Values*, p. 94. Dunmore Press, Palmerston North.

12. Blood associated with menstruation and childbirth is considered obnoxious to most Māori. It is tapu—polluted, dangerous and forbidden.

13. To a Māori, a fish in the sea is a child of the god Tangaroa, and watched over by potent local guardians. Māori have a responsibility to protect its life forever.
    The resources of the natural world are not to be abused. Even essential food resources are to be approached with care and used with respect.
    Patterson, op. cit., p. 145.

14. A Kōaitau is a kind of flute, made of flax, wood or bone.

Chapter 2

1. *Just as tribes are closely linked by a network of genealogical connections, so are the peoples related spiritually to their ancestral lands. And these relations have ethical implications.*
    Patterson, J., 1992, *Exploring Māori Values*, p. 88. Dunmore Press, Palmerston North.

2. A traditional pā is a fortified village. Many pā sites were surrounded by very high fences, usually milled from local timber. In addition, deep ditches were often dug close to a water course, to provide access to freshwater springs during times of siege. Pā were always near rich food sources, such as shellfish beds, and land suitable for growing kūmara.

3. Girls and boys traditionally had different chores to do around the home. For the most part, boys did the fishing and pig hunting, while girls did the food processing and cooking.
    Girls generally had more domestic responsibilities and were drawn to women's work activities. Boys were permitted to roam farther from home, take more risks, and appeared to assert more authority within the peer group. In effect, the pattern of sex role specialization is as much a consequence of peer influences as of parental modeling.
    Ritchie, J., and Ritchie, J., 1989, *Violence in New Zealand*, p. 109. Allen and Unwin, Wellington.

4. Heeni is referring to a sense of self-esteem which comes from personal adherence to the authority and law of the ancestors:
    The behavioral guidelines of the ancestors were monitored by the living relatives, and the wishes of an individual were constantly balanced against the greater mana and concerns of the group.

Jackson, M., 1988, 'The Māori and the Criminal Justice System: A New Zealand Perspective', *He Whaipānga Hou. Part 2.* Department of Justice, Wellington. From Patterson, op. cit., p. 81.

5. With no written language, Māori tribal history was passed on not only through storytelling, but also through a rich tradition of song and dance. Māori musical tradition is full of allusions to mythology, past and present.

> *If ever humans sang and made music to fulfill themselves, it was the Maori, and any man or woman who could do both well was assured of respect... Every song had its point—an orator could drive home an argument, a pleader could sway his listeners into compliance, each one with a culminating point; a telling illustration; a flash of revelation.*

Siers, J., 1967, *The Maori People*, pp. 17, 20. Sevenseas Publishing Ltd, London.

6. Even though Heeni is contemplating what appears to be a Christian concept, she is using two gods in the Māori pantheon as focal points.

> *Tangaroa is the god of the sea, lakes, and rivers, with dominion over all creatures which live in them. ...Tāne is lord and master of the forests and the birds of Rēhua (caretaker of bird life).*

Barlow, C., 1991, *Tikanga Whakaaro: Key Concepts in Māori Culture*, pp. 11–12. Oxford University Press, Auckland.

7. Magnanimity and kindness are character traits of the rangatira class of Māori people.

8. A Māori belongs to a particular marae according to ancestral lineages linked to iwi and hapū ties. Indeed, it is possible to view the intricate network of marae across all of New Zealand as the infrastructure which sophisticatedly maintains the solidarity of Māori culture.

> *The marae is central to the concept of Māoritanga. Māoritanga consists of an acknowledgement of and pride in one's identity as a Māori. While Māoritanga has a physical base in ethnic identity, it also has a spiritual and emotional base derived from the ancestral culture of the Māori. Māori oratory, language and values and social etiquette are given their fullest expression in the marae setting at tangi and hui.*

Walker, R., 1987, *Nga Tau Tohctohe: Years of Anger*, pp. 28–9. Penguin Books, Auckland. Marae activities still unite Māoridom in myriad ways. For example, all Māori decision making, which is conducted according to rules that promote consensus building, and much of Māori entertaining, celebrating and grieving, are still conducted on ancestral marae or in auxiliary meeting houses.

9. *On the one hand, your body is tapu and so you must treat it with respect, and on the other hand there are various external tapu that must be observed.*

Patterson, op. cit., p. 84.

10. Heeni has a traditional view of the role of men and women in Māori society. On the surface this seems paradoxical, because she carries so much of her own mana. But her mana is both powerful and passive. For example, as she is one of the senior matriarchs of her people, her presence is sought at ceremonial events such as tangi and hui, yet it is rare for her to serve an active vocal role on these occasions. However, she does remain quite visible, sitting quietly and humbly as a symbol of all that it means to be a Māori woman.

> *To me she portrays and embodies all that is wonderful in womanhood. She's the living personification of human humility. She certainly never pushed herself in front of things, but has always been there in the background, to help, to advise, and to counsel. We know that things are well because of her presence. By sitting in the meeting house, she keeps us warm. From my perception, the role that she has with Te Arikinui is like a confidante, someone who's there but isn't there. Heeni is someone Dame Te Ata can turn to and talk with at any time. One of the queen's daughters was named after her. She, the eldest. So that's the kind of mana Heeni's holding, the queen's first born named after her, called Heeni.*

Personal interview with Dave Tūmōkai Pānapa, 1993.

11. *It is through genealogy that kinship and economic ties are cemented and that the mana or power of a chief is inherited. Whakapapa is one of the most prized forms of knowledge and great efforts are made to preserve it. All of the people in a community are expected to know who their immediate ancestors are, and to pass this information on to their children so that they too may develop pride and sense of belonging through understanding the roots of their heritage.*

Barlow, op. cit., p. 174.

12. Reverend Whiteley won much prestige among local Māori for defending them against the New Zealand government, whose land policies were considered a betrayal of the Treaty of Waitangi. He was murdered in a freak accident when he went to meet a war party in the hope of restraining them and reasoning with them.

> *As he rode up the sunken roadway near the Blockhouse, he was challenged and warned to go back, but replied that he could not do so when his children were doing wrong. At this a*

shot was fired, by whom is not clear, and his horse fell under him. Realising the crisis, Whiteley dropped to his knees in prayer, when further shots rang out and this fine old servant and friend of the Maoris was killed. The story has been told and retold but the full details will never be completely clear. What is clear however, is that the advance party of Maoris returned to report to the main body under Wahanui at Awakino that the road was open. . . . The Apostle of peace who had mediated so many tribal confrontations had at last become a victim of the unleashed bitterness rising from the clash of the two peoples, and from the long succession of wrongs and misunderstandings that had led to the flare up. The spread of the news among the Maori communities was met by the shamed and saddened tangi of the women in every settlement.

Laurenson, G., 1972, *Te Hahi Weteriana: Three Half Centuries of the Methodist Maori Missions 1822–1972,* pp. 173–4. Proceedings of The Wesley Historical Society of New Zealand, 27(1 and 2).

13. Heeni could not have known at the time she was given over to the Methodist Church, 60 years after Whiteley's murder, that as an adult she would in some ways pick up where Whiteley's work had left off. She was to become a missionary of peace herself, a church leader who would build important bridges between two races in order to heal some of the legacies of the often misguided colonial programme.

Part Two

1. Personal interview with Professor Jim Ritchie, University of Waikato, August 1993.
2. Ritchie, op. cit.
3. The rest of the male members of the family faced a disinherited life or they joined the church or military to escape indigence.
4. Orange, Claudia. 1987. *The Treaty of Waitangi.* Wellington: Allen and Unwin, p. 22.
5. Ward, Alan. *Shadow of the Land.*
6. Orange, op. cit., p. 56.
7. Orange, op. cit., p. 57.
8. Laurenson, op. cit., 1973.
9. Laurenson, op. cit., p. 49.
10. Laurenson, op. cit.
11. Laurenson, op. cit., 127.
12. Laurenson, op. cit., 56.
13. Orange, op. cit., 177.
14. Laurenson, op. cit., 163.
15. Orange, op. cit., p. 209.
16. Fry, Ruth. 1987. *Out of the Silence: Methodist Women of Aotearoa 1822-1985.* Methodist Publishing, Christchurch, p. 175.
17. Laurenson, op. cit., p. 223.

Chapter 3

1. After Te Kūiti, Heeni made the move to Auckland, where she was to serve a leadership role in the newly established Kurahuna Māori Girls' School. This school had the primary goal of reaching potential Māori mothers to teach them various aspects of domestic work, the rudiments of hygiene and something of the care of babies.
2. At this time, some churches were connected to the Education Department.
3. Maharāia Winiata was born in Tauranga in 1912 of Ngāi Te Rangi and Ngāi Ranginui lineage. He went to Edinburgh on a Nuffield Fellowship, gaining his PhD in 1952. He wrote an influential thesis on Māori leadership, and was subsequently on the organising committee of a round of young leaders' conferences set up under the auspices of the Department of Continuing Education at Auckland and Victoria Universities. Through his recognition of the national and historic importance of the Kīngitanga, he became a close associate of 'Princess' Te Puea, Tainui leader and champion of the Kīngitanga, and an advisor to King Korokī, father of the present Māori queen. He died in 1960.

Chapter 4

1. The New Zealand Methodist Order of Deaconesses was established in 1907 in Christchurch. Deaconesses were trained to help women better care for their children and families. They

reached out to the poor, the old, the sick and the derelict. They were trained to work in the rural areas as well. 'In Maori communities it was felt that women had a pastoral role to play.' Fry, R., 1987, *Out of the Silence: Methodist Women of Aotearoa 1822–1985,* p. 101. Methodist Publishing, Christchurch.

Part Three

1. Personal Interview with Dr. Michael King, August 1993.
2. Fourth world peoples are those who live on or near their original homeland, culturally and economically disadvantaged within a wider, dominant society whose government is increasingly transnational in its economic activities. Fourth world peoples are those whose cultural traditions are in jeopardy while they seek economic self-determination in a disproportionate context of social problems. See Ritchie, J. 1992. *Becoming Bicultural.* Wellington: Huia Publishers.
3. Personal interview with Dr. Michael King, August 1993.
4. Personal interview with Professor Jim Ritchie, August 1993.
5. Personal interview with Dr. Anthony Rogers, hostel physician.
6. Personal interview with Michael King, August 1993.
7. Heeni was one of four of Te Puea's trusted drivers. "Being a chauffeur for Te Puea meant two things. First it meant that Heeni was literally trustworthy because the life of such an important person was in her hands. But it also meant that Heeni was someone Te Puea liked to have around her. And that meant you had to be one of two types of people. You either had to be a complete minion, or someone who would just shut up and do what they were told and not make a fuss—and Te Puea used quite a lot of people like that. Or, you had to be someone like Heeni, who would basically do what they were told but who was also confident and assertive enough to stand up to her—and who would actually discuss things with her, too. Heeni had that kind of relationship with her, although she always speaks of Te Puea with great respect. I know that Heeni was on of the few younger women that Te Puea would actually ask for an opinion."
8. Personal interview with the late Dave Tumokai Panapa, May 1993.
9. King, Michael. 1977. *Te Puea: A Biography.* Auckland, NZ: Houghton and Stodder, p. 22.
10. King, op. cit., p. 22.
11. King, op. cit., p. 23.
12. King, op. cit., p. 26.
13. King, op. cit., p. 27.
14. Although reserved, he did lead a delegation to England to petition the Crown, regarding the confiscated waikato lands and the Treaty of Waitangi.
15. King, op. cit., p. 66.
16. King, op. cit., p. 66.
17. MacDonald, Charlottte, Penfold, Meremeri, and Williams, Bridget, eds. 1991. *The Book of New Zealand Women. Ko Kui Ma Te Kaupapa.* Wellington: Bridget Williams, p. 665.
18. MacDonald, C. 1991. *New Zealand Women.* Wellington: Bridget Williams Books, p. 665.
19. MacDonald, op. cit., p. 665.
20. King, op. cit., p. 94 .
21. King, Michael. 1977. *Te Puea: An Autobiography.* Auckland, NZ: Hodder and Stoughton, p. 243.
22. King, op. cit., p. 163.
23. King, op. cit., p. 163.
24. King, op. cit., p. 115.
25. MacDonald, Penfold, Williams, op. cit., p. 666.
26. MacDonald, Penfold, Williams, op. cit., p. 665.
27. Personal interview with the late Dave Tumokai Panapa, August 1993.
28. King, op. cit., p. 151.
29. King, op. cit., p. 156.
30. King, op. cit., p. 182.
31. Personal interview with Michael King, August 1993.
32. Personal Interview with Dr. Michael King, August 1993.
33. King, Michael. 1984. *Te Puea Herangi: From Darkness to Light.* Wellington: School Publications Branch NZ Department of Education, p. 66.
34. King, op. cit., p. 249.
35. Personal interview with Dr. Michael King, August 1993.

36. Personal interview with Dr. Anthony Rogers, August 1993.
37. Personal interview with Dr. Anthony Rogers, August 993.
38. Personal interview with Michael King, August 1993.
39. Personal interview with Dr. Anthony Rogers, August 1993.
40. King, 1977, op. cit., p. 284.
41. Personal interview with Dr. Michael King, August 1993.

Chapter 5

1. By the time Heeni had completed her deaconess training, she'd been thoroughly exposed to the best of both Māoritanga and Pākehātanga. Indeed, after 15 years steeped in each culture, Heeni emerged a bicultural woman—fluent in both cultures and languages and ready to undertake her life's work.

2. Heeni was 30 when she arrived in Hamilton, at the height of the Second World War. At this time, Hamilton had achieved the status of city, which required a population of 20,000. However, most people living there were Pākehā and knew very little about the aristocratic side of Māori culture to which Heeni belonged.

    ...Hamilton...was established on the site of an old Māori community called Kirikiriroa. But it was...on land that had been confiscated after the Waikato land wars by the very people who fought those wars. They were given land grants in return for fighting the Māori. So it meant that Hamilton grew up not only without any Māori in it, but that the Māori were for a long time hostile to the very existence of the city itself, right up until the 1950s.
    Personal interview with Michael King, 1993.

3. Tahupōtiki Wiremu Rātana was a Māori from a Methodist family who became something of a messiah to his people when, in 1918, he had a prophetic vision of divine healing. This vision immediately allowed him to perform curing miracles, which drew him a large following. He founded a new religious movement which incorporated Christian as well as traditional Māori elements. People came from all over New Zealand to Rātana pā to hear his teachings and to receive the grace of a cure.

    By 1924, Rātana followers who had begun ministering their own weddings and baptisms were putting pressure on the Reverend Seamer to help them create their own legitimate church. Rātana leaders, like Heeni's koro, were chosen as lay ministers. They came from very different folkways and backgrounds, and their preaching drew upon the traditions from which they individually came. By the late 1920s, the Rātana Church, based on Christian and Māori teachings with the official backing of the Methodists, had become the church of choice for a high proportion of Māori people.

4. King Korokī's daughter Piki (later Te Arikinui Dame Te Atairangikaahu, the present Māori queen) was a student at Heeni's hostel. The future queen of Māoridom was not to receive any special treatment. Te Puea insisted that she was to work as hard as possible and to learn as much as she could, but never to forget her Māori roots.

    This education was for the benefit of the people, not themselves; the one thing she did not want in the Kāhui Ariki as a result of education was a replacement of Māori communal sensitivity by a strongly individualist, competitive, money-grubbing instinct.
    King, M., 1977, Te Puea: A Biography, p. 249. Hodder and Stoughton, Auckland.

5. Up until the 1950s, there was very little contact between most Māori and Pākehā. They didn't share the same institutions, such as hospitals or schools. Heeni therefore found herself a bicultural woman in a monocultural environment, which meant that, as a bridge-builder, she had her work cut out.

6. E kuhuna ai te miro mā, te miro pango, te miro whero. I muri kia mau ki te aroha, ki te ture me te whakapono.

7. Princess Te Puea visited the Rāhui Girls' Hostel, quite often in the beginning, lending her support and strength while Heeni adjusted to her new role. Te Puea was a mentor to Heeni. In time, Heeni became one of Te Puea's protégées, and their relationship, characterised by much aroha and confidence, ultimately grew into a deep and lasting friendship.

    Heeni was utterly devoted to Te Puea, and to Te Puea's teachings. They were both kindred spirits. Heeni used to chauffeur her around, and in the process she became Te Puea's confidante. Heeni was someone Te Puea could bounce ideas off, and she needed a sounding board. You need people around you that will tell you the truth. I would like to suggest that Heeni was one of those.
    Personal interview with Dave Tūmōkai Pānapa, 1993.
    Heeni was one of four of Te Puea's trusted drivers.

Being a chauffeur for Te Puea meant two things. First it meant Heeni was literally trustworthy because the life of such an important person was in her hands. But it also meant that Heeni was someone Te Puea liked to have around her. And that meant you had to be one of two types of people. You either had to be a complete minion, someone who would just shut up and do what they were told and not make a fuss—and Te Puea used quite a lot of people like that. Or you had to be someone like Heeni, who would basically do what they were told but who was also confident and assertive enough to stand up to her—and who would actually discuss things with her, too. Heeni had that kind of relationship with her, although she always speaks of Te Puea with great respect. I know that Heeni was one of the few younger women that Te Puea would actually ask for an opinion.

Personal interview with Michael King, 1993.

8. Ranginui Walker has pointed out that bodily wellbeing among traditional Māori is dependent on the social world, which is governed by the laws of tapu. Becoming too close to the royal family was a breach of tapu.

Any transgression of the laws of tapu led to withdrawal of divine protection. [One's life force] was then exposed to the influence of malevolent spirits. Illness with a non-observable physical cause was attributed to an attack on the life force by those spirits.

Walker, R., 1987, *Nga Tau Tohetohe: Years of Anger*, pp. 136–7. Penguin Books, Auckland.

9. Heeni was one of three visitors allowed to be with Te Puea in her dying moments in 1952.

All day on Sunday, 12 October, Te Puea lay semiconscious, her eyes closed, breathing with difficulty. Her feet, legs and back were cold. Memo [a friend] rubbed them for a while in the morning and was relieved by sister Heeni. Nobody else dared touch the old lady.

King, op. cit., p. 284.

Chapter 6

1. Te Puea displayed extraordinary compassion during the great influenza outbreak of 1918. More than 720 million people worldwide died in this epidemic, 20,000 of whom were New Zealanders. It is unknown how many of these were Māori. However, it is known that many of those who died were young people in their prime, aged 20–40, parents who were looking after both the young and the old.

This meant that in the aftermath, whole communities found themselves without mothers and fathers, primary wage earners and active leaders. Te Puea not only organized the nursing of the sick, but single-handedly adopted many of the orphans and elderly left behind in the wake of the death of their parents.

King, M., 1977, Te Puea: A Biography, p. 115. Hodder and Stoughton, Auckland.

2. Danny was extremely wealthy by New Zealand standards, and of course Heeni enjoyed this, albeit with some ambivalence.

3. It would be incorrect to say Heeni opposed marriage, nor was she so busy with some kind of artificial marriage to the Church that she wouldn't have made room for it. It is probably more accurate to say that Heeni never found the right man. Perhaps she never found him because of Te Puea's instructions that she not marry.

Father Seamer's only reason for why she never married wasn't that she was married to the Church, or the Kīngitanga, which was perhaps true in a way; but that she certainly never found anyone—someone that might live up to the expectations required of such an extraordinary woman.

Personal interview with Dr Anthony Rogers, 1993.

Danny Smith came close. But, in addition to the obstacle posed by his wealth, a marriage to him would have meant Heeni leaving her people, and as Michael King has said, tribal people just can't do that.

Part Four

1. Personal interview with Robert Mahuta, brother of the Māori Queen, August 1993.
2. Personal interview with Dr. Anthony Rogers, August 1993.
3. Personal interview with Dave Tumokai Panapa, August 1993.
4. Cajete, Gregory. 1994. *Look to the Mountain*. Durango, CO: Kivaki Press.
5. *Waikato Times,* January 1993.
6. *Waikato Times,* February 1993.
7. *Waikato Times,* February 1993.

8. Melbourne, Hineani, ed. 1995. *Maori Sovereignty: The Maori Perspective.* Auckland: Hodder Moa Beckett Publishers Limited.
9. Melbourne, op. cit., p. 146.
10. Personal interview with James Ritchie, 1993.
11. Walker, Raninui. "The Treaty of Waitangi as the Focus of Maori Protest." In *Waitangi: Maori and Pakeha Perspectives on the Treaty of Waitangi,* Kawharu, I. H., ed. New York: Oxford University Press, pp. 263–269.
12. Walker, op. cit., p. 263.
13. *The Treaty of Waitangi,* 1840.
14. *Te Tirititi o Waitangi,* 1840.
15. Dennehy, Personal Communication, 1993.
16. Orange, Claudia. 1987. *The Treaty of Waitangi.* Wellington: Allen and Unwin, p. 41.
17. Walker, op. cit., p. 264.
18. Orange, op. cit., p. 41.
19. *The Treaty of Waitangi,* 1840.
20. *Te Tirititi o Waitangi,* 1840.
21. Walker, op. cit., p. 265.
22. Orange, op. cit., p. 246.
23. Orange, op. cit., 250–251.
24. Archie, Carol, ed. 1995. *Maori Sovereignty: The Pākehā Perspective.* Auckland: Moa Beckett.
25. Archie, op. cit., p. 7.
26. Archie, op. cit., p. 143.
27. Melbourne, op. cit., p. 119.
28. Melbourne, op. cit., p. 143.
29. Personal interview with Dr. Michael King, 1993.
30. Personal interview with Jim Ritchie, 1993.
31. Personal interview with Robert Mahuta, 1992.
32. Interview with the late Dave Tūmōkai Pānapa, August 1993.
33. Melbourne, op. cit., p. 146.
34. "The Endowed Colleges Proposal—A Tainui Special." He Ra Whakahirahira. Maori Studies and Research Center Newspaper. University of Waikato, September 1995.
35. Melbourne, op. cit., p. 148.
36. Personal interview with Jim Ritchie, 1993.

Chapter 7

1. The poukai is the annual round of visits Te Arikinui makes to the loyal marae of the Kīngitanga. It is a royal progress, during which the monarch is seen by the people with the people.
2. Māori and Pacific Islanders are disproportionately represented in all of the socioeconomic indices of social stress. For example, the 1991 New Zealand census shows a New Zealand national unemployment rate of 11 percent, while the Māori and Pacific Islander rates are 24 percent and 20 percent respectively. Likewise, almost two-thirds of Māori have no official school certification. Māori and Pacific Islanders also have lower median annual household incomes than the New Zealand national average. Māori make up 13 percent of the New Zealand national average. Māori make up 13 percent of the New Zealand population, but represent 65 percent of the country's prison population. Source: *1991 New Zealand Census Report.* Department of Statistics, Wellington.

GLOSSARY

āpōtoro: minister, apostle

Aotearoa: The Māori name for New Zealand, of which the most commonly quoted meaning is Land of the Long White Cloud.

aroha: love, compassion, sympathy, pity

haka: dance with males to the fore and accompanied by words recited in rhythm. Haka have many themes, e.g., welcome, challenge, derision, politics, war.

hāngi: food or meal cooked in an earth oven; the oven itself (see **oumu**)

hapū: subtribe, clan

hara: sin, crime

hui: gathering, meeting

iwi: tribe, people, nation; bone

kahu kiwi: kiwi-feather cloak

Kāhui Ariki: the name of the Māori royal family (literally, gathering of nobles)

karakia: incantation, church service

kaumātua: elder, adult, old person

kēhua: ghost, apparition

Kīngitanga: The name, meaning kingship, given to the Māori monarchist movement.

kōrero: conversation, narrative, news

koro: grandfather, father figure, old man

korowai: (chiefly) cloak

kuia: matron, old lady

kūmara: sweet potato *(Ipumoea batatas)*

mahi: job, work, function

mākutu: bewitch(ed), cast a spell

mana: integrity, prestige

Māoritanga: Māori culture/perspective

marae: meeting house (and associated buildings) and the land on which it stands; area in front of a meeting house where guests are welcomed, the dead farewelled, important issues discussed and celebrations held (weddings, birthdays, etc.)

mauri: life principle

mihi: greeting, welcome

mōkai: person who gives dedicated service

muru: absolve, cleanse

oumu (omu, umu): oven

pā: stockade, stockaded village

Pai Mārire: a 19th-century religious creed—Christianity purified of missionary error— now unique to the **Kīngitanga** (literally, goodness and peace)

Pākehā: non-Māori, European, Caucasian

Pākehātanga: Pākehā culture/perspective

pātaka: storehouse, pantry, cupboard

piupiu: flax skirt

poukai: the annual round of visits the Māori monarch makes to the loyal **marae** of the **Kīngitanga**; royal progress

ponga: tree fern *(Cyathea dealbata)*

pūhā: sow-thistle *(Sonchus* species)

puhi: virgin, girl of eligible status (usually highborn)

rangatira: chief, leader, noble

Rātana: The religious movement founded by Tahupōtiki Wiremu Rātana after he had a vision of divine healing in 1918. The movement incorporates Christian and traditional Māori elements.

rourou: small basket for food

ruru: small spotted owl *(Ninox novaeseelandiae)*. The common name morepork
echos the owl's call. Ruru are believed to be heralds of important news.

Tāne Mahuta: guardian spirit of the forest, one of the many gods who personify natural
phenomena (see also **Tangaroa**)

Tangaroa: guardian spirit of the sea, one of the many gods who personify natural
phenomena (see also **Tāne Mahuta**)

tangi: mourning, wake, funeral gathering

taonga: property, treasure

tapu: sacred, forbidden, confidential, taboo

te runga rawa: the creator, the supreme being (a term coined only after the arrival of
Pākehā)

tiki: neck pendant, usually a primal human figure carved out of greenstone or bone
tohunga: priest, expert

utu: price, revenge

wāhi: place, area, position

wairua: spirit, soul, mood

waka (taua): (war) canoe; the people (and their descendants) who came to **Aotearoa** in
one of the ancestral canoes

whakapapa: genealogy, family tree, cultural identity

whakaruru: shelter

whakataukī: proverb, motto, slogan

Appendix

DOC.1 THE TREATY OF WAITANGI
(Official English Version Conceived by
James Buzby and Lieutenant Hobson in 1840)

The English text uses the word "sovereignty". The Māori equivalent is "Mana", but that word was not used in the Māori text. The word that was used was "governorship", which was a new word and concept for Māori people, and therefore ambiguous.

DOC.1 THE TREATY OF WAITANGI
(Official English Version Conceived of By James Buzby and Lieutenant Hobson in 1840)

Preamble:

Her Majesty, Victoria Queen of the United Kingdom of Great Britain and Ireland regarding with Her Royal Favor the Native Chiefs and Tribes of New Zealand and anxious to protect their just Rights and Property and to secure to them the enjoyment of Peace and Good Order, has deemed it necessary in consequence of the great number of Her Majesty's subjects who have already settled in New Zealand and the extension of Emigration both from Europe and Australia which is still in progress, to constitute and appoint a Functionary properly authorized to treat with the Aborigines of New Zealand for the recognition of Her Majesty's Sovereign Authority over the whole or any part of those islands—Her Majesty therefore being desirous to establish a settled form of Civil Government with a view to avert the evil consequences which must result from the absence of the necessary laws and Institutions alike to the Native population and to Her subjects, has been graciously pleased to empower and authorize me William Hobson, a Captain in Her Majesty's Royal Navy, Consul and lieutenant-Governor of such

parts of New Zealand as may be or hereafter shall be ceded to her majesty, to invite the Confederated and independent chiefs of New Zealand to concur in the following Articles and Conditions.

ARTICLE THE FIRST:

The Chiefs of the Confederation of the United Tribes of New Zealand and the separate and independent chiefs who have not become members of the confederation cede to Her Majesty the Queen of England absolutely and without Reservation all the Rights and Powers of Sovereignty which the said Confederation or Individual Chiefs respectively exercise or possess, or may be supposed to exercise or possess over their respective Territories as the sole sovereigns thereof.

ARTICLE THE SECOND:

Her Majesty the Queen of England confirms and guarantees to the Chiefs and Tribes of New Zealand and to the respective families and individuals thereof, the full and exclusive and undisturbed possession of their lands and Estates, Forests, Fisheries and other properties which they may collectively or individually possess so long as it is their wish and desire to retain the same in their possession; but the Chiefs yield to Her Majesty the exclusive right of Pre-emption over such lands as the Proprietors thereof may be disposed to alienate at such prices as may be agreed upon between the respective Proprietors and persons appointed by Her Majesty to Treat with them in that behalf.

ARTICLE THE THIRD:

In Consideration of thereof her Majesty the Queen of England extendes to the Native

193

of New Zealand Her Royal Protection and imparts to them all the Rights and Privileges of British Subjects.

> Exclusive Right of Pre-emption (to buy) to the Crown was not mentioned in the Māori Text.

> Article III granted British citizenship, which was very soon negated with respect to Māori land interests, and the right to participate in parliament.

> About 500 of the 540 Chiefs who signed the treaty, signed the Māori text version. It was also signed by Captain Hobson.

DOC.2 Tititi O Waitangi
(Official Māori version written by Henry Williams, 1840)

DOC.2. Te Tirititi o Waitangi
(Literal English Translation of the Maori Text)

Preamble:

Victoria, Queen of England, in her *kind (gracious) thoughtfulness* to the Chiefs and Hapus of New Zealand, and her desire to preserve to them their chieftainship and their land, and that peace and quietness may be kept with them, because of a great number of the people of her tribe have settled in this country and more will come, has thought it right to send a chief (an officer) as one who will make a statement, to negotiate with the Maori people of New Zealand. Let the chiefs accept the *governorship* of the Queen over all parts of this country and the islands. Now, the Queen desired to arrange the *governorship* lest evils should come to the Maori people and the Europeans who are living here without law. Now, as the Queen has been pleased to send me, William Hobson, a Captain in the Royal Navy, to be Governor for all the places of New Zealand which are now given up or which shall be given up to the Queen. And she says to the Chiefs of the Confederation of the Hapus of New Zealand and the other Chiefs, these are the laws spoken of.

This is the First:

The Chiefs of the Confederation, and the rest of the chiefs, as well as those who have not become members of the confederation, have truly given to the Queen of England forever the Governorship over all their lands.

> The Māori word *"Kawanatanga"* signifies much less than the English word "sovereignty".

This is the Second:

The Queen of England agrees and consents to give to the Chiefs, the Hapus, and all the people of New Zealand the full chieftainship of their lands, their villages and all their possessions. But the Chiefs of the Confederation and all the other Chiefs give to the Queen the purchasing of those pieces of land which the owner is willing to sell, subject to the arranging of payment which will be agreed to by them and the purchaser who will be appointed by the Queen for the purpose of buying for her.

> "Possessions" was translated as "o ratou taonga katoa" meaning *"everything which the people value"*. This included lands, fisheries, villages, forest food sources, possessions, their language, spirituality and health practices.

This is the Third:

This is the arrangement for the consent to governorship of the Queen. The

Queen will protect all the Māori people of New Zealand and give them all the same rights as those of the people of England.

This protection is understood as an *active protection* in light of the preamble above.